Choosing Peace

Choosing Peace

The Catholic Church
Returns to Gospel Nonviolence

edited by

MARIE DENNIS

ORBIS BOOKS
Maryknoll, New York 10545

Founded in 1970, Orbis Books endeavors to publish works that enlighten the mind, nourish the spirit, and challenge the conscience. The publishing arm of the Maryknoll Fathers and Brothers, Orbis seeks to explore the global dimensions of the Christian faith and mission, to invite dialogue with diverse cultures and religious traditions, and to serve the cause of reconciliation and peace. The books published reflect the views of their authors and do not represent the official position of the Maryknoll Society. To learn more about Maryknoll and Orbis Books, please visit our website at www.maryknollsociety.org.

Manufactured in the United States of America

Manuscript editing and typesetting by Joan Weber Laflamme.

Library of Congress Cataloging-in-Publication Data

Names: Dennis, Marie, editor.
Title: Choosing peace : the Catholic Church returns to Gospel nonviolence / Marie Dennis, editor.
Description: Maryknoll : Orbis Books, 2018. | Includes bibliographical references and index.
Identifiers: LCCN 2017043168 (print) | LCCN 2017044588 (ebook) | ISBN 9781608337361 (e-book) | ISBN 9781626982703 (pbk.)
Subjects: LCSH: Peace—Religious aspects—Catholic Church. | Nonviolence—Religious aspects—Catholic Church.
Classification: LCC BX1795.P43 (ebook) | LCC BX1795.P43 C48 2018 (print) |
     DDC 261.8/73088282—dc23
LC record available at https://lccn.loc.gov/2017043168

Contents

Acknowledgments

This book is the collective gift of many storytellers and authors whose participation in the process toward a deeper Catholic understanding of and commitment to nonviolence and just peace has made it a truly fruitful undertaking. Where the reflection or writing is the contribution of a single person, he or she is identified, but much of the thinking and many of the words that follow are the result of a truly collective effort to share the richness and depth of this endeavor. Each person who was actively involved in planning the April 2016 conference, who participated in the conference, or who serves in leadership of the Catholic Nonviolence Initiative should be listed as a co-author of this book.

In particular, Judy Coode played a central role in organizing the conference itself and in managing many details as the Catholic Nonviolence Initiative formed following the conference, including basic descriptions of the initiative for the webpage that are adapted for the Introduction that follows. Others on the Catholic Nonviolence Initiative Executive Committee and Steering Committee also contributed in significant ways to the writing of this book, although most are not specifically named as an author of a given piece: Ken Butigan (US), Loreta Castro (Philippines), Pat Gaffney (UK), Jose Henriquez (El Salvador), Filo Hirota (Japan), Sheila Kinsey (US), Ann Lanyon (Australia), Gerry Lee (US), Felix Mushobozi (Tanzania), Eli McCarthy (US), Ann Scholz (US), Greet Vanaerschot (Belgium), and Teresia Wamuyu Wachira (Kenya).

The active participation of Cardinal Peter Turkson, Dr. Flaminia Giovanelli, and the staff of the Pontifical Council for Justice and Peace (now the Dicastery for the Promotion of Integral Human

Development) in preparations for the conference and in the conference itself helped make the gathering in Rome in April 2016 an extraordinary event. Since the conference, Archbishop Silvano Tomasi also has been enormously helpful.

Every participant in the April 2016 conference brought rich experience and deep commitment. Of tremendous importance was the presence of so many people from regions of violent conflict or war. Their reflections focused our conversations as nothing else could. At the same time, our commitment to diversity of experience among conference participants made it impossible to extend invitations to many people, especially from the global North, who would have made a significant contribution to our reflections. We believe they will do just that as the process continues.

The papers prepared for the conference (many referenced in this book) are available at www.nonviolencejustpeace.net.

A Message to the Conference

POPE FRANCIS

**MESSAGE OF HIS HOLINESS POPE FRANCIS
TO CARDINAL PETER K. A. TURKSON ON
THE OCCASION OF THE CONFERENCE
ON "NONVIOLENCE AND JUST PEACE:
CONTRIBUTING TO THE CATHOLIC
UNDERSTANDING OF AND COMMITMENT TO
NONVIOLENCE" [ROME, 11–13 APRIL 2016]**

6 April 2016

Your Eminence,

I am delighted to convey my most cordial greetings to you and to all the participants in the Conference on *Nonviolence and Just Peace: Contributing to the Catholic Understanding of and Commitment to Nonviolence,* which will take place in Rome from the 11th to 13th of April 2016.

This encounter, jointly organized by the Pontifical Council for Justice and Peace and Pax Christi International, takes on a very special character and value during the Jubilee Year of Mercy. In effect, mercy is "a source of joy, serenity and peace",[1] a peace which is essentially interior and flows from reconciliation with

---

[1] *Misericordiae vultus,* n. 2.

the Lord.[2] Nevertheless, the participants' reflections must also take into account the current circumstances in the world at large and the historical moment in which the Conference is taking place, and of course these factors also heighten expectations for the Conference.

In order to seek solutions to the unique and terrible 'world war in installments' which, directly or indirectly, a large part of humankind is presently undergoing, it helps us to think back in time. Let us rediscover the reasons that led the sons and daughters of a still largely Christian civilization in the last century to create the Pax Christi Movement and the Pontifical Council for Justice and Peace. From their example we learn that to bring about true peace, it is necessary to bring people together concretely so as to reconcile peoples and groups with opposing ideological positions. It is also necessary to work together for what persons, families, peoples, and nations feel is their right, namely, to participate on a social, political, and economic level in the goods of the modern world.[3] Further, the "unceasing effort on the part of that higher creative imagination which we call diplomacy"[4] must be continuously nourished; and justice in a globalized world, which is "order in freedom and conscious duty,"[5] must constantly be promoted. In a word, humanity needs to refurbish all the best available tools to help the men and women of today to fulfill their aspirations for justice and peace.

Accordingly, your thoughts on revitalizing the tools of non-violence, and of active non-violence in particular, will be a needed and positive contribution. This is what as participants in the Rome Conference you propose to do. In this message I would like to remind you of some further points which are especially of concern to me.

The basic premise is that the ultimate and most deeply worthy goal of human beings and of the human community is the abolition

---

[2] Ibid., n. 17.

[3] *Gaudium et spes*, n. 9.

[4] Pope Paul VI, Message for the celebration of the day of peace 1976, *The Real Weapons of Peace.*

[5] Ibid.

of war.[6] In this vein, we recall that the only explicit condemnation issued by the Second Vatican Council was against war,[7] although the Council recognized that, since war has not been eradicated from the human condition, "governments cannot be denied the right to legitimate defence once every means of peaceful settlement has been exhausted."[8]

Another cornerstone is to recognize that "conflict cannot be ignored or concealed. It has to be faced."[9] Of course, the purpose is not to remain trapped within a framework of conflict, thus losing our overall perspective and our sense of the profound unity of reality.[10] Rather, we must accept and tackle conflict so as to resolve it and transform it into a link in that new process which "peacemakers" initiate.[11]

As Christians, we also know that it is only by considering our peers as brothers and sisters that we will overcome wars and conflicts. The Church tirelessly repeats that this is true not merely at an individual level but also at the level of peoples and nations, for it truly regards the International Community as the "Family of Nations." That is why, in this year's [2016] Message for the World Day of Peace, I made an appeal to States' leaders to renew "their relations with other peoples and to enable their real participation and inclusion in the life of the international community, in order to ensure fraternity within the family of nations as well."[12]

Furthermore, we know as Christians that, in order to make this happen, the greatest obstacle to be removed is the wall of indifference. Recent history justifies using the word 'wall' not in a figurative sense alone, for unhappily it is an all too tangible reality. This phenomenon of indifference touches not only our fellow hu-

---

[6] *Address to the Fourth Course for the Formation of Military Chaplains on International Humanitarian Law*, 26.10.2015.

[7] Cfr. *Gaudium et spes*, nn. 77–82.

[8] *Gaudium et spes*, n. 79.

[9] *Evangelii gaudium*, n. 226.

[10] Ibid.

[11] Ibid, n. 227.

[12] Pope Francis, *Message for the World Day of Peace 2016, Overcome Indifference and Win Peace*, n. 8.

man beings but also the natural environment, with often disastrous consequences in terms of security and social peace.[13]

Nevertheless, we can succeed in overcoming indifference—but only if, in imitation of the Father, we are able to show mercy. Such mercy is so to speak 'political' because it is expressed in solidarity, which is the moral and social attitude that responds best to the awareness of the scourges of our time and of the inter-dependence of life at its different levels—the connections between an individual life, the family, and the local and global community.[14]

In our complex and violent world, it is truly a formidable undertaking to work for peace by living the practice of nonviolence! Equally daunting is the aim of achieving full disarmament "by reaching people's very souls,"[15] building bridges, fighting fear, and pursuing open and sincere dialogue. The practice of dialogue is in fact difficult. We must be prepared to give and take. We must not assume that the others are wrong. Instead, accepting our differences and remaining true to our positions, we must seek the good of all; and, after having finally found agreement, we must firmly maintain it.[16]

We can joyfully anticipate an abundance of cultural differences and varied life experiences among the participants in the Rome Conference, and these will only enhance the exchanges and contribute to the renewal of the active witness of nonviolence as a "weapon" to achieve peace.

Finally, I would like to invite all those present to support two requests I addressed to governmental authorities in this Jubilee Year: to abolish the death penalty where it is still in force, and to consider the possibility of an amnesty; and to forgive or manage in a sustainable way the international debt of the poorer nations.[17]

---

[13] Cfr. ibid, n. 4.
[14] Cfr. ibid, n. 5.
[15] Pope John XXIII, *Pacem in terris*, n. 113.
[16] *Address to Representatives of Civil Society*, Asunción, 11.07.2015.
[17] *Message for the World Day of Peace 2016*, n. 8.

I warmly wish Your Eminence and all the participants fruitful and successful labors, and I extend to you all my Apostolic Blessing.

FRANCISCUS

In the Presence of the Spirit

HILDEGARD GOSS-MAYR

Holy Spirit, our source of light and strength, we thank you for having inspired the call to peacemakers from all over the world to meet in the dramatic situation of humanity to reconsider our responsibility, to deepen and promote the liberating and healing nonviolence of Jesus.

Merciful God, our Father and Mother, you sent your Son Jesus, our brother, to reveal through his life and teaching your divine, self-giving Love and so incarnate in our world the power of nonviolence, able to overcome ALL forms of violence and to reconcile humanity in justice and peace.

We confess that for centuries our church, people of God, has betrayed this central message of the gospel many times and participated in wars, persecution, oppression, exploitation, and discrimination.

Holy Spirit, as we meet as peacemakers, we count on your light and your strength to help revive in the theology of peace the nonviolent message of Jesus in which there is no place for violence and to offer to all Christians the arms of peacemaking, pardon, and reconciliation.

Hildegard Goss-Mayr, whose witness to the power of active nonviolence has inspired around the world courageous and effective nonviolent activities toward just and sustainable peace, wrote "In the Presence of the Spirit" in preparation for the conference.

Holy Spirit, we trust in your light and strength that this conference may mark a new step for our church, on its way to becoming a church of peace, in the spirit of our brother Jesus and so respond to the cry of humanity for life in dignity and peace.

Introduction

A Catholic Reflection
on Nonviolence and Just Peace

Conflict cannot be ignored or concealed. It has to be faced. But if we remain trapped in conflict, we lose our perspective, our horizons shrink and reality itself begins to fall apart. In the midst of conflict, we lose our sense of the profound unity of reality. . . . The message of peace is not about a negotiated settlement but rather the conviction that the unity brought by the Spirit can harmonize every diversity.

—*EVANGELII GAUDIUM*, nn. 226, 230

Nonviolence and Just Peace Conference

From April 11 to April 13, 2016, the Pontifical Council for Justice and Peace (now the Dicastery for Promoting Integral Human Development) and Pax Christi International brought together more than eighty people to discuss the Catholic Church's history of and commitment to nonviolence. Additional organizers of Nonviolence and Just Peace: Contributing to the Catholic Understanding of and Commitment to Nonviolence included prominent Catholic organizations already deeply engaged in peacebuilding: the Justice and Peace Commission of the Union of International Superiors General/Union of Superiors General, the Conference of Major Superiors of Men, the Leadership Conference of Women Religious, the Maryknoll Office for Global Concerns, St. Columban's Mission Society, and Pace e Bene.

The conference focused on the experience of those from the global South and areas of conflict. Participants were members of the clergy (including one cardinal, two archbishops and three bishops), women religious, academics, and peace practitioners from around the world. Countries represented were the Philippines, Sri Lanka, Pakistan, Afghanistan, South Africa, Croatia, Iraq, Thailand, Democratic Republic of the Congo, El Salvador, South Sudan, Colombia, Burundi, Guatemala, Uganda, Kenya, Zambia, Mexico, Northern Ireland, Uruguay, and Palestine, as well as South Korea, Australia, Japan, Italy, Germany, Luxembourg, France, Switzerland, Belgium, the Netherlands, the UK, and the United States.

We heard from Catholic leaders involved in negotiating with violent armed actors in Northern Uganda and Colombia and from an Iraqi sister calling for an end to the militarization and bombing of her country. We heard from a bishop in South Sudan who founded a peace village and who has the deep trust of all the armed actors. We heard about peace education in the Philippines, a university of nonviolence in Lebanon, the search for truth in Sri Lanka, and loving an enemy in the midst of war in Croatia.

A creative process that allowed each participant to share his or her experience shaped the two and one-half day gathering. In each of four sessions a small group sat in a "fishbowl" formation; every person would speak for a few minutes. Other participants were welcome to approach the "fishbowl" and take a turn to respond or to address the given topic. After each large session the participants broke into seven small, language-specific groups to share more fully. This led to deep, serious, and respectful conversations.

The four main topics addressed:

1. *Experiences of nonviolence.* Participants from countries immersed in violent conflict were asked to share about

their experience of nonviolence as a spiritual commitment of faith and as a practical strategy in violent situations and different cultural contexts. What might we learn from such experience to provide soil for theological reflection and action planning?

2. *Jesus's way of nonviolence.* Participants were asked to share how recent experiences of nonviolence help deepen our understanding of Jesus's way of nonviolence and engaging conflict. How does Jesus help illuminate the roots of nonviolence? What has the latest scholarship and praxis revealed about Jesus's approach and practices for nonviolence and engaging conflict? How might we appropriate recent theological reflection on nonviolence? How can we integrate these insights into present-day contexts?

3. *Nonviolence and Just Peace.* Participants were asked how Catholic communities already embody and practice just peace. What are the developments in theological reflection on just peace, and how do they build on scripture and the trajectory of Catholic social thought? How would a turn to just peace impact our moral analysis of conflicts, practices, and engagement with the broader society, including policymakers?

4. *Moving beyond unending war.* Participants were asked to address the reasons for and the ramifications of the Catholic Church making an explicit rejection of the language, or even the concept, of just war. They discussed some key elements of a more fruitful ethical framework for engaging acute conflict and addressing the responsibility to protect by developing the themes and practices of nonviolent conflict transformation, nonviolent intervention, and just peace.

Nonviolence was the primary focus of the conference, but the just war theory was discussed with nuance and depth. Participants were committed to peacemaking and nonviolence, but many were not opposed to the use of armed force or violence under any circumstances. In dialogue, participants challenged the centrality of the just war tradition and affirmed active, nonviolent approaches to peacemaking at all levels.

Repeatedly, participants who live in areas of conflict said, "We are tired of war." The need for the church to promote non-violence—to deepen its understanding of and commitment to nonviolence—seemed obvious and essential.

Nonviolence and Just Peace

The wide-ranging and ongoing conversation upon which this book is based has developed around two important concepts, *nonviolence* and *just peace*, neither of which is well understood in the Catholic community or fully developed in the Catholic tradition. The following chapters present some basic definitions and foundational ideas that we hope will contribute to a broader Catholic ownership of nonviolence and of just peace. We who have been guiding the Catholic Nonviolence Initiative, which was launched at the April 2016 conference as a project of Pax Christi International, believe that both are essential to faithful discipleship in the context of a violent world.

We have used *nonviolence* to mean a method that, while clearly rejecting violence, is also a positive and active approach and a dynamic for creating peace and justice. Fundamentally, we understand *active nonviolence* as a spirituality, a way of life, a positive and powerful force for social change, and a means of building a more just, peaceful, and sustainable global community. Active nonviolence is a method for challenging and transforming the innumerable forms of direct, cultural, structural, and systemic violence; a path for resolving interpersonal, social, and international conflict; and a way to protect the vulnerable without resort to violence or lethal force.

In "An Overview of Gospel Nonviolence in the Christian Tradition," an essay prepared for conference participants, Ken Butigan and John Dear, leaders of Campaign Nonviolence, add:

The word *nonviolence*, while it has a long history in other traditions, is a relatively new term in Christianity. Increasingly, however, theologians, church leadership, and Christians in many parts of the world have come to see that this word effectively characterizes Jesus's way—a way that combines *both* an unmistakable rejection of violence *and* the power of love and truth in action for justice, peace, and integrity of creation. Nonviolence is a clearer way to understand Jesus's vision than even *love* or *peace* by themselves, because we can use these terms but at the same time support violence and war. This is more difficult with nonviolence. The word *nonviolence* illuminates the heart of the Gospel— the proclamation of the Reign of God, a new nonviolent order rooted in God's unconditional love.

Just peace is a Christian school of thought and set of practices for building peace at all stages of acute conflict—before, during, and after. It draws on three key approaches for building a positive peace—principles and moral criteria, practical norms, and virtue ethics, which emphasizes the development of a person's character as key to ethical thinking.

This book is about both nonviolence and just peace, their relationship to the Gospel, and their usefulness in the twenty-first century. Further development and a much wider embrace of these interrelated approaches to Christian life in the public arena can help expand the tools available for addressing some of the most serious moral questions around security and the protection of vulnerable people, basic rights and liberation from oppression, access to scarce resources and budget priorities, and other critical issues that the global community faces in these times.

Rooted in Experience

As Pope Francis teaches, theory and abstract ideas must be rooted in practice and tested in real life. Therefore, the reflections and experiences of conference participants from regions of war and violent conflict, as well as of other participants, are essential here and in the following chapters. They bring shape and color to our exploration of active nonviolence and just peace and give added impetus to the dynamic results of the conference.

For example, Bishop Paride Taban from South Sudan spoke about his experience during the long years of civil war that engulfed Sudan, north and south, from 1955 to 1972 and 1983 to 2005. In a peaceful January 2011 referendum, 99 percent of the South Sudanese voted for independence, establishing the Republic of South Sudan in July 2011, but a round of vicious violence began in the new country in December 2013. Bishop Taban, in a preconference essay, writes of active nonviolence:

> The best example I can give you is the Holy Trinity Peace Village Kuron (www.kuronvillage.net). The Peace Village came out of my dream during the civil war. I wanted to create a village where individuals and communities could interact and relate without threat and fear. The village was created in 1997 and has grown ever since. It brings together people from diverse ethnic and cultural backgrounds and offers social and economic services including peace education that are meant to sustain peaceful coexistence among the various people. The Peace Village has the potential to offer people from Sudan, the region, and the world a model for reconciliation that is grounded on sound spiritual and human values. . . .
>
> One should know oneself and find out whether one has true will to engage in this difficult complex work. Peace is a risk; it needs sacrifice. One must learn how to live in difficult times with the whole mind, body, and soul. Take care of yourself and say the twenty-eight Words every day: love, joy, peace, patience, compassion, sympathy, kindness, truthfulness, gentleness, self-control, humility, poverty, forgiveness, [mercy, friendship,] trust, unity, purity, faith, hope, I love you, I miss you, thank you, I forgive, we forget, together, I am wrong, I am sorry.

In the months following the Rome conference, Cardinal Peter Turkson repeatedly affirmed the importance of the focus on nonviolence and just peace that emerged. In an April 22, 2016, interview with journalist Christopher Lamb, he said:

> "Pax Christi's proposal is very legitimate. In the worldwide Catholic network, it is an important voice among many. Pope Francis is working for collegiality, following the teaching of Vatican Council II. It will be of utmost importance to initiate a broad, open, qualified, deeply felt, and widespread debate. A possible encyclical is plausible only as the fruit of much dialogue, not as a starting point."[1]

A few months later, in an interview by Joshua McElwee, Cardinal Turkson said that Pope Francis was giving "very strong recognition" to the conference, that the "pontiff's decision to focus his message for World Peace Day in 2017 on nonviolent strategies to prevent and stop global violence was partly caused by the discussions at the conference." He noted that "the participants of the conference asked the church to reexamine the concept of just war, first enunciated by fourth-century bishop St. Augustine," and "slightly begin to move away from that." Cardinal Turkson continued: "From the point of view of us Christians, and talking as Christians, our master also taught us a way of dealing with violence. . . . Is it worth following what our master taught us? What he taught us is this nonviolence."[2]

Pope Francis's 2017 World Day of Peace message (see Chapter 10), "Nonviolence: A Style of Politics for Peace," is an extremely hopeful sign that the Catholic Church is deepening its reflection on active nonviolence. The Catholic Nonviolence Initiative, a project of Pax Christi International in collaboration with the many other

---

[1] See Christopher Lamb, *The Sunday Times*, April 24, 2016.

[2] Cardinal Peter Turkson, in Joshua McElwee, "Cardinal Turkson: 'We Do Not Stop War by Starting Another War,'" *National Catholic Reporter*, September 20, 2016.

Catholic organizations, is making a significant contribution to this critical transition.

At Session 1 of the conference, Mairead Maguire, Nobel Peace Laureate from Northern Ireland, said:

"We live in cultures of violence, but we're not born violent, we're born peaceful. To have a culture of violence requires that the institutions continue with the myth that the only way to solve problems is through military and war. The challenge is for us to have a new consciousness—literally, for us to have a new awareness that violence is wrong, that we can live in peace, that peace works, that peace is possible, indeed that peace is the only way for the human family to live and to survive. So, we're talking about a huge transformation, a quantum leap from a way of militarism to a way of non-killing, nonviolence, and solving our problems without killing each other in the process. So if we have to leap to a new consciousness, we need to involve everyone—from all the sciences, all the religions, right across the world. And we have to declare very clearly our vision of stopping militarism and war and building institutions and structures that reflect the diversity of the human family. It has, in a sense, to be articulated at many levels. I think that churches have a tremendous opportunity at this point in history, to turn around our history and to declare our vision of a demilitarized, peaceful world, which is what we long for. And if churches give that kind of visionary, prophetic leadership, the people are ready for it. All over the world, people are ready for it. We've had enough of war, of killing each other, destroying. People are ready for the vision if we can articulate it from the heart of Rome, through the church, through an encyclical on nonviolence and peace. It's going to be a long, long work, transforming a cultural mindset. But we can do it. We're turning history. This is historic, we're turning history. And it's doable."

Conference participants are committed to keeping alive a conversation on the many complex issues related to the meeting and will look for ways to support the church's work "to integrate Gospel nonviolence explicitly into the life, including the sacramental life, and work of the church through dioceses, parishes, agencies, schools, universities, seminaries, religious orders, voluntary associations, and others." We hope this book will contribute to that effort.

1

An Appeal to the Catholic Church

Humanity needs to refurbish all the best available tools to help men and women of today to fulfill their aspiration for justice and peace.

—POPE FRANCIS, APRIL 11, 2016

Introduction

The harsh consequences of war and extreme violence—especially in the past century—are increasingly obvious: huge numbers of precious lives lost, both military and civilian; devastating physical, psychological, and spiritual wounds that will last a lifetime, affecting individuals, their families and their communities; moral injury and wounds from remote and virtual battles; people displaced and on the move seeking refuge around the world; catastrophic environmental damage; ongoing violence permeating societies engaged in long wars where generation after generation have known only the tools of violence for dealing with conflict at whatever level.

This tragic reality has set the stage for a fresh appraisal of the challenge of peace and the role of the institutional Catholic Church and the wider Catholic community in pointing out and promoting a route to a just and sustainable peace that is most consistent with the gospel.

The rich and concrete experience of people making peace around the world—especially those in extremely violent circumstances who are living witnesses to the power of nonviolence—can help enrich a Catholic theology of positive peace and encourage Catholics to engage energetically in the development of more and more effective nonviolent practices for protecting vulnerable communities, avoiding violent conflict, transforming structures of violence, and promoting cultures of peace.

The just war tradition can no longer claim center stage as *the* Christian approach to war and peace. After more than fifteen hundred years and misuse of the just war criteria too often to sanction war rather than to prevent war, the Catholic Church, like many other Christian communities, is rereading the text of Jesus's life and reappropriating the Christian vocation of active peacemaking.

Emphasizing the need to work for a just peace, the church is moving away from the acceptability of calling war "just." While clear ethical criteria are necessary for addressing egregious attacks or threats in a violent world, moral theologians and ethicists should consider no longer referring to such criteria as the just war theory, because that language undermines the moral imperative to develop tools and capacity for nonviolent conflict.

Many are deeply concerned that continued use of the term *just war* in our tradition gives license to the Catholic community to prepare for and support war rather than to discourage war and look for other solutions to actual or potential conflict, violent or not. At the same time, the effectiveness of strategic nonviolent practices in many situations of violent conflict has been demonstrated in different ways throughout history, but especially in the past century. Yet nonviolence is often misrepresented, misunderstood, or too narrowly defined. Rarely is there sufficient human or financial investment in developing effective nonviolent practices useful in the sociopolitical arena.

Concepts like nonviolence, structural violence, culture of violence, JustPeace, and culture of peace are not widely known or well understood in the Catholic community. Where discussion about these concepts takes place, it has tended to be a theoretical or intellectual discussion among moral theologians, ethicists, academics, and peace activists. Among many, though not all Catholic bishops, within schools of theology and seminaries, the movement from a just war framework to a just peace framework is neither understood nor accepted. The pastoral implications of such a shift to nonviolence have not been developed at all, and there is very little grassroots Catholic education or preaching about Catholic teaching on war and peace.

Yet, in 2007, Pope Benedict XVI said, "For Christians, nonviolence is not merely tactical behavior but a person's way of being, the attitude of one who is so convinced of God's love and power, [who is] not afraid to tackle evil with the weapons of love and truth alone. Love of one's enemy constitutes the nucleus of the 'Christian revolution.'"[1]

During the April 2016 conference, participants wrote an *Appeal to the Catholic Church to Re-commit to the Centrality of Gospel Nonviolence*, urging the church to move beyond the language of just war that has been central to Catholic theology on war and peace for centuries and to "integrate Gospel nonviolence explicitly into the life, including the sacramental life, and work of the Church through dioceses, parishes, agencies, schools, universities, seminaries, religious orders, voluntary associations, and others." We asked Pope Francis to write his World Day of Peace message, and someday an encyclical, on nonviolence.

Testimony to the Potential of Active Nonviolence

Central to our conversations during the conference on nonviolence and just peace were the voices of people promoting active nonviolence in the midst of violence. Many participants came from countries that have been at war or dealing with serious violence for decades. Their testimony was extremely powerful.

At Session 1, during the language-specific group discussion "Experiences of Nonviolence," Iraqi Dominican Sister Nazik Matty, whose community was expelled from Mosul by ISIS, said,

---

[1] Pope Benedict XVI, *Angelus*, St. Peter's Square, February 18, 2007.

"We can't respond to violence with worse violence. . . . It's like a dragon with seven heads. You cut one and two others come up."

Ogarit Younan, who co-founded the Academic University for Nonviolence and Human Rights in Lebanon, shared her positive experience of equipping youth, educators, and community leaders throughout the Middle East with nonviolent skills to end vicious cycles of violence and discrimination.

At Session 3, during the plenary discussion "Nonviolence and Just Peace," Jesuit Francisco DeRoux told the story of Alma Rosa Jaramillo, a courageous woman and audacious lawyer who had joined their team in the Magdalena Medio region of Colombia to support displaced small farmers. She was kidnapped by the National Liberation Army, the ELN, and finally released. Then she was captured by the paramilitaries. "When we managed to recover Alma Rosa," Francisco told us, "she was lying in the mud, dead; they had cut off her arms and legs with a chainsaw." Immediately, another woman stepped in to take her place, as did Alma Rosa's son, Jesus. The team continued to talk with the guerrillas, the paramilitaries, and the army, searching for a nonviolent solution a war that had gone on for *fifty* years. Over and over again they heard from *campesinos*, native people, Afro-Colombians—people whose youngsters had joined the guerrilla groups, the paramilitary groups, and the army: "Stop the war, stop the war now, and stop the war from all sides!"

We heard similar stories from many of the other conference participants—courageous people in local communities living with unimaginable danger who said stop the militarization, stop the bombing, stop the proliferation of weapons, and rely on nonviolent strategies to transform conflict.

Their witness led to a deep conversation that lasted long after the conference about the significance of active nonviolence and the meaning of just peace in Catholic thought and theology. Encouraged by the Vatican, the Catholic Nonviolence Initiative prepared to work with bishops' conferences, moral theologians, ethicists, academics, politicians, peace activists, and the Catholic community at large to understand the implications of "love your enemy" in the twenty-first-century political context. The conversation would include

- theologians to help develop a new moral framework for Catholic theology on war and peace, a rich theology of nonviolence, and excellent scriptural exegesis around the theme of nonviolence;
- politicians and social scientists to help articulate effective nonviolent strategies to use in a dangerous world;
- peacebuilding practitioners to design nonviolent practices to protect vulnerable communities;
- leaders in Catholic schools, Catholic universities, seminaries, and parishes to teach active nonviolence to the people of God and generate creative thinking about what makes for just peace locally and globally;
- activists to bring Catholic values to the public debate on the use (or not) of violent force in specific situations; and
- citizens who will insist that resources be devoted to meeting basic human needs and protecting the integrity of the natural world, not building more weapons for war.

The conference made clear the importance of specifically including in this process those who have lived in war and violent conflict—sometimes for their whole lives—and, of course, women, whose voices are too often muted in the institutional Catholic Church.

What If . . . ?

For Christians, nonviolence is a way of life, a positive and powerful force for social change, and a means of building a global community committed to the well-being of all. Active nonviolence is a multilayered approach that is fundamental to the teaching of Jesus and recognizes the humanity of every person, even our sons and daughters who are perpetrators of terrible violence. If carefully developed based on the evidence now available about what sustains peaceful societies as well as on future research—and if nonviolent practices are sufficiently scaled up—these strategies may well help prevent egregious violence, transform violent conflict, and protect vulnerable people and their communities.

Behind preparations for the conference, the *Appeal to the Catholic Church to Re-commit to the Centrality of Gospel Nonviolence*, and the energetic process of discussion and discernment at the conference and following it were two simple questions: What if Catholics were formed from the beginning of life to understand and appreciate the power of active nonviolence and the connection of nonviolence to the heart of the gospel? What if the Catholic Church committed its vast spiritual, intellectual, and financial resources to developing a new moral framework and nonviolent tools to prevent atrocities, to protect people, and to safeguard the planet in a dangerous world?

An Appeal to the Catholic Church to Re-commit to the Centrality of Gospel Nonviolence

As Christians committed to a more just and peaceful world we are called to take a clear stand for creative and active nonviolence and against all forms of violence. With this conviction, and in recognition of the Jubilee Year of Mercy declared by Pope Francis, people from many countries gathered at the Nonviolence and Just Peace Conference sponsored by the Pontifical Council for Justice and Peace and Pax Christi International on April 11–13, 2016, in Rome.

Our assembly, people of God from Africa, the Americas, Asia, Europe, the Middle East, and Oceania included lay people, theologians, and members of religious congregations, priests, and bishops. Many of us live in communities experiencing violence

---

This statement, crafted in a consensus process, was released at the end of the conference and has since been endorsed by thousands of individuals and organizations around the world. For commentaries and discussion, see http://www.nonviolencejustpeace.net.

and oppression. All of us are practitioners of justice and peace. We are grateful for the message to our conference from Pope Francis: "your thoughts on revitalizing the tools of nonviolence, and of active nonviolence in particular, will be a needed and positive contribution."

Looking At Our World Today

We live in a time of tremendous suffering, widespread trauma and fear linked to militarization, economic injustice, climate change, and a myriad of other specific forms of violence. In this context of normalized and systemic violence, those of us who stand in the Christian tradition are called to recognize the centrality of active nonviolence to the vision and message of Jesus; to the life and practice of the Catholic Church; and to our long-term vocation of healing and reconciling both people and the planet.

We rejoice in the rich concrete experiences of people engaged in work for peace around the world, many of whose stories we heard during this conference. Participants shared their experiences of courageous negotiations with armed actors in Uganda and Colombia; working to protect Article 9, the peace clause in the Japanese Constitution; accompaniment in Palestine; and countrywide peace education in the Philippines. They illuminate the creativity and power of nonviolent practices in many different situations of potential or actual violent conflict. Recent academic research, in fact, has confirmed that nonviolent resistance strategies are twice as effective as violent ones.

The time has come for our Church to be a living witness and to invest far greater human and financial resources in promoting a spirituality and practice of active nonviolence and in forming and training our Catholic communities in effective nonviolent practices. In all of this, Jesus is our inspiration and model.

Jesus and Nonviolence

In his own times, rife with structural violence, Jesus proclaimed a new, nonviolent order rooted in the unconditional love of God.

Jesus called his disciples to love their enemies (Matthew 5:44), which includes respecting the image of God in all persons; to offer no violent resistance to one who does evil (Matthew 5:39); to become peacemakers; to forgive and repent; and to be abundantly merciful (Matthew 5—7). Jesus embodied nonviolence by actively resisting systemic dehumanization, as when he defied the Sabbath laws to heal the man with the withered hand (Mark 3:1–6); when he confronted the powerful at the Temple and purified it (John 2:13–22); when he peacefully but determinedly challenged the men accusing a woman of adultery (John 8:1–11); when on the night before he died he asked Peter to put down his sword (Matthew 26:52).

Neither passive nor weak, Jesus's nonviolence was the power of love in action. In vision and deed, he is the revelation and embodiment of the Nonviolent God, a truth especially illuminated in the Cross and Resurrection. He calls us to develop the virtue of nonviolent peacemaking.

Clearly, the Word of God, the witness of Jesus, should never be used to justify violence, injustice, or war. We confess that the people of God have betrayed this central message of the Gospel many times, participating in wars, persecution, oppression, exploitation, and discrimination.

We believe that there is no "just war." Too often the "just war theory" has been used to endorse rather than prevent or limit war. Suggesting that a "just war" is possible also undermines the moral imperative to develop tools and capacities for nonviolent transformation of conflict.

We need a new framework that is consistent with Gospel nonviolence. A different path is clearly unfolding in recent Catholic social teaching. Pope John XXIII wrote that war is not a suitable way to restore rights; Pope Paul VI linked peace and development, and told the UN "no more war"; Pope John Paul II said that "war belongs to the tragic past, to history"; Pope Benedict XVI said that "loving the enemy is the nucleus of the Christian revolution"; and Pope Francis said "the true strength of the Christian is the power of truth and love, which leads to the renunciation of all violence. Faith and violence are incompatible." He has also urged the "abolition of war."

We propose that the Catholic Church develop and consider shifting to a Just Peace approach based on Gospel nonviolence. A Just Peace approach offers a vision and an ethic to build peace as well as to prevent, defuse, and to heal the damage of violent conflict. This ethic includes a commitment to human dignity and thriving relationships, with specific criteria, virtues, and practices to guide our actions. We recognize that peace requires justice and justice requires peacemaking.

Living Gospel Nonviolence and Just Peace

In that spirit we commit ourselves to furthering Catholic understanding and practice of active nonviolence on the road to just peace. As would-be disciples of Jesus, challenged and inspired by stories of hope and courage in these days, we call on the Church we love to:

- continue developing Catholic social teaching on nonviolence. In particular, we call on Pope Francis to share with the world an encyclical on nonviolence and Just Peace;
- integrate Gospel nonviolence explicitly into the life, including the sacramental life, and work of the Church through dioceses, parishes, agencies, schools, universities, seminaries, religious orders, voluntary associations, and others;
- promote nonviolent practices and strategies (e.g., nonviolent resistance, restorative justice, trauma healing, unarmed civilian protection, conflict transformation, and peacebuilding strategies);
- initiate a global conversation on nonviolence within the Church, with people of other faiths, and with the larger world to respond to the monumental crises of our time with the vision and strategies of nonviolence and Just Peace;
- no longer use or teach "just war theory";
- continue advocating for the abolition of war and nuclear weapons;
- lift up the prophetic voice of the church to challenge unjust world powers and to support and defend those nonviolent

activists whose work for peace and justice put their lives at risk.

In every age, the Holy Spirit graces the Church with the wisdom to respond to the challenges of its time. In response to what is a global epidemic of violence, which Pope Francis has labeled a "world war in installments," we are being called to invoke, pray over, teach, and take decisive action. With our communities and organizations, we look forward to continue collaborating with the Holy See and the global Church to advance Gospel nonviolence.

Only the Violence of Love

Bishop Kevin Dowling, CSsR

"We open our doors to everyone—even to those who might come in to kill us." I heard those powerful words from a soft-spoken Syrian Jesuit with pain-filled eyes during a ceremony in a church in Sarajevo, Bosnia-Herzegovina, on Sunday evening, June 8, 2014. That evening I was privileged to give the Jesuit Refugee Service Syria the 2014 Pax Christi International Peace Award together with my Pax Christi International co-president, Marie Dennis from the United States. The two Jesuit recipients, accompanied by a member of their leadership team from Rome, were Fr. Mourad Abou Seif and Fr. Ziad Halil.

Earlier that day in Sarajevo we had listened to Fr. Mourad and Fr. Ziad describe the terrible suffering in that protracted war and their work with the Jesuit Refugee Service in Homs and Aleppo, where both of them remained in spite of the assassination of Fr.

In the aftermath of the conference, Bishop Kevin Dowling, CSsR, from Rustenburg, South Africa, co-president of Pax Christi International, further elaborated the extremely challenging questions that we as followers of Jesus face in the real, yet violent, world. This document is adapted from his address to the Denis Hurley Peace Institute, November 8, 2016.

Frans van der Lugt, a brother Jesuit priest, in Syria in April 2013. Yes! They did come in and they killed him, but yes! those Jesuit priests stayed with their people and witnessed to nonviolence and peace together with groups of Muslim and Christian peace activists with whom they worked in providing humanitarian relief, education, healthcare, and above all, hope, which few know about. But, as Fr. Mourad said: "We open our doors to everyone—even though they might come in to kill us. And we will never stop opening our doors. We can only find our safety in God." . . .

This is an example of church personnel fulfilling the witness of *presence*, of *staying with in solidarity*, of responding to human need in a situation of horrendous suffering, fraught with danger.

Appalling experiences like that in Syria have driven Pope Francis to state that we are in the midst of a *third world war in installments*. Our whole world—from the international arena right down to experiences at the local level in many countries in the world, including our own in South Africa—seems to be trapped in a cycle of never-ending violence.

Atrocities and wars, the use of violence to force through whatever one wants to get, the destruction of property, the violation of the human rights of others, the culture of impunity, and so on and so on . . . has this to be accepted as the norm today in our world, and here in South Africa?

Surely there *has to be* another way to deal with divisions and conflict between nations without going to war and killing thousands of innocent children and people? Surely there *is* another way here (in South Africa) to seek objectives like a wage increase or to solve issues like municipal demarcations without resorting to violent protests and destruction of property? There is a great, *great* need for healing in our land. But even with the analysis of all the reasons why people opt for violence, and the causes behind their anger and despair about change, does that justify violence—and if not, what is to be done about this?

Surely at all levels of society and the world we need to promote and consolidate another mindset, another way of thinking based on real values and on a commitment to respectful encounter and dialogue as the first step in conflict resolution. . . .

Oscar Romero, Denis Hurley, Pope Francis, Mahatma Gandhi—and in my own faith, the person of Jesus—give me hope that there *is* another way. . . . All of them were or are the very antithesis of the violence that this world seems committed to consign to the children of the future, and indeed to the planet.

In March 2005 I was privileged to participate in a week-long reflection in El Salvador to commemorate the twenty-fifth anniversary of the assassination of Archbishop Oscar Romero, killed by a single shot from a sniper. I listened to fascinating theological reflections by great theologians like Gustavo Gutiérrez. But we also listened to the witness of the *campesinos*, the poor peasant farmers and families who suffered horrendous atrocities and massacres at the hands of the notorious Salvadoran National Guard and death squads, whose officers were allegedly trained at Fort Benning in Georgia in the United States at the School of the Americas, which gained notoriety and was then renamed the Western Hemisphere Institute for Security Cooperation. I prayed at the altar where Romero fell while celebrating mass—everything the same except for the inscription on the wall: "At this altar Monsignor Oscar A. Romero offered his life for his people." I visited the simple rose garden at the University of Central America where the six Jesuits and their housekeeper and her daughter were shot to death by an elite unit of the Salvadoran National Guard and the site where the three religious sisters and a lay missionary were raped and murdered by these extremely violent military personnel.

Archbishop Romero, from the perspective of his context, analyzed violence in our world thus:

The church does not approve or justify bloody revolution and cries of hatred. But neither can it condemn them while it sees no attempt to remove the causes that produce that ailment in our society. . . . I will not tire of declaring that if we really want an effective end to violence we must remove the violence that lies at the root of all violence: structural violence, social injustice, exclusion of citizens from the management of the country, repression. All this is what constitutes the primal cause, from which the rest flows naturally.[2]

And we could add to his list of examples of structural violence.

In many ways, the Catholic Church in South Africa during the struggle against the structural violence of apartheid tried to tread that difficult and challenging path of Monseñor Romero—being constructively supportive through our solidarity and action with the poor, the suffering and oppressed; actively engaging in the quest for change and for a peace based on justice; and committing to the protection and promotion of human rights and the rights of the people's movements and organizations on the ground. In a situation that was always so volatile and unpredictable, it was not easy for the bishops to maintain a consistent and thought-through prophetic stance. But as the oppression became more brutal especially in the late 1970s and 1980s, the bishops took an increasingly principled stand—their call for justice and change became ever clearer.

We had our prophet in the person of Archbishop Denis Hurley, who invited and inspired our church leadership and people toward more conscious and committed involvement in the struggle for justice, without which there could be no resolution to the impasse. He was one of many prophetic church-based and faith-based leaders who shared in the struggle of the oppressed people, and their leaders and organizations, through protest marches and courageous witness and action on behalf of human rights . . . all in the quest for change and justice that would open the way to a different future. We all remember that iconic photo of Archbishop Hurley together with other church and faith leaders walking arm in arm in peaceful protest. . . .

Pope Francis, as I indicated earlier, has described the present reality of wars, atrocities, and violence all over the world as a "third world war in installments." "We never tire of repeating that the name of God cannot be used to justify violence. Peace alone,

---

[2] Oscar A. Romero, "Homilias, 12 February 1978," and "Homilias, 23 September 1979," in *The Violence of Love* (Maryknoll, NY: Orbis Books, 2004), 36–37 and 166, respectively.

and not war, is holy!" the Pope said on September 20, 2016, at the closing ceremony of an interreligious peace gathering in Assisi. "I am thinking of the families, whose lives have been shattered; of the children who have known only violence in their lives; of the elderly, forced to leave their homeland. All of them have a great thirst for peace," he said. "We do not want these tragedies to be forgotten."

Violence

I move now to a sub-theme in my reflection, namely, the articulation in Catholic Church theology of the just war theory, and the proposition of the use of violence as a last resort to overcome atrocities, oppression, and structural injustice, that is, injustice and violence against an entire people or nation, or groups, or classes of people.

In El Salvador, in the face of massacres, assassinations, and unspeakable atrocities against the people, there arose a coalition of guerrilla groups called the Farabundo Martí National Liberation Front (FMLN). The FMLN engaged in an armed struggle against the government in a twelve-year civil war from 1979 to 1992—during which Romero was assassinated in 1980. We have seen something similar to this on several occasions and in different contexts, for example, the uprising of the people in South Sudan against decades of war and oppression by the Al Bashir Khartoum Regime in the north, and eventually the waging of a liberation war against the north by the Sudan People's Liberation Army and Movement. Just two examples among so many others in the world arena.

Romero fiercely condemned all forms of violence and oppression against innocent people. He also affirmed the right of people to oppose a regime that caused untold destruction and suffering to ordinary citizens. He wrote:

> The church condemns structural or institutionalized violence, the result of an unjust situation in which the majority of men, women, and children in our country find themselves deprived of the necessities of life (cf. Third Pastoral Letter). The church condemns this violence not only because it

is unjust in itself, and the objective expression of personal and collective sin, but also because it is the cause of other innumerable cruelties and more obvious acts of violence."[3]

The Medellín document on peace, quoting a text from Paul VI's encyclical *Populorum progressio,* mentions the legitimacy of insurrection in the very exceptional circumstances of an evident and prolonged tyranny that seriously works against fundamental human rights and seriously damages the common good of the country, whether it proceeds from one person or from clearly unjust structures. It immediately goes on, however, to warn of the danger of occasioning, through insurrection, new injustices . . . new imbalances . . . new disasters—all of which would justify a condemnation of insurrection (Medellín Documents, *Peace,* #19).[4]

I sense from what Romero often said that he was aware of the potential in revolutionary violence and armed struggle to degenerate into the use of violence to achieve power as an end in itself, or that armed struggle and wars could bring about new forms of injustice, violence, and destruction—as has happened in El Salvador, a very violent society with multiple mostly gangland murders each day. But I also think it would have pained Archbishop Romero in the depths of his being that people and communities were "driven," as it were, to take an option for violence because of a despair that anything would change in their situation; in other words, he would have been understanding towards them, while always calling on them to choose the way of nonviolent peacemaking for the common good.

On November 27, 1977, he said:

---

[3] Oscar Romero, "Fourth Pastoral Letter: The Church's Mission and the National Crisis," August 6, 1979, in *Voice of the Voiceless,* trans. Michael J. Walsh (Maryknoll, NY: Orbis Books, 1985), 70.

[4] Oscar Romero, "Third Pastoral Letter: The Church's Moral Judgment on Violence," August 6, 1978, in *Voice of the Voiceless,* 105–10.

"We have never preached violence, except the violence of
love, which left Christ nailed to a cross, the violence that we
must each do to ourselves to overcome our selfishness and
such cruel inequalities among us. The violence we preach
is not the violence of the sword, the violence of hatred. It is
the violence of love, of brotherhood, the violence that wills
to beat weapons into sickles for work."[5]

Romero was not an absolute pacifist, in the sense of being
passive in the face of aggression and not acting in any way in
self-defense. This is what he wrote in his Third Pastoral Letter:

The church allows violence in legitimate defense, but under
the following conditions: (a) that the defense does not exceed
the degree of unjust aggression (for example, if one can adequately defend oneself with one's hands, then it is wrong to
shoot at an aggressor); (b) that the recourse to proportionate
violence takes place only after all peaceful means have been
exhausted; and (c) that a violent defense should not bring
about a greater evil than that of the aggression—namely, a
greater violence, a greater injustice.[6]

These are criteria used in the just war theory, . . . but the question
is: is this applicable today in the face of the totally disproportionate effects of modern war and extreme violence? . . .
   What emerged during our [conference] discussions was a
questioning of the just war theory as an accepted teaching in the
Catholic Church and a move to a more inclusive challenge and
call to active peacemaking, that is, seeking a just peace especially
through giving space for the consideration of multiple nonviolent
methods of peacemaking, as opposed to a continued commitment
to wars and violence as a method to achieve objectives. Not all
participants were on the same page; there were committed pacifists in the group, a few who still believed in the just war theory

---

[5] Romero, "Homilias, 27 November 1977," in *The Violence of Love*, 12.
[6] Romero, "Third Pastoral Letter," in *The Voice of the Voiceless*, 108.

in certain circumstances, but a large group who were consciously committed to finding how to respond to wars through active non-violence and peacemaking.

In recent decades church leadership and faith activists have increasingly realized that the just war theory does not go far enough. Its focus is on war, not peace. The just war theory sets out to distinguish what could be regarded as a justified war from unjustified wars, but the massive, indiscriminate violence and destruction of modern wars call this into question.

As analysts have noted, some key criteria of the theory, namely, proportionality and protection of noncombatants, are never met by modern wars. . . . By the very criteria of the just war theory, in our era it is difficult to see how there can be such thing as a justified war, and the conference in Rome made its declaration: "There is no just war" today, it stated, while recognizing that we face huge and very difficult challenges in the face of what to do and how to respond when war and massive violence breaks out—how to stop this, and then begin the process of peacemaking, including striving for justice for the victims. Complex issues, and there are no easy answers, especially given what some world powers are doing. But the conference wanted to introduce a different type of thinking in the discussion around wars and violence, and to carry this through into advocacy. . . .

So, are there practical alternatives to the cycle of violence, wars, and atrocities that characterize our present world? In fact, there is a compelling story of nonviolent action over the sixty years since Gandhi—and not nearly enough of this story I believe has been brought into discussions around modern wars, and possible alternatives both to such wars and all other forms of violence, and indeed the violence being meted out on our planet.

And symbols, gestures are important to keep hope alive in the search for peace. There was that moment when Pope Francis called for his vehicle to stop and he got out and gently leaned his head in prayer against the wall dividing Palestinian from Israeli. . . . Well, that gesture would have spoken more than thousands of words to the Palestinians about his active and caring solidarity with their suffering. But later on the same visit, he was inclusive of those in

Israel who had suffered in the Holocaust, and this was followed by his call to President Abbas and President Peres to come to Rome to meet each other as fellow human beings, to pray together for peace, the symbol of which was planting an olive tree. A small step . . . but the search must go on. . . .

Recently, a small group of Israeli women began a march to Jerusalem from northern Israel to demand that the Israeli government restart a peace process with the Palestinians. After they reached the Palestinian city of Jericho on the West Bank, the core group of twenty women was joined by more than three thousand others, including around one thousand Palestinian women. And, even though the Palestinian women could not proceed beyond the barrier that separates the West Bank from Israel, the Israeli women headed for the prime minister's residence, where they held an emotional rally. Liberian peace activist Leymah Gbowee, a 2011 Nobel Peace Prize laureate, addressed the group: "I say to my sisters in Israel, that this is your time to stand up and say no to war and yes to peace. When you stand firm for what you believe, the men with guns are afraid of you."[7] Those women witnessed to the call that peace has to be *built* from *within* the affected communities everywhere, and peacemaking strategies must, therefore, be varied and adapted to each situation—including here in South Africa.

But because the agenda for peacemakers is clearly so complex and challenging, a vision—and indeed *an inner strength of spirit*—is needed to inspire and match the scope of that agenda. For Christians, that vision can be discovered in the New Testament, particularly through what Jesus proclaimed in the Sermon on the Mount in Matthew 5: "Blessed are the peacemakers, blessed are those who hunger and thirst for what is right; blessed are the gentle, the merciful; blessed are those persecuted in the cause of right"—and so on.

Reflecting on the cultural, economic, political, and religious context of Jesus's time, it seems clear that Jesus's life was one of nonviolent resistance to the structural evil in his situation. He

---

[7] Ruth Eglash, "These Israeli Women Marched from the Lebanese Border to Jerusalem. Here's Why," *The Washington Post*, October 19, 2016.

invited everyone, especially the excluded, into an inclusive community; he struggled to relieve the suffering of his people, both their physical suffering as a healer and the grinding suffering from an unjust political system that was breaking the spirit of the people; . . . but he stood against the growing violence that was emerging in response to this.

He stood up to and engaged the "powers" of his time, but he also wept over the city of Jerusalem because he understood the great anger and violence that was building up in the people. He could foresee that, unless the people took a different direction, that anger would play out in a violent revolt against Rome, which would lead to their destruction, as it did.

He taught, therefore, an alternative way to respond to the "enemy," the way of nonviolence. "Love your enemies. Do good to those who persecute you." Utopian? Maybe. But his teaching reflected his life and calls someone like myself to think in other terms about how to respond to war and violence. Archbishop Romero commented:

> The gospel's advice to turn the other cheek to an unjust aggressor, far from being passivity and cowardice, is evidence of great moral strength that can leave an aggressor morally defeated and humiliated. *The Christian can fight, but prefers peace to war,* was what Medellín said about this moral force of nonviolence (Medellín Documents, *Peace,* #15).[8]

This is all about a choice, a decision every person, group, and organization can make—what Romero, Hurley, Pope Francis chose to do, and what others of different faiths, like Mahatma Gandhi, and others who ascribe to no faith at all have done and continue to do. The choice, the decision is to be peacemakers who work to relieve peoples' suffering, try to change the economic and political structures that bring so much suffering to the vulnerable, and remove or transform the underlying causes of violence, conflict, and war so that there can be sustainable peace and economic justice,

---

[8] Romero, "Third Pastoral Letter," in *The Voice of the Voiceless,* 107ff.

especially for the excluded and the victims of conflict—but, to do all this without any form of violence. But, what is to be done when the rule of law and the human rights of others are violated? The challenge is to introduce the power of nonviolent responses to nations and communities, groups and individuals—to prevent wars and violence if possible, or to limit the effects of war and violence, and to bring healing, hope, and new beginnings after wars and violence have ended.

2

A Broken World

A broken world: While the last century knew the devastation of two deadly World Wars, the threat of nuclear war and a great number of other conflicts, today, sadly, we find ourselves engaged in a horrifying world war fought piecemeal. . . . We know that this "piecemeal" violence, of different kinds and levels, causes great suffering: wars in different countries and continents; terrorism, organized crime, and unforeseen acts of violence; the abuses suffered by migrants and victims of human trafficking; and the devastation of the environment.

—POPE FRANCIS, WORLD DAY OF PEACE MESSAGE 2017

Time and again Pope Francis has referred to what he calls a "third world war in installments"—bloody conflicts tied to a specific context such as South Sudan, Syria, or Iraq; violent attacks by extremist groups and individuals, whether in Pakistan or Paris, New York or Nigeria; and the overt violence of systematized repression as in the occupation of Palestine, the violations against the Rohingya in Myanmar, attacks against opposition groups by the Ethiopian government, or unrelenting street violence in Chicago and Baltimore. But also part of the violence that comprises a "third world war in installments" is structural or systemic violence: forced migration and the abuse or rejection of people seeking refuge; excessive expenditures on weapons systems, including nuclear weapons, or on preparations for war; cyber warfare; economic violence that causes or exacerbates poverty; and ecological violence.

The Many Expressions of Violence

The World Health Organizations's *World Report on Violence and Health* defines violence as "the intentional use of physical force or power, threatened or actual, against oneself, another person, or against a group or community that either results in or has a high likelihood of resulting in injury, death, psychological harm, maldevelopment, or deprivation."

Rajkumar Bobichand writes, "Violence is any physical, emotional, verbal, institutional, structural, or spiritual behavior, attitude, policy or condition that diminishes, dominates or destroys others and ourselves."[1] Norwegian sociologist Johan Galtung understands violence as

the avoidable impairment of fundamental human needs or, to put it in more general terms, the impairment of human life, which lowers the actual degree to which someone is able to meet their needs below that which would otherwise be possible. The threat of violence is also violence.[2]

In other words, Galtung said, "Violence is here defined as the cause of the difference between the potential and the actual, between what could have been and what is. Violence is that which increases the distance between the potential and the actual, and that which impedes the decrease of this distance."[3]

---

[1] Rajkumar Bobichand, "Understanding Violence Triangle and Structural Violence," kanglaonline.com, July 30, 2012.

[2] Johan Galtung, "Kulturelle Gewalt," in *Der Bürger im Staat* 43, no. 2 (1993), 106. In English, in Ragnar Müller, "Violence Typology by Johan Galtung" (n.d.), available online.

[3] Johan Galtung, "Violence, Peace, and Peace Research" (International Peace Research Institute, Oslo, 1969), available online.

Galtung's analysis of violence considers, for example, distinctions between physical and psychological violence, as well as between negative and positive violence. He asks whether violence is present when there is no "object that is hurt" (for example, the testing of nuclear weapons) or in which there is no subject (person) committing direct violence. Galtung refers to the type of violence when there is an actor that commits the violence as personal or direct and to violence in which there is no such actor as structural or indirect.

> In both cases, individuals may be killed or mutilated, hit or hurt in both senses of these words, and manipulated by means of stick or carrot strategies. But whereas in the first case these consequences can be traced back to concrete persons as actors, in the second case this might is no longer meaningful. . . . The violence is built into the structure and shows up as unequal power and consequently as unequal life chances.[4]

Galtung identified three types of violence: direct, cultural, and structural violence.

> Direct violence can take many forms. In its classic form, it involves the use of physical force, like killing or torture, rape and sexual assault, and beatings. Further, we understand that verbal violence, like humiliation or put downs, is also becoming more widely recognized as violence.[5]

> Structural violence exists when some groups, classes, genders, nationalities, etc. are assumed to have, and in fact do have, more access to goods, resources, and opportunities than other groups, classes, genders, nationalities, etc., and this unequal advantage is built into the very social, political, and economic systems that govern societies, states, and the world. These tendencies may be overt such as Apartheid or

---

[4] Ibid.

[5] Bobichand, "Understanding Violence Triangle and Structural Violence."

more subtle such as traditions or tendency to award some groups privileges over another.[6]

Cultural violence should be understood as those aspects of culture that can be used to justify or legitimate the use of direct or structural violence. The Stars and Stripes, Hammer and Sickle, flags, hymns, military parades, portraits of the leader, inflammatory speeches, and posters are all included in this category.[7]

The Latin American Catholic Bishops meeting in Medellín, Colombia, in 1968 wrote about what they called "institutionalized violence," another term for structural violence.

Justice is a prerequisite for peace. . . . In many instances Latin America finds itself faced with a situation of injustice that can be called institutionalized violence, when, because of a structural deficiency of industry and agriculture, of national and international economy, of cultural and political life, "whole towns lack necessities, live in such dependence as hinders all initiative and responsibility as well as every possibility for cultural promotion and participation in social and political life" [Paul VI, *The Development of Peoples*, no. 30], thus violating fundamental rights.

Many participants in the April 2016 conference on nonviolence and just peace were personally and painfully familiar with contemporary violence in all of its forms.

Living the Reality of Direct Violence and War

The Philippines

In her short paper submitted prior to the conference, Jasmin Nario-Galace, president of Pax Christi Pilipinas and executive director

---

[6] Ibid.

[7] Johan Galtung, in "Violence Typology by Johan Galtung."

of the Miriam College Center for Peace Education in Quezon City, wrote about the direct violence of war that has devastated the southern Philippines.

> The war in Mindanao is more than four decades old. The human cost is enormous: 120,000 people dead for the duration of the conflict; economic loss of twenty billion pesos (about US$400 million) on a daily basis; 982,000 people displaced from the all-out war in 2000 alone. The armed conflict has also led to the disruption of children's schooling; trauma, insecurity, and fear; the loss of livelihood or economic dislocation; and multiple burdens for women, among others. Women bear the pain and the brunt of keeping a family when men in the family are in the battlefield or have died in armed conflict. Women suffer from lack of facilities such as health and sanitation facilities when in evacuation centers. Women have also reportedly suffered from sexual harassment. An account from Kalinaw, Mindanao, for example, told of armed men who had raped and sexually violated women, "groped their breasts while allegedly searching for grenades." Women and their communities are normally reluctant to report rape and other cases of sex and gender-based violence out of fear and "because it was taboo to 'dishonor' the family."

South Sudan

Several participants in the conference live in South Sudan. After decades of war that set the context for Bishop Paride Taban's Kuron Peace Village, South Sudan finally gained its independence from the North in 2011. In less than two years, however, the country had fallen back into war, with tribal animosities and personal ambition making progress toward lasting peace seem impossible. In April 2017, members of the Religious Superiors' Association of South Sudan wrote:

> We have heard from our brothers and sisters some shocking and disturbing news. The country is immersed in violence and in a deep economic crisis. There have been many

killings, raping, burning of houses, and looting. Innocent people, including children, have been brutally killed. The rights and dignity of people have been grossly violated. Hundreds of thousands are internally displaced or refugees. Famine is a sad reality and the economic crisis increases hunger. Hatred, bitterness, and divisions have also increased. People feel traumatized and helpless. We are concerned that often church personnel have been harassed, intimidated, detained, and some have been killed. This civil war that keeps on revolving is evil and has claimed the lives of too many brothers and sisters and inflicted endless suffering on our people. What have we done to our humanness and the sacredness of life?[8]

During the first session of the April 2016 conference Fr. James Oyet Latansio, general secretary of the South Sudan Council of Churches, introduced himself in the following way:

"I come from the Republic of South Sudan. I serve the Lord in the South Sudan Council of Churches. I am a Catholic priest, from the Catholic Diocese of YEI. I was born in war; I grew up in war; I went to school in war. I was ordained a priest during war—the bishop hesitated as he was imposing the hand on me because there were artillery bombs flying over the Cathedral. So, my life has been always surrounded by violence. I live in a violent situation. I live by violence. I think violence. I look at things violently. If you ask me to draw something here, I will draw a violent image. This is true for me and for most of my South Sudanese brothers and sisters.

"Before I came here a small girl about nine years asked me, 'Father, where is your Jesus? Where is your Jesus? We are born in a violent situation, why are we not getting peace?

---

[8] Religious Superiors' Association of South Sudan, "Active Nonviolence: A Way to Build Lasting Peace In South Sudan" (April 28, 2017), available online.

You preach at the pulpit about peace, the peace of Jesus, but I say, where is it? I needed an answer because I'm also am in a crisis. I needed an answer."

Mexico

In the same session during the conference Pietro Ameglio, co-founder of the Mexican Peace and Justice Service and the Movement for Peace with Justice and Dignity said:

"In Mexico we have a very badly named drug war. It really is a war against people. It's a kind of war where everywhere there are people of the government, there are people from the gangs, and there are businessmen. It's not a war of government against organized crime, it's a war of groups, of gangs, where in every gang there are these different sectors. So society sees itself in the middle. 103,000 people have been killed in the last six years and 32,000 people are disappeared. To be disappeared is much worse than to be killed. In that situation the family stops living. Every phone call, every time something rings, you think it is your disappeared loved one. So, it devastates social organization.

"In the middle of a war in Mexico, we are not afraid, we are terrorized. It's different to be afraid than to be terrorized. And it's not so easy to struggle in the middle of terror. When you are terrorized, you lose the capacity to think, to reflect. Our society is terrorized. I work with victims and I also work in resistance for the land. It's a different situation. In land disputes, there are community victims, but in our drug war there are individual victims, families."

Croatia

Katarina Kruhonja, co-founder of the Center for Peace, Non-violence, and Human Rights in Osijek and recipient of the Right Livelihood Award, spoke during Session 1 about the violence that engulfed her community in 1991:

"For us ordinary people the war in Croatia, the violent dis-integration of Yugoslavia came suddenly, unexpectedly. We were confused, and the war, the logic of war, was spreading like wild fire. The growth of nationalism and enemy-making and the armed attacks were overwhelming. I found myself surrounded by Serbian forces that were bombing us. I started to think like everyone else that there was no other way. It is them or us. What we can do? And while we were praying in a small group, we thought and talked about what love your enemies might mean in this very concrete situation. Some-one said maybe the love for enemy in this situation is to kill him or them, to prevent him or them from committing more atrocities. That hit me very hard. I started to think every day what would it be to love my enemy in the middle of the war? I couldn't find an answer, but I made a decision. I said that killing my enemy is surely not how Jesus would love his enemy. So I chose to love my enemy as Jesus would. I didn't know what that would mean, but the choice itself re-ally was my Passover from the logic of the violence. I would be able to live again."

Sri Lanka

On May 18, 2009, the Sri Lankan government declared victory and an end to the civil war fought for twenty-six years with the Liberation Tigers of Tamil Eelam, the Tamil Tigers. For many Sri Lankans, however, the physical, emotional, and psychological wounds of war—the experiences of violence—have remained. Fr. Ashok Stephen, OMI, director of the Centre for Society and Religion in Colombo shared with other participants at Session 1:

"Sri Lanka was at war for the last twenty-six years. The war ended in 2009 but still the remnants of war are here and there. Still people are suffering. One thing people, especially from the north, are asking is what happened to the people who were surrendered to the government when the war was over in 2009. Fifteen buses of people were surrendered to the army, the armed forces, and to date the government has not said what had happened to them."

South Korea

In the reflection paper submitted by Columban Father Patrick Cunningham prior to the conference, he described the violence to earth and local communities by the construction of a naval base on Jeju Island, South Korea, and the militarization it represents.

Since 2011, the main focus of my work as the Columban Justice Peace and Integrity of Creation coordinator in Korea has been to highlight the issue of the Gangjeong Naval Base construction on the Island of Jeju (Island of World Peace) and to help promote and build international solidarity in opposition to the base and the militarization of Jeju Island.

With the installation of the base perimeter fence in September 2011 and the subsequent blasting of Gureombi Rock in March 2012, I have engaged in numerous protests, prayer vigils, and direct actions to help highlight the adverse environmental impact of the construction on the UNESCO designated biosphere reserve which includes soft coral communities located near Beom Island.

It is widely acknowledged that the base is a US-driven project aimed at containing China rather than enhancing South Korean security. In July 2012, the South Korean Supreme Court upheld the base's construction. It is expected to host US aircraft carriers, nuclear submarines, and US Navy Aegis destroyers, which are warships outfitted with nuclear defense systems (a key element of US first strike strategy).

Therefore, what was once labeled by the Korean government as an absolute preservation area and a national cultural asset, the Gangjeong Village, the living rocky coast and offshore waters were conveniently delisted to make way for the base construction. Official environmental designation has been literally washed away in the quest to build a naval base to facilitate the US military and its China containment policy in the Asia Pacific region.

President Obama's 2012 announcement of a "pivot" and the projection of US foreign and military power into the Asia Pacific region serves as the backdrop to the doubling of US military operations in the region as well as the deployment of US troops to Darwin, Australia, and base expansions in Guam, the Philippines, and Okinawa—all with the goal of strategically encircling and containing China. Since the United States is unable to contain and compete with China economically, it will use military might to control China's importation of vital resources such as oil, natural gas, and minerals needed to fuel its vast economic engine. This is a highly dangerous and provocative strategy by the Pentagon with the prospect of Gangjeong village not only acting as a port of call for US warships but also potentially becoming a target in this superpower war game.

On September 2, 2011, the beautiful Geurombi Rock and the Gangjeong coastline were closed off to Gangjeong villagers in order to prepare the coastline for demolition and lay the groundwork for base construction. A massive crackdown operation was undertaken by approximately 1,000 police mostly deployed from the mainland, resulting in thirty-six arrests and three people imprisoned. Access to Gureombi Rock was closed off once and for all, and a fifteen-foot-high wall was subsequently constructed to keep villagers away from the proposed base.

United States and Peru

Maryknoll Sister Joanne Doi lived in the altiplano of Peru among the Aymara people as the internal terrorism reached its peak (1983–94). Between 1980 and 2000, according to Peru's Truth and Reconciliation Commission, the political violence claimed almost seventy thousand lives, most of them indigenous. Joanne wrote prior to the conference the following reflection on her encounter as a US Japanese American with the underside of history.

Even as I was in pastoral ministry in Peru as a Maryknoll sister during those years, the resonance and affinities with the unknown world of the Aymara began to challenge and encourage me to enter into my own unknown world as a Japanese American woman, to enter into our "underside of history" during the WWII Internment period 1942–1946. My parents' and grandparents' generations were swept up into the "evacuation and relocation" to ten "internment camps" of those of Japanese ancestry who lived in the designated military security zone of exclusion (California, the western parts of Oregon and Washington, and the southern part of Arizona). Two-thirds were US citizens and more than half were children.

Uganda

Archbishop John Baptist Odama, archbishop of Gulu and former chairman of the Acholi Religious Leaders Peace Initiative (ARLPI), spoke to the conference in Session 3 about the years of violence in Northern Uganda:

> "For twenty-three years we were in war. The rebel group called the LRA, Lord's Resistance Army, and then the Government of Uganda, were engaged in war. As the common saying at home is, when two elephants are fighting, it is the grass which is under the feet of these elephants that is suffering.
>
> "So the civil population, the poor, especially children, and their mothers and their fathers and so on, they suffer. So we came to the sense that we must work for peace and promote harmony. I want to end with a statement of Pope St. John Paul II. He said, 'War is a lie, war is a lie. Why? Because it destroys what it says it wants to defend.' And I saw this happen under my eyes. And so I said no more war in this area. Let us move humanity to accept peace and not war anymore."

Afghanistan

Merwyn DeMello, a Mennonite Central Committee international service worker based in Kabul, Afghanistan, wrote a reflection paper he submitted prior to the conference:

> From 1994 to 2013 I served as a Maryknoll lay missionary in Japan, Tanzania, Zimbabwe, and the United States. Since 2014 and presently as Mennonite Central Committee international service worker based in Kabul, Afghanistan I am an Advisor to the peacebuilding project of a reputed organization with a long-term presence in country. I humbly venture that my life journey and work as a peacebuilder are intertwined within the principles of nonviolent presence and living. It is in my current role and experience that I present this reflection paper.
>
> In the Magnificat, Mary grounds herself within the community of the oppressed, of which she is a member. Mary is the beacon for God's plan to turn upside down the social hierarchy of the world order, of wealth and poverty, power and subjugation. God's covenant of love and mercy is an assurance of this new world order. Mary, prophet for the new age, heralds the new order—she is spokesperson for God's restorative justice. The question before me and us all called to be peacebuilders and co-creators of this vision is "What are the means toward this end?"
>
> My journey in faith brought me to Afghanistan, plagued by war over the last four decades. Shows of strength and power exacerbate and protract the cycles of violence that have direct, structural, and cultural manifestations. Direct violence is most visible in the active fighting between government forces and/or local security forces and armed opposition groups in many of Afghanistan's provinces. In the Afghan capital, Kabul City, where I live, interspersed with the periods of quiet are the suicide bombers' explosions targeting government officials, Afghan National Security Forces, international forces, foreign NGO and security sector

individuals and guest houses, and more recently civilians. Afghanistan's third largest city, Heart, whose founding dates back to 550–330 BC, has experienced in 2014–15 over fifty targeted shootings of individuals, including the 2015 abduction of a Jesuit priest, subsequently released. Currently swathes of territory in Baghlan province to the north are under siege from opposition forces—damage from raging battles has severely restricted the supply of electricity to all of Afghanistan.

At the interpersonal and community levels, violence rates, particularly for women, are high. The Afghan Independent Human Rights Commission (AIHRC) reported that in a nine-month period from September 2014 to June 2015 there were 4,250 reported cases of violence against women in Afghanistan; however, it is assumed that many more cases go unreported. Oxfam reports that 87 percent of Afghan women experience some form of abuse or forced marriage in their lifetime. The following types of violence against women have been reported: beatings, torture, rape, murders, forced self-immolations, forced marriage, giving Bad (retribution of a woman for a murder, to restore peace), and verbal/psychological abuse. In 2013, AIHRC reported 240 cases of honor killings.[9]

Structural violence can be defined as "the disabilities, disparities, and even deaths that result when systems, institutions, or policies meet some people's needs and rights at the expense of others."[10] One example would be in the justice realm where certain laws rather than being a deterrent allow impunity for perpetrators of violence against women or the plague of corruption within the justice system which allows impunity for perpetrators of violence of all kinds.[11]

---

[9] See the websites of the Revolutionary Association of the Women of Afghanistan, Oxfam, and the Afghan Independent Human Rights Commission.

[10] Lisa Schirch, *The Little Book of Strategic Peacebuilding: A Vision and Framework for Peace with Justice* (Intercourse, PA: Good Books, 2004), 22.

[11] Human Rights Watch, "Today We Shall All Die: Afghanistan's Strongmen and the Legacy of Impunity" (March 2015).

A recent example could be the secret meeting in Kabul of justice officials that overturned the death sentences for the four men charged with the murder of Farkhunda, a young woman brutally killed by a mob near a Kabul shrine after being falsely accused of burning the Koran. This occurred after the completion of a long public trial.

A second example is the corruption in several governmental institutions where power and wealth is consolidated into the hands of a few powerful people who then determine how the needs of others with less power are met. This contributes to widening disparities between rich and poor.

A third example of structural violence would be the unequal distribution of resources particularly between urban and rural areas. This can be the result of powerful individuals bestowing favors on some areas and not on others; fighting that prevents humanitarian aid organizations from reaching impoverished areas; development organizations that do not follow conflict-sensitive Do No Harm principles; or armed groups that deliberately block the flow of resources into certain areas. Included in this would be lack of schools in rural areas, particularly for girls.

A fourth example of structural violence impacting Afghanistan is the way global development policies bring benefits to richer nations exacerbating the unequal distribution of wealth, making recipient nations even poorer.[12]

Cultural violence includes the attitudes and beliefs that legitimize direct and structural violence and teach us about the power and necessity of violence.[13] In Afghanistan, because of the four decades of intense violence that people have experienced, those under forty years of age have not known a time their country has not been at war. Violent solutions to conflict are witnessed daily. Those who kill are made into

---

[12] Asia Pacific Forum on Women, Law, and Development, "The Road to Development Justice," video.

[13] Johan Galtung, "Cultural Violence," *Journal of Peace Research* 27, no. 3 (August 1990): 291–305.

heroes or martyrs by both sides in the current conflict. Guns are a common and acceptable feature of life in most areas of Afghanistan. Impunity is also a symptom of the cultural violence prevalent in Afghan society—a collective fear and acceptance of the rights of the powerful.

Cultural violence is evident in the way people internalize or normalize the violence or systems of violence around them. For example, a UNICEF study showed that 92 percent Afghan women believe that husbands have the right to beat their wives in specific instances.[14] The violence is legitimized through the attitudes, the patriarchal beliefs, and the structure of society, as well as how those attitudes translate into law, whether secular or religious.

We recognize that the perpetration of violence does not happen in isolation but is often linked directly to the experience of violence. Individuals, communities, and whole societies can be caught up in cycles of violence, unless deliberate steps are taken to break out of the cycle.[15]

Economic and Political Drivers of Violence

For much too long, powerful people and political decision makers have been promoting a paradigm that justifies enormous loss of human life and widespread destruction of the planet in pursuit of an elusive peace, false security, national geopolitical interests, and tremendous profits for a few people and companies. The consequences of this framework have been front and center in the lives of millions of people around the world. Hundreds of thousands in Afghanistan, Iraq, Pakistan, Yemen, Syria, Libya, and elsewhere have been killed or maimed; millions have been displaced; trauma, psychological damage, and moral injury are endemic; and violence is increasingly multidimensional as

---

[14] Donna Clifton, "Most Women in Afghanistan Justify Domestic Violence," Population Reference Bureau.

[15] See Carolyn Yoder, *The Little Book of Trauma Healing: When Violence Strikes and Community Is Threatened* (Intercourse, PA: Good Books, 2005).

racism, Islamophobia, and "othering" lead to war, street violence, and mass shootings.

Fear has been globalized. Every day we are reminded that violent extremism is spreading. Gang violence, organized crime, and militarized security forces hold many communities hostage. Rather than meeting treaty obligations to disarm, as agreed in the Nuclear Non-Proliferation Treaty nuclear-weapons states are spending fortunes to refurbish their nuclear arsenals.

War, preparations for war, trade in weapons—from handguns to extremely sophisticated delivery systems—and the sale of munitions are big business. World military expenditures in real terms for 2016 were US$1.7 trillion. As long as wars continue, tremendous contracts for weapons to replace bombs dropped and planes, drones, and other military equipment destroyed in conflict will be awarded to munitions companies. The Middle East, Africa, Mexico, and the "Northern Triangle" of Central America are awash in weapons that continue to fuel treacherous situations; a very dangerous arms race is under way in Asia; and the United States is struggling with a breathtaking epidemic of gun violence.

In the midst of war, traders and profiteers often manipulate prices, preying on desperate communities trying to survive. And in too many mineral-rich countries vicious warlords, unscrupulous corporations, and corrupt governments are fueling violence rather than trying to quell it.

Toward the end of the first session of the conference, having listened to many stories of direct violence experienced by participants from different countries and regions of the world, Chris Cole from England, founder of Drone Wars UK, said:

> "It is very inspiring for those of us who live in the North or West, to hear about the situation in South Sudan and Palestine and South Africa. All the very moving contributions that we've heard about humility and the audacity of the people are very inspiriting. But it would be a mistake, I think, if we focused our work on the visible signs of the violence in the world. There are major structures, invisible structures, global structures of violence that we also need to focus on,

particularly those of us in the West. We are not living in these situations, but we are part of the structures of violence that are casting many to their deaths around the globe and we need to challenge those structures as well. Pope Francis mentioned the war of indifference. We need to get involved, to challenge indifference and these structures of violence."

In an essay submitted prior to the conference, Chris Cole, Pat Gaffney, and Valerie Flessati, all from the UK, wrote:

The UK is a highly militarized country. We have the world's fourth largest military budget. We are a nuclear state, looking to renew our independent nuclear deterrent. We are the sixth largest arms exporter in the world. We have recently developed our own independent capability for drone warfare. We have been a key "coalition" member of various military interventions over the past sixteen years and have particularly strong military and political links in the Middle East, with Saudi Arabia and Israel, and Palestine in particular. We are deeply involved in the fuelling of war and conflict.

As well as projecting military force overseas, many UK citizens themselves experience violence that is related to poverty, exclusion, and racism. This manifests itself in knife and gun crime, especially among young people, or through acts of community or domestic violence.

A climate of fear is fostered, whether around the idea of terrorist threats or from the projection of "the other," refugees, and migrants, as threats to our way of life, economy, and more. This cultivation of fear could lead to more communal violence and more militarized approaches to domestic security policies.

Jean Stokan, from the United States, works with the Sisters of Mercy of the Americas and serves on the National Council of Pax Christi USA. She added that US policy also has caused or contributed to so much damage—from the first bombs in Iraq to Palestine and to Colombia—that we have to confess our sin as a country. Following Pope Francis and Archbishop Romero, the church needs to have a prophetic voice that is not afraid to talk about the arms race, the economic roots of violence, unbridled capitalism that is driving so many wars, the killing of those who are standing up for basic rights.

Violence is pervasive, both within and, at times, between nations. Its root causes are many, different, sometimes multidimensional, often interconnected. A wide array of manifestations—from war and preparations for war to street violence and terrorism—and their devastating personal and societal consequences present researchers and peace practitioners in these times with ever-increasing challenges. Why is just, enduring, sustainable peace so elusive? How can we humans fruitfully engage the complex systems that drive war and violence and build the peaceful world we all seek?

3

Nonviolence in a Violent World

As Christians we remain deeply convinced that the ultimate aim, that most worthy of the person and of the human community, is the abolition of war. We must therefore always commit ourselves to building bridges that unite rather than walls that separate; we must always help to find a small opening for mediation and reconciliation; we must never give in to the temptation of considering the other as merely an enemy to destroy, but rather as a person endowed with intrinsic dignity, created by God in his image.

—POPE FRANCIS,
OCTOBER 2015

Active, Courageous Nonviolence

During the April 2016 conference in Rome, participants from war zones and areas spoke about unrelenting violence, but they also shared stories about active nonviolence and courageous work for peace in violent contexts. Speaking from their own experience (not attempting to articulate a universal opinion), their testimony provided a solid foundation for the ultimate insistence of the conference that creative, well-planned, scaled-up, strategic nonviolence could play a more significant role in quelling the violences of our world.

Afghanistan

During the third session of the conference, Merwyn DeMello said:

"When I knew that I was coming to this conference I consulted with my Afghan colleagues and one of the things I said, 'What message should I take? I wish one of you, as a practitioner of Islam, as a practitioner of peacebuilding, as an individual who professes to Islam that embodies nonviolence, that embodies peacebuilding, you should be the one going. You have the legitimacy to talk about Afghanistan, to talk about Islam, and peacebuilding and nonviolence.' So they said to me, 'Convey to your friends there how proud we are to be Afghan.'

"Therefore, I thought the least I could do is greet you with the greeting of peace, which is *as-salaam-aleikum*, and then speak a few word in Dari to you.

"One of the most beautiful aspects of this culture is greeting and being greeted back. People cannot fail to respond to me if I say *as-salaam-aleikum*. There's a smile on their face, and if they're eating something, they are bound to invite me to join them. I've often sat with people right on the sidewalk and eaten a piece of naan or, if it happens to be lunchtime, I've eaten their lunch with them. Or, if it's during Ramadan, I fast with them as a sign of solidarity and therefore live just peace and nonviolence.

"My greatest inspiration is a man called Abdulla. He was my first encounter with a vendor. Every Wednesday evening I carry two bags in my hand and go grocery shopping. Abdulla has a small cart on which he sells onions, potatoes, tomatoes, and whatever vegetable is in season. Abdulla is the kindest man I have ever met. He not only sells me his vegetables, but I work with him on a credit basis. Money has no significance in Afghanistan; it's the relationship behind the money that matters. That comes from my African roots as well. Abdulla has an old kind of scale on which I set one kilo of tomatoes and one kilo of something else, but they only add up to one-and-a-half kilos; he tilts the scale in such a way that it looks even, and he gives me whatever I want. And then, because I'm at the beginning of a pretty long walk through the market, he allows me to store my bag on his cart.

"Abdulla has been for me the channel to meeting leaders in society where he lives. I may not ever achieve anything in my formal work—we make plans and then things are postponed and nothing happens—but I will have the legitimacy of relationships and maybe, maybe somewhere down the line I will have *lived* just peace and nonviolence. Thank you."

Experience in Nonviolent Strategies

Listening to the diversity of ways that nonviolence was effective, those assembled at the conference also were convinced that the institutional Catholic Church could help build humanity's understanding of the potential for nonviolence to both shape the hearts of people immersed in violence and support the development of evidence-based nonviolent strategies more consistent with Jesus's words and witness.

Important research, analysis of case studies, and ongoing dialogue among activists and academics, peacemakers, and policymakers are beginning to reveal important lessons about what makes for lasting and just peace—what some in the United Nations are now referring to as "sustaining peace."[1] For example, Mary Anderson and Marshall Wallace examined thirteen case studies of communities that opted out of war, including the Jaghori district in Ghazni, Afghanistan; Tuzla in Bosnia; the peace villages in Colombia; Gaza province in Mozambique; the Muslim community in Rwanda; Fiji; Burkina Faso; Manipur state in India; four communities in Kosovo; the Ukwa region in Nigeria; zones of peace in the Philippines; the village of Lawana in the Moyamba district of Sierra Leone; and Madhu in Sri Lanka. Their conclusion was:

---

[1] Youssef Mahmoud and Anupah Makoond, "Sustaining Peace: What Does It Mean in Practice?" *International Peace Institute* (April 8, 2017).

The prevention of violent conflict is doable. Normal people living normal lives have the option to say no to war. Normal leaders in systems that already exist can respond to and support their people in nonengagement. This kind of conflict prevention does not require special training, new leadership, or special funding. It occurs repeatedly and around the world in different types of conflict, and we can learn from it.[2]

They have begun to identify crucial common characteristics in the different communities that deliberately avoided being drawn into war.[3]

The Philippines

Pax Christi-Pilipinas leader Jasmin Nario-Galace wrote clearly in an essay submitted before the conference about the need to end the forty-year-old war in Mindanao and the role of active non-violence in the tedious process toward peace which, despite the failure of the Philippine Congress to pass the Bangsamoro Basic Law, continues.

War in Mindanao and everywhere else must be put to an end. This is the reason why we, at the Center for Peace Education-Miriam College and Pax Christi Pilipinas, have ardently supported the peace process in Mindanao. The peace process is a nonviolent approach to ending the war that has caused misery to many.

What are the strengths of this nonviolent approach? One, it has allowed the participation of many to look collaboratively at the prospects for ending a war, the negotiating parties, the civil society, the academe, the religious leaders, people in the community directly affected by armed conflict, and the international community, among others. The Center

---

[2] Mary B. Anderson and Marshall Wallace, *Opting Out of War: Strategies to Prevent Violent Conflict* (Boulder, CO: Lynne Rienner Publishers, 2015).
[3] Ibid., 10.

for Peace Education, for example, led many consultations among women in conflict-affected communities, asking them what they wanted to see in the Bangsamoro Basic Law (BBL) meant to establish the political entity and structure of government of the Bangsamoro people.[4] These perspectives we submitted to those in charge of drafting and adopting the law. Hence, this peace process has given that space for those in the margins to be heard. Additionally, this nonviolent conflict resolution approach is both an ethical and a practical choice. The ceasefire that is in effect gave the people a chance to experience a situation of "no war," a respite from the running and hiding caused by air strikes when armed conflict was still raging.

This peace process has given a space to the majority of the Filipinos to know who the Bangsamoro people are, a people whose narrative is almost absent from Philippine history textbooks. The peace process has presented to us an opportunity to transform mindsets replete with stereotypes and attitudes that are intolerant. It has given hope to many that soon they will be leading a life of normalcy and stability. For the women we spoke with, this process has given them hope that doors will open for them to meaningfully participate in the public space particularly in political affairs. It gave them a chance to dream: "Our children will soon be able to go to school uninterrupted." "We will soon have gainful employment and have the ability to provide for the needs of the family." "The episode of running for our lives will now come to an end." The peace process has also paved the way to bustling socioeconomic activities and the development of infrastructure in a region which is the

---

[4] Bangsamoro people are defined in the BBL as "those who at the time of conquest and colonization were considered natives or original inhabitants of Mindanao and the Sulu archipelago and its adjacent islands including Palawan, and their descendants, whether of mixed or of full blood, shall have the right to identify themselves as Bangsamoro by ascription or self-ascription. Spouses and their descendants are classified as Bangsamoro" (http://www.rappler.com).

poorest in the country. Most important, it presents the opportunity to correct a historical injustice committed against the Bangsamoro people. Correcting such injustice can help pave the way for healing and reconciliation.

South Sudan

The war continued in South Sudan, beginning in December 2013, less than three years after the new nation's independence. Women were viciously attacked, including in the capital, Juba, when they ventured out to find food or water for their families. Hundreds of thousands were displaced and famine reared its ugly head. But even as the violence escalated, the South Sudan Conference of Catholic Bishops in June 2016 echoed the appeal from the Rome conference in its "Statement of Encouragement and Hope." Without suggesting simplistic solutions to the urgent need to protect vulnerable people, the bishops wrote:

> We must protest at the ethic of violence in our country. We reiterate the message of the Pontifical Council for Justice and Peace and Pax Christi International April 2016 conference on Nonviolence and Just Peace, that violence is never the solution and simply leads to more violence. We wish to challenge the militaristic culture in South Sudan, where even civilians carry assault rifles. We condemn the arms trade which provides these weapons and we stress the need for peaceful disarmament of civilians. We abhor the fact that thousands of young men are carrying arms when we don't have enough money to provide basic services to our own people; this is a misuse of our national resources. We are appalled to hear reports that there are still many child soldiers. We beg that the lives of our children be spared; let them prepare for their future through education rather than being trapped in violence.

During Session 1 of the conference John Ashworth, who works with the churches in South Sudan, said:

"I arrived in South Sudan thirty-three years ago, one month before the civil war started. I've now seen the end of that civil war and the beginning of a new civil war. So again, that ties in with what Maria [Stephen] said, that violent conflict doesn't solve the problem. Violent conflict leads to more conflict.

"I want to pick up very briefly on two points I've heard this morning. One is about the ordinary people. In our experience in South Sudan, the ordinary people do not want war, and that's been said about other countries too. Of course there are people who want war. There are vested interests. There are young men for whom fighting is a very exciting way of life. As our brother from Japan [Bishop Taiji Katsuya] said, there are people who perhaps haven't been directly affected, who haven't realized there's a crisis, and so they're not antiwar. But the ordinary people don't want war, the ones who are affected. And that's why much of the work of the church in South Sudan has been at the grassroots. It's a question of empowering the ordinary people to find a way of stopping their leaders from making war. And also, they're often being manipulated by their leaders, so it's a way of empowering them to resist the manipulation of their leaders to take them to war.

"We, I think, are probably the ones who coined the phrase 'people to people.' We did a lot of what we call people-to-people dialogue. People to people, peace and reconciliation at the grassroots. . . . We started all this before we'd ever heard of peacebuilding, these technical terms and all these wonderful academics you know who've actually written about it. But we learned later about John Paul Lederach's pyramid model, where you've got the grassroots, the middle level, and the high level. We don't neglect the high level, as the bishop said. Our leaders talk to the president and the head of the rebels and others, but our main concentration is at the grassroots level to empower those people to put pressure on the next level and the next level. . . .

"The other thing I've picked up on is trauma. I don't know whether the word has been mentioned, but it's certainly been implied in some of what's been said. After what is effectively six decades of conflict in South Sudan, from the 1950s to the early 1970s, then from the 1980s through to 2005, and now again since 2013, trauma features broadly in everybody's life experience. I'm not a trauma expert, so there may be different types of trauma—long-term trauma, short-term trauma, immediate exposure, secondary exposure, all these things, experts will tell you. But the reality is, if a country has been in conflict for sixty years, then everybody in that country has been born into trauma, has been traumatized by their parents who were born into trauma. The culture of the country is one of violence, so even if you aren't actually exposed to physical violence, you're in this violent, traumatized culture. And so, in fact, to be honest, even in some of the people who've spoken today, you can detect trauma, and probably in the way I'm speaking as well.

"If we want to bring peace, and in a nonviolent way, then we also have to face trauma. Again, Bishop Taban gave us an example; our leaders are afraid, they are traumatized also. And they're afraid of what's going to happen to them if they make peace. And what do we do? Probably we'll threaten them with the International Criminal Court. Is that a non-violent solution? How is that going to affect a traumatized person to say, 'Hey, if you make peace we're going to punish you?' The young men who are doing the killing, what are we going to do about them? Child soldiers in many places, what are we going to do about them? We have a traumatized community."

Mexico

Pietro Ameglio spoke in Session 1 from a very different but also extremely violent context about the challenge of promoting nonviolence:

"We have the experience in Chiapas of a ceasefire. It's a very hard job to keep a ceasefire. It's an art, nonviolence, because the sides continuously provoke the spiral of violence. There is a continuous push to violence, to vengeance, to different provocations. In Mexico there is a deep culture of violence because people normalize violence, think that it's the only way. We have made a big cultural mistake by putting the word *security* over peace. People think that peace is security, but security is a military concept, not a peaceful concept. It comes from the army. And everybody wants security—it's not only a way of speaking, it's a reality every day in the streets. They don't think of peace in the sense of justice. How can you make people understand that militarization, even if it seems to provide more security, really is the provocation of war, continuous war. I don't know how you challenge that."

Croatia

Katarina Kruhonja reflected in Session 1 on how she would defend life without taking life:

"My next step was to realize that to kill is not to love. But what would that mean for instance if I were to be in the situation to defend my life? My next answer: I would defend life but not by killing. And then, but what would happen if I had to defend the lives of my children? So I said again, I would defend life but not by killing another. So it was a very radical pacifistic point, and fortunately I was not ever in this situation. I don't know what I would do, actually, in such a situation. But this passover from the logic of violence very quickly opened up my mind and my heart to figure out what I could do for peace in the middle of war. Soon I met someone who was an ethicist and a conscientious objector. We started to think together about what we could do for peace in the middle of the war. That was the beginning of the peace movement, of peace activism in Croatia in the middle of the war."

South Korea

In his essay submitted prior to the conference Patrick Cunningham continued his story about nonviolent attempts to protect Gureombi Rock:

> Contrary to government expectations, the people rose up. They began to occupy the land and use their bodies to get in the way of construction equipment in order to protect sacred Gureombi Rock. There are stories of peace activists, villagers, Catholic priests, and supporters sleeping on the rocks for months at a time and stories of others having been arrested for obstructing construction equipment. Priests and supporters celebrating mass on Gureombi Rock have become a potent symbol of nonviolent resistance and their witness is a continuation of the centuries-long reverence for the rocky coast as a sacred site and an integral part of the communal life of the village.
>
> With daily mass being celebrated in front of the naval base, many peace activists have been joining in, speaking out, sitting in, fasting, praying, and taking nonviolent action to stop the destruction of this beautiful and pristine coastline.
>
> Inspired by Jeju's Bishop Peter Kang U-il's prophetic stance in voicing opposition to the base from the very beginning, Father Mun Jeong Hyen's brave witness and constant presence at the gate, and Professor Yang Yoon Mo, a Catholic and Jeju native who was first arrested in April 2011 for pitching his tent on Gureombi and living there for years in order to impede construction work, many others have followed suit and joined the peace movement in Gangjeong.
>
> Throughout the nine years of struggle and opposition to the base there has been a strong spirit of collaboration among the various faith groups. International delegations and solidarity visits from international activists have been a mainstay of the struggle. This support continues to arrive and will help sustain the nonviolent resistance to the militarization of Jeju island now that the base has been completed.

United States and Peru

In her preconference reflection paper, Maryknoll Sister Joanne Doi shared deeply about her experience of living in Peru at the height of the internal terrorism experienced by that Andean country. The creativity and spiritual practices that formed the responses of so many indigenous communities to the violence of extremist groups and government forces, as well as to the violence of extreme poverty illustrate dimensions of active nonviolence that are often overlooked. Joanne wrote:

> Instead of resignation, retaliation, or capsizing from fear, I witnessed defiant hope and a tenacity of life embodied in spiritual practices and gestures of solidarity whether it be struggling against a frost or terrorist attack or the economic crisis. The Solidarity Office of the Prelature worked together with such popular religious practices and the cosmology that understands all peoples and the earth as interrelated. Reaching out to the local police to provide a space to reflect on their experiences of trauma, violence, and escalating fear proved helpful in reconnecting them to their own local communities and treatment of their own people. Festivals for Peace with *pasacalles* (parades for peace) and contests for peace songs counteracted the climate of fear and isolation. Maintaining their popular religious practices of pilgrimage to sacred sites strengthened their identity, resilience, and hope across time as they touched the deep memory of the earth and their ancestors. . . .
>
> I reconnected with my own heritage by participating in the annual Manzanar Pilgrimage, a return to the site of the Japanese American concentration camp. Such pilgrimages revisit shadowed ground, uncovering sacred traces of suffering and hope. The land holds memory. The cemetery obelisk at Manzanar expresses the message: "This is the place of consolation for all of humanity." It is about reconnection with each other, with our ancestors, with mystery and the depth of life. It is not an escape like tourism, but a

return to the center of pivotal events that have marked us and to narratives implanted in the land itself. The pilgrim's journey seeks a restoration of wholeness by a re-centering, a re-entering, recovery of history, and recovering from history. It is a rediscovery that we are part of a living and vital collective memory. It creates a space for community to mourn and honor our dead and our losses, as the losses endured that cannot be recovered require the ability to mourn, a measure of our humanity, rather than be forgotten or compromised. The pilgrimage practice engenders compassionate relatedness and solidarity with those facing similar conditions today: Arab Americans in a post 9/11 world, undocumented immigrants, family detention centers (for women and children fleeing violence), Syrian refugees. It begs the question and concern for reparations for African Americans and Native Americans in the United States.

In Lima, the capital of Peru, there is a garden with a stone that symbolizes *El Ojo que Llora,* the Crying Eye, in remembrance and mourning for those who suffered and died during the terrorism years. Although it is still a contested space, because many want to forget those years, the desire to remember so that it "never happens again" is in the background. This sentiment is also expressed at the Manzanar Pilgrimages. There has been a realization however, that such dynamics are often happening and we fail to perceive them. Simply remembering and mourning will not deter such dynamics but may teach a healthy vigilance and strong interrelatedness in order to respond in compassion, to break the cycle of violence. How are these kinds of popular religious practices considered practices of active nonviolence? How do we learn from the wisdom of cultures that have lived through cycles of violence or centuries of oppression? . . . How do we deepen our Catholic sacramental practices by connecting them to our Catholic social teachings and practice of nonviolence?

Afghanistan

Merwyn DeMello continued his preconference reflection on the strengths and opportunities created by active nonviolence in the challenging context of war-torn Afghanistan:

> The culture and philosophy of active nonviolence shaped our Peacebuilding Project activities dedicated to the goal of greater peace and stability in Afghan homes, communities, and organizations. We look at opportunities and gateways for peace that exist in the Afghan culture and traditions and that lie embedded in the Islamic faith. The pathways created by active nonviolence give voice to and build the capacity of the majority who choose the path of active nonviolence. . . .
>
> Participants value diversity in their communities, accept, appreciate and celebrate it! The Afghan society is characterized by diversity. Afghanistan is made up of seven major ethnic groups—Pashtun 42 percent, Tajik 27 percent, Hazara 9 percent, Uzbek 9 percent, Aimaq 4 percent, Turkmen 3 percent, and Balochand 2 percent. These percentages are a point of contestation among ethnic groups as there is not an independently conducted census that is reliable. Pashai, Nuristani, Gujjar, Arab, Brahui, and Pamiri are additional ethnic groups present in smaller numbers. The main languages are Pashtu and Dari but there are also numerous minority languages such as Aimaq, Arabic, Ashkun, Baluchi, Gujari, Hazaragi, Kazaki, Moghili, Uzbeki, Turkmani, Pashai, Nuristani, and Pamiri. Islam is the national religion, although Sikhism, Hinduism, Judaism, and Sufism are also present. Among the Muslims, the majority are Sunni Muslims of the Hanafi school, a smaller number of Shi'a, and few Twelver (Imamis) and Ismaili Muslims.
>
> Afghanistan has been able to hold its ethnic diversity in balance for centuries, possibly through oppressive means, but also through networks of relationships that emerge when people live in close proximity. Civil society groups also speak about the importance of rising above ethnic divisions.

In our work, we are sensitive to the need to build a language and a culture of diversity in Afghanistan. We challenge ourselves and others to answer the question: "How can we promote diversity within our current work?" Our educational programs try to build trust and reduce prejudice . . . raising awareness about cycles of violence and trauma healing and the importance of those concepts in building peace.

The last forty years of war have had an impact on the mental health of Afghans. In one of the only mental health surveys conducted in Afghanistan, research from 2002 found that 62 percent of the respondents experienced at least four trauma events in the previous ten years.[5] These trauma events included lack of food and water, lack of shelter, imprisonment, serious injury, sudden fleeing, forced separation from family, murder of family members, and rape, to name a few. Over 60 percent reported that they were experiencing depression and anxiety. Over 40 percent had symptoms of Post Traumatic Stress Disorder. Feelings of hatred were high for over 80 percent of the respondents.

Our work integrates concepts of trauma healing and cycles of violence into our peacebuilding curriculum. At the same time we look for ways to partner with organizations that have community mental health programming so as to make closer connections between addressing mental health issues and healing collectively from historical trauma.

Participants use conflict resolution skills in their day to day life. Tensions between traditional and modern cultural norms contribute to conflict in Afghanistan. These conflicts can emerge at different levels in society from the family level, as younger generations challenge the older generations, to the national level as armed groups rooted in the

---

[5] Barbara Lopes Cardozo, "Mental Health, Social Functioning, and Disability in Postwar Afghanistan," *The Journal of the American Medical Association* 292, no. 5 (August 4, 2004).

traditional culture threaten those who are attempting to change the culture.

Five cultural tensions impact people's lives:

1. The emphasis on shame and honor, though this is slowly changing. New generations are more interested in right/wrong beliefs.[6]
2. The clash between traditional and modern norms in the expression of views and opinions.
3. The power exerted by the lens of religion and religious beliefs. This influences people's life actions and their response to conflict. Everything is evaluated through the filter of religion. However, for those who are not educated or who live in rural areas, these religious beliefs may stem more from the beliefs of the local mullah, who holds a lot of power in rural and traditional areas. The people the mullah leads may not know that they are not following the true teachings of Islam. In modern cultures people practice Islam according to their own readings of the Qur'an and the Hadith, but they may not understand the essence of why they are doing it or how they should do it. Islamic principles of nonviolence and peacebuilding are a religious framework for rooting practice within the context of a nonviolent response.
4. Traditional beliefs value family, but the modern culture is more interested in power and money.
5. In the traditional culture government and religion should be closely linked; in the modern culture, people are calling for a separation between the two.

The goal of our activities is to provide tools, resources, spaces, and processes that contribute to a just peace. In a society that has over its history of forty years been embedded in conflict, a just peace calls for establishment of mecha-

---

[6] See Roland Muller, "Honor and Shame in a Middle Eastern Setting," Nabataea.net (2000).

nisms that will promote a culture of nonviolent resolution of conflict. Our project promotes practices that apply indigenous methods and tools that are culturally and religiously appropriate in teaching about and resolving conflicts. It is deliberate in creating, promoting, and facilitating these methods for peace education and peacebuilding strategy. The project incorporates Islamic principles of nonviolence into its peacebuilding work—Islamic nonviolence principles exhort adherents to nonviolent practice and living. The project seeks to understand and build upon this platform in the performance of its work. It promotes the incorporation of peacebuilding processes into Shuras and Jurgas, community-based institutions that are intertwined with the lives of people in Afghanistan.

Uganda

During the third session of the conference Archbishop Jean Baptiste Odama shared some of his experience with Joseph Kony and the Lord's Resistance Army in Northern Uganda:

"One basic underlining point is this one: Human beings want to be listened to. Second, they want to be loved. Third, yesterday Bishop Taban said they want to be trusted. . . . An interreligious group of Muslims, Orthodox, Anglicans, and Catholics started to promote that sense of trusting the government, the rebels. . . .

"And we became like a bridge, linking them. That was the first thing we did. Second, we began to do advocacy to rally other people to support this idea of dialogue between these two people. And we went to many, many, many countries, including the Sudan, especially South Sudan, who participated. . . . The process of our negotiations took about two years. And in the end, the two sides disarmed themselves in our region, particularly in the northern part of Uganda, where I am. The rebels put down their arms, the government put down its arms, and they decided to agree not to continue this war in Uganda. Unfortunately, the final peace agreement was not signed. Up to now it's not signed."

Kenya

Writing before the conference, Elizabeth Kanini Kimau shared how nonviolence was key to transforming the Rendille-Borana conflict in Northern Kenya:

The Leyai IDP camp was inhabited by Rendille community. While there, I observed that the Rendille and Borana communities were deeply divided and never interacted. Each community used its own source of water, means of transport and never traded with each other. They perceived each other as an enemy and whoever killed an enemy was praised and termed as a hero. I witnessed situations where people were killed and cattle were raided. The pain of loss, bitterness, anger, was temporarily "relieved" after revenge.

As I interacted with the children I learned that the enmity and hatred had been passed from generation to generation leaving the conflict in a vicious cycle. Whenever I asked the children to draw, they all drew guns, people killing each other, and cattle being raided. I asked different questions at different times. What will you do when you grow up? "I will go kill Borana and take back our cattle." Who created your parents? "God." Who created parents of Borana children? "The Devil." When I bring Borana children what will you do with them? "We will kill them." My interaction with the pupils informed me of an urgent need to cut the chain of enmity and hatred.

The hatred and enmity between Rendille and Borana communities was a big obstacle to any dialogue or attempt to solve disputes constructively. I heard from the local communities that many peace meetings ended up violently. In addition I observed that any act of violence was reacted to with excessive violence. If cattle were raided and a person killed, revenge was immediate, and it was doubled in many cases.

Many victims of revenge were innocent people, especially from Songa and Jaldesa locations at the border of the two communities. The revenge mission escalated the violence to a very high magnitude, leaving the area very insecure.

The deep-rooted culture of violence and revenge could only be transformed if people changed the way they perceived each other and communicated. Consequently their violent actions will change. I met a team from Germany who were training on nonviolent communication. Together, we introduced nonviolence between Borana and Rendille communities. We began by training the elders, who are the key decision makers. They were taken away from the violence zone to a peaceful area (more than 600km [over 370 miles]). The elders started to interact, listen to each other; and perceive each other as human beings. They were able to sit and discuss the violence which has enslaved them. The elders went back to Marsabit as a team and when people saw them together in Marsabit town they asked, "When did Rendille and Borana elders start talking together?" These elders visited various villages to ask people to unite and take responsibility to build their own peace. Secondly, a team of Morans/warriors (key perpetrators to the conflict) were trained in nonviolent communication. Some confessed how they were to kill each other during several violent attacks. They decided to remain friends. When they went back they resolved to preach peace to their peers and keep them from raiding or killing. The women whose children and husbands had been killed by the bloody conflicts were also trained. All these people became agents of peace in their region.

The language of nonviolence changed the perception of an enemy to a human being whom they can collaborate with in development activities. Consequently the elders who are key decision makers started holding dialogues and resolving disputes before they escalated to violence.

Incidences of killing and raids have been highly reduced. People living in IDP camps like Leyai have gone back to their farms and resumed agricultural activities. In May 2014, they contributed 5,000 kgs [11,000 pounds] of maize to areas affected by drought in Marsabit County. There was enhanced communication where each community started alerting the other in case they sensed any danger. The two communities started trading together and using the same means of transport. Some Rendille started working as casual workers in Borana farms. Elders started tracing raided cattle and returning them to the owners. Criminals are punished with no regard for which group they are. The elite youth took responsibility for promoting interaction between Rendille and Boran youth through sports and parties, which has promoted good relationships among the young people. Consequently the Rendille and Borana have now lived in a peaceful environment for the last three years after many years of bloody conflict.

United Kingdom

Chris Cole, Valerie Flessati, and Pat Gaffney of Pax Christi UK described in a preconference paper some of the ways in which communities and organizations in the UK have directly challenged the culture of militarism using strategies of nonviolent social change:

- Working to reframe security, away from the dominant military model towards one that sees human security in terms of food, health, education, spiritual well-being, just and loving relationships. We have produced ecumenical briefings/teaching resources and a DVD, *Give Peace a Budget,* on this and use the Global Day of Action on Military Spending as one tool to engage communities in critical thinking/decision making about priorities and budgets for war or for peace.
- Campaigning and advocacy work against policies of military violence, for example, the renewal of the Trident nuclear program and the UK's involvement in and profiteering from the global arms trade from a moral,

humanitarian, and legal perspective. Our distinctive contribution to this is to promote Catholic Social Teaching and the words and messages of Pope Francis.

- Working with teachers/young people to help them resist the marketing of the armed forces in our schools and communities. We do this through workshops, talks, resources, and cooperation with groups such as Veterans for Peace.
- Taking our vision, liturgy, and prayer to places that prepare for war, such the Ministry of Defense, military bases, arms-producing companies, and arms fairs and exhibitions. This is another distinctive contribution which we offer, surfacing the language, symbols, direct actions that name, expose, and confront militarism. In this way we keep alive and affirm the tradition of nonviolent witness and civil disobedience.
- Attempting to engage the church and bishops' conference in all of the above, recognizing that there is often a very ambiguous relationship between the church and the military in the UK. An example of this is the role of military chaplains.

Education and formation in peace and active nonviolence.

- We have trained in and offered the *From Violence to Wholeness* program, adapting it for use in the UK with the title *In the Direction of Nonviolence.* We produce resources that celebrate and promote the success of nonviolence including our brochure/exhibition *60 Nonviolent Victories of the Past Century.*
- We seek out and promote the witness of Christian peacemakers in order to better understand the various approaches to peacemaking. For example, to explore the place of conscience and objection to war we use the life of Franz Jägerstätter and of Veterans for Peace today.
- To explore the place of nonviolent accompaniment in peacemaking we support and promote the Ecumenical Accompaniment Program in Palestine and Israel and Christian Peacemaker Team programs in Palestine. Members of Pax Christi UK have been Ecumenical Accompaniers who share their invaluable experiences on their return.

- We have worked with families bereaved through knife violence who have chosen to reject anger and revenge. We have been able to offer them some support and create opportunities for them to share their experiences with teachers and young people. We hope that this may avert street/youth violence, offering young people, their families and teachers skills and language to better respond to provocation and threats.

Ongoing Conversation

Peter Prove, director of the World Council of Churches Commission of the Churches on International Affairs

"I want to ask all the panelists, but maybe especially Francisco and the archbishop, about some of the built-in assumptions we have about whether or not it's possible to dialogue with certain actors. In the current context we think especially of ISIS as being fundamentally not amenable to dialogue and how to deal with that. But when we hear the testimony that Francisco gave about the sort of atrocity that he described it's really not a million miles from what ISIS does. The same can be said about the LRA (Lord's Resistance Army), and so I would like to invite them to reflect more and to encourage us not to assume that there is no possibility of dialogue with even those who seem not amenable to it."

Archbishop Odama, Northern Uganda

"Thank you for the question. With the LRA and the government of Uganda, particularly the LRA, there was no place that we could talk with them. My argument all the time was, Are there people the LRA will talk to and trust? Why don't we find these people and address the issues for all concerned through those the LRA trusts and are willing to talk to? And indeed that was at the end our entry point. Then, we began to ally ourselves with those whom they trust and they can talk to, to be their friends. That was making LRA our friends. But we took the principle, as an interreligious group, that the LRA and the government were our children. So we love them both. We don't hate any of them. What we are not happy about is their fighting. And that was how we entered in. Thanks be to God."

Fr. Francisco DeRoux, SJ, founder of the Magdalena Medio Peace and Development Program and highly respected advocate for peace in Colombia

"My conviction is that dialogue transforms people everywhere. I know five people, for instance, I met them for the first time thirty years ago, who are totally different now because of dialogue. But this is different in any culture. In Colombia, where we have a Catholic country, going to see the guerrillas immediately after a massacre, immediately after an attack they had done. It was just after they've acted we've gone to see them. And we tried to respect them always, to tell them that we don't understand what they are doing, but we believe they are doing that because they think this is the best thing they can do for mankind or for the Colombian people. Then we start the dialogue, inviting them to be consistent with humanity, with human dignity in order to get the transformation of the conscience. It is always possible. I know that."

Eli McCarthy, justice and peace director for the Conference of Major Superiors of Men, author of Becoming Nonviolent Peacemakers: A Virtue Ethic for Catholic Social Teaching and US Policy

"These are really great examples; they are hopeful for whatever situation. We do have examples of ISIS actually negotiating with other groups, for example, around hostages, prisoners, and humanitarian-aid access. They are talking to people, and I think this point about identifying people they trust, people with credibility, is huge. We've seen that principle also to be effective with the Cure Violence model for preventing gang violence in Honduras, the United States, and elsewhere."

In April 2017, responding to a context that was quite different but extremely violent and very difficult, Pope Francis sent a message to Cardinal Blase Cupich of Chicago:

Please convey to the people of Chicago that they have been on my mind and in my prayers. I know that many families have lost loved ones to violence. I am close to them, I share in their grief, and pray that they may experience healing and reconciliation through God's grace. I assure you of my support of the commitment you and many other local leaders are making to promote nonviolence as a way of life and a path to peace in Chicago. . . . I urge all people, especially young men and women, to respond to Dr. King's prophetic words—and know that a culture of nonviolence is not an unattainable dream, but a path that has produced decisive results. The consistent practice of nonviolence has broken barriers, bound wounds, healed nations—and it can heal Chicago.[7]

At the same time, Cardinal Cupich pledged a quarter of a million dollars and established a venture philanthropy fund called the Instruments of Peace to support grassroots antiviolence initiatives. He also announced that more parishes would invest in social services and youth programs to reduce poverty and violence throughout the city with one of the highest homicide rates in the United States.

---

[7] Manya Brachear Pashman, "'Never Lose Hope' Pope Writes to Chicago Families Stricken by Violence," *Chicago Tribune*, April 4, 2017.

4

Jesus and Nonviolence

Scriptural Evidence

TERRENCE J. RYNNE

*To be true followers of Jesus today also includes em-
bracing his teaching about nonviolence. As my predecessor Benedict XVI observed [February 18, 2007],
that teaching "is realistic because it takes into account
that in the world there is too much violence, too much
injustice, and therefore that this situation cannot be
overcome except by countering it with more love, with
more goodness. This 'more' comes from God."*
—POPE FRANCIS, WORLD DAY OF PEACE MESSAGE 2017

*Introduction: What evidence do we have that Jesus was radically
nonviolent? The following paper, written for background in ad-*

Terrence Rynne is teacher of peace studies at Marquette University (Milwau-
kee, Wisconsin, USA) and author of *Jesus Christ, Peacemaker: A New Theology of Peace* (Maryknoll, NY: Orbis Books, 2014) and *Gandhi and Jesus:
The Saving Power of Nonviolence* (Maryknoll, NY: Orbis Books, 2008). This
paper was published for the April 2016 Conference on Nonviolence and Just
Peace under the title "Overview of Contemporary Scriptural Exegesis and
Ethics on Jesus' Nonviolence." It has been slightly adapted for this volume.

vance of the nonviolence and just peace conference provides an overview of Jesus's nonviolence from contemporary scriptural exegesis of the roots, significance, principles, ethical approaches, and core practices of Jesus's nonviolent way in the context of first-century Palestine. The emphasis is on scriptural witness and draws on the revolution of exegetical and theological research over the past half century on the centrality of nonviolence to the life and message of Jesus.

For the past fifty years the stream of scholarship on the nonviolence of Jesus, and its relationship to the church's teaching on war and peace, has widened and deepened—and the current continues to pick up speed.

Numerous seminal works by theologians and scripture scholars illuminating the nonviolence of Jesus have been published since the mid-twentieth century, from Lisa Sowle Cahill to James Douglass, from Leonardo Boff to John Dominic Crossan, from Albert Nolan to Eileen Egan, from John Dear to Ched Myers, and from Rev. Emmanuel McCarthy to Eli Sasaran McCarthy. Here are a few highlights of this contemporary research.

Robert Daly, SJ, in his article on nonviolence in the New Testament and the early church[1] concludes that there is little scholarly doubt that the message of nonviolence is central to Jesus's life and teaching as well as part and parcel of the faith in early Christianity. He cites the survey work of Rene Coste: "Rene Coste, for example, is summarizing a broad consensus of gospel criticism when he affirms: 'It is an incontestable fact that Christ did preach nonviolence, both as a condition and a consequence of the universal love that he taught us. To pretend, as is sometimes done, that his directives are only meant to be applied to individual . . . relationships is a supposition nowhere to be found in the New Testament.'"

---

[1] Robert Daly, SJ, "The New Testament and the Early Church," in *Nonviolence: Central to Christian Spirituality*, ed. Joseph Culliton (New York: Edwin Mellen Press, 1982), 41.

Many influential moral and systematic theologians have incorporated this New Testament scholarship into their work. Edward Schillebeeckx, for example, wrote a two volume study, the first of which entitled *Jesus* was a summary of contemporary scripture scholarship and the second, *Christ,* translated that scholarship into a systematic Christology.[2] Schillebeeckx concluded that based on scripture scholarship Jesus died because of the way he lived—with nonviolent resistance.

Bernard Häring's 1986 volume, *The Healing Power of Peace and Nonviolence*, is a clarion call to Christians to embrace nonviolent action.[3] Fr. Häring, recognized as the finest moral theologian of the twentieth century, rooted his research in the work of a set of scripture scholars who helped him to see vividly the nonviolent Jesus. These scholars included Rudolph Schnackenburg, Rudolph Pesch, Norbert Lohfink, and Heinrich Spaemann. They found that nonviolence is at the heart of the gospel.

Another important contribution to this area of study was the publication in 1972 of John Howard Yoder's *The Politics of Jesus*,[4] called by the eminent theologian Stanley Hauerwas "the most important work of theology of the twentieth century." Using the latest tools of historical and critical biblical scholarship, bridging the gap between scripture studies and moral and systematic theology—and drawing on the work of C. H. Dodd; Hans Conzelmann; Rudolph Schnackenburg; John L. McKenzie, SJ; Robert Margenthaler; Robert North, SJ; Krister Stendhal; and Hans Dieter Betz—Yoder concluded that Jesus taught an ethic informed by the sociopolitical realities of first-century Palestine whose content consisted most importantly of nonviolence and love of enemy and that this is normative for Christians.

---

[2] Edward Schillebeeckx, *Jesus: An Experiment in Christology* (New York: Vintage Books, 1981); idem, *Christ: The Experience of Jesus as Lord* (New York: Crossroad, 1980).

[3] Bernard Häring, *The Healing Power of Peace and Nonviolence* (Mahwah, NJ: Paulist Press, 1986).

[4] John Howard Yoder, *The Politics of Jesus*, 2nd ed. (Grand Rapids, MI: Eerdmans, 1994).

The moral theologian Richard Hays, exploring the moral vision of the New Testament, recognizes that the call to nonviolent peacemaking, while not easy, stretches people beyond what is typically considered "realistic" or "natural." He writes: "God broke through the borders of our standard definition of what is human and gave a new formative definition in Jesus."[5]

Scripture scholar and theologian Walter Wink also made definitive contributions to a revitalized understanding of the nonviolence of Jesus. Through careful exegesis of New Testament texts—including the "hard sayings" of Jesus like "Turn the other cheek" (Matt 5:38–41)—he illuminated Jesus's "third way" of nonviolence as an active and transformative alternative to either violence or passivity.[6] Wink's pioneering exegesis and theological analysis have dramatically underscored the centrality of Jesus's programmatic nonviolence.

The growing consensus of contemporary scriptural and theological research is that Jesus proclaimed and lived nonviolence.

Jesus's Nonviolence

To illuminate, recover and live Jesus's nonviolence today, it is critical that we understand the context in which he lived and ministered.

Jesus was born into a land seething with violence. The people of Galilee at the time of Jesus's birth were murderously angry. They were angry at the Roman occupiers who squeezed them for tribute to fight their wars, angry at Herod and his sons for bleeding them dry with taxes to build their glorious buildings and towns, angry at their priests for sending thugs into the countryside to steal their grain, their only source of meager wealth. It was not surprising that after Herod died in 4 BCE (just after Jesus's birth) Judas the Galilean was able to tap that anger and spark a violent revolt. He and

---

[5] Richard Hays, *The Moral Vision of the New Testament* (San Francisco: Harper San Francisco, 1996), 105.

[6] Walter Wink, *Engaging the Powers: Discernment and Resistance in a World of Domination* (Minneapolis: Fortress Press, 1992), 175ff.

his followers attacked the capital of Galilee, Sepphoris, the home of wealthy landowners allied with the Temple priesthood, and raided the armory there. The Roman general in the region, Varus, sent part of his army into the countryside. Josephus writes: "They caught great numbers of them. . . . Those who were the most guilty he crucified; these were in number about two thousand."[7]

Sepphoris was four miles from Jesus's hometown of Nazareth. Jesus no doubt grew up hearing the story of the "Day the Romans Came" when Rome used its favorite tool to strike terror into the hearts of a people, crucifixion. Two thousand rebels nailed or tied, naked, to crosses for all to see, slumping, pulling themselves up again and again, slowly, painfully, asphyxiating, gasping for breath, and at last giving up their spirits. The constant threat of blood and violence was in the air that Jesus breathed. The city of Sepphoris was rebuilt by Herod Antipas during the years of Jesus's youth.

Before Jesus's lifetime, during his life, and for decades after, uprisings and rebellions continued, escalating each time in violence until the final, fateful destruction of Jerusalem and the Temple in the year 70 CE and the end of the Jewish people in their own country.

His people were an oppressed people—kept in line by the threat of violence. Jesus could see what was going to come down on their heads if they stayed on the path of escalating violence. He wept over the city of Jerusalem. "Oh, Jerusalem I wanted to take you under my wings as does a hen her chicks" (Luke 13:34) and "Oh Jerusalem, if only today you had known the ways of peace" (Luke 19:42). He imagined what was likely to happen and described what did happen quite accurately—"not a stone will be left on a stone" (Matt 24).

So what did Jesus do about it?

He did two things. One, he gave them a powerful alternative to violence, and two, he worked to change the underlying causes

---

[7] Josephus, *War of the Jews*, trans. William Whiston (1737), Book 2, Chapter 5, http://www. sacred-texts.com.

of their suffering—the structural violence built into their political system.

One: Jesus's Powerful Alternative to Violence

It was thought at the time that there were only three ways forward: flight, fight, or accommodate. The Essenes, the faction of the Jews that we learned about from the Dead Sea Scrolls, chose flight. They fled into the desert to build their own version of the Jewish religion and refused contact with any outside their fold. The priests and the Herodians had chosen accommodation; collaborating with the Romans meant they could continue to practice their religion and as long as they did what the Romans wanted, they could wield a degree of power and even build some wealth for themselves. The Pharisees, later the party of violent resistance, chose to resist, maintain their identity against the pagans, keep it clear that they were enemies, and eventually to fight.

Jesus pointed out a fourth way for Israel. Build an inclusive community, even including so-called enemies, by using the power of nonviolent, loving, willing-to-risk-suffering action. Later it will be called the Way of the Cross. Instead of a way of narrow exclusion, Israel could practice the way of arms-wide-open inclusion and be the city on the hill that the rest of the world was looking for: "Love your enemies and pray for those who persecute you" (Matt 5:44). It is at the same time a warning that the way they are choosing will be a dead end. As Albert Nolan writes: "Jesus's message was to persuade the Jews that their present attitude of resentment and bitterness is suicidal. . . . The only way to be liberated from your enemies is to love your enemies."[8]

Jesus expands on his recommendation in the Sermon on the Mount when he says:

> "You have heard it said, an eye for an eye and a tooth for
> a tooth, but I say to you, 'Do not violently resist one who

---

[8] Albert Nolan, *Jesus before Christianity* (Maryknoll, NY: Orbis Books, 2008), 13.

does evil to you. If anyone strikes you on the right cheek,
turn to him the left; if someone goes to court to take your
coat, give him your cloak as well; and if anyone presses you
into service for a mile, go a second mile.'" (Matt 5:39–41)

Many people have read this passage and concluded that Jesus
is counseling passivity in response to violence. Contemporary
exegesis shows that Jesus is recommending just the opposite—creative, nonviolent resistance. Gerhard Lohfink writes: "There is a
widespread consensus in New Testament exegesis that in this text
we hear Jesus himself."[9] Jesus lays out three very tightly drawn
examples of violence that his disciples very well might recognize,
namely, an abusive superior insulting an inferior with a backhand
slap on the face *(right* cheek is the clue); a person taking another
to court to sue for his last stitch of security, the cloak that a poor
person, reduced to homelessness, wrapped himself in at night to
keep out the cold; and a Roman soldier pressing a Jew to carry his
sixty-pound service pack for a mile.

The function of this kind of language, a series of examples, one
after another, is to invite the listener to think of still more examples
of everyday violence. The language is evocative, inviting thought
and imagination. Jesus is not laying down a law. As Robert Tannehill writes: "The language arouses moral imagination, enabling
hearers to see their situation in a new way and to contemplate new
possibilities of action."[10]

Jesus invites his hearers to think what they would do if someone
slapped them backhanded on the right cheek. Instead of striking
back, might there be a nonviolent, more productive response?
Imagine the inferior in the situation looking the one who has
committed the insult in the eye and then turning to that person
the other cheek—saying in effect, "I am not cowed. And you are

---

[9] Gerhard Lohfink, *Jesus and Community* (Philadelphia: Fortress Press,
1984), 50–51.

[10] Robert Tannehill, "The 'Focal Instance' as a Form of New Testament
Speech: A Study of Matthew 5:39b—42," *Journal of Religion* 50, no. 4
(1970): 382.

acting in a way that is beneath yourself. So go ahead, if you really want to lower yourself, now punch me in the face. You still will not intimidate me. But I will not strike you back. I will maintain my dignity." Such a response is not a surefire way to avoid further trouble, but it is a response that just might work. The one insulted does not respond to the violence with violence but with a gesture that says, "I am willing to endure additional pain to reach you with a message about our common humanity." Jesus is certainly not counseling rolling over passively in a situation of violence. He is saying instead, "Stand up for yourself, but don't respond in kind." He is suggesting that his followers act as he acted—with creative nonviolence.

To place the second example in historical context—debt and exorbitant interest in Jesus's time led to loss of ancestral lands and homelessness. Deuteronomy 24:10–13 stipulates that a creditor could take the cloak as collateral but would have to return it every night so a poor man in the cold could sleep. Staying out of debt and securing one's daily ration of bread are the two central issues in the life of peasants in Jesus's day—as reflected in the Lord's prayer. What if, in response to being dragged into court and handing over your cloak, you handed over your coat, what is under the cloak, next to the skin, an undergarment, as well. Perhaps your creditor will recognize that his actions have led another human being to this state, defenseless as the day he was born. The legal system that countenances such a lawsuit that leaves a person in such dire straits is also called into question. As Walter Wink comments: "Such an action unmasks the cruelty embedded in the structures of the society and its pretenses of justice."[11]

The background for the third example is Rome's occupation of the country. The Roman soldier had the right, according to Rome's code, to press into service at any time a member of the occupied country to carry his pack of sixty to eighty-five pounds. To limit resentment from the local population, the code stipulated that impressment of an individual could be only for one mile. Forcing someone to carry the pack more than a mile could warrant pun-

---

[11] Walter Wink, *Powers That Be* (New York: Doubleday, 1998), 104.

ishment from the centurion. Jesus says imagine when you come to the end of the first mile, you take the initiative and make the choice to carry the pack a second mile. In that action you would be saying to the soldier—you see me as a person without power, a veritable beast of burden. I am letting you know I am a person who can make choices.

With these examples Jesus is putting forth an alternative way to the presumed limited choices of an oppressed people, a direction that is not fight or flight or accommodation. It is instead a way to resist without being infected by the very violence that one is resisting. People have an unlimited array of possibilities once they are able to see their way past the violent response. Jesus calls on his disciples to act against domination using their imaginations, courage, and strength.

The Sermon on the Mount is Jesus's summons to us to act as he acts, which in turn is to act as his Father acts—who "sends the rain on the just and the unjust alike." His disciples have observed him. They have heard him speak of his Father as one who approaches humans with a free offer of love and grace—unearned. And they have seen him deal with people in the same way—none is outcast, none is beyond the pale. All are embraced—even when they choose to turn away from him, he does not give up on them. So living the Sermon on the Mount is to live in a different way—beyond the way people "naturally" act. Act not because of laws but out of love that gives strength and knows no bounds. It is to live in the free air of those who know they are loved without limit and who as a result can pass that spirit on to others. It is no wonder that Mahatma Gandhi, after first reading the Sermon on the Mount as a young man, said that it went straight to his heart. It confirmed for him the best of his tradition and made him admire Jesus as the "Prince of the Satyagrahis" (practitioners of nonviolence), a person of creative, nonviolent action. It is also no wonder that Pope Benedict XVI said:

"Love your enemies. . . . This page of the Gospel is rightly considered the 'magna carta' of Christian nonviolence: it does not consist in surrendering to evil—as claims a false interpretation of 'turn the other cheek' (Luke 6:29)—but in responding to evil with good (Romans 12:17–21), and thus breaking the chain of injustice. It is thus understood that nonviolence, for Christians, is not mere tactical behavior but a person's way of being, the attitude of one who is convinced of God's love and power, who is not afraid to confront evil with the weapons of love and truth alone. Loving the enemy is the nucleus of the 'Christian revolution.'"[12]

Pope Benedict moreover said this of the nonviolent Jesus:

"He was always a man of peace. It could be expected that, when God came to earth, he would be a man of great power, destroying the opposing forces. That he would be a man of powerful violence as an instrument of peace. Not at all. He came in weakness. He came with only the strength of love, totally without violence, even to the point of going to the Cross. This is what shows us the true face of God, that violence never comes from God, never helps bring anything good, but is a destructive means and not the path to escape difficulties. He is thus a strong voice against every type of violence. He strongly invites all sides to renounce violence, even if they feel they are right. The only path is to renounce violence, to begin anew with dialogue, with the attempt to find peace together, with a new concern for one another, a new willingness to be open to one another. This is Jesus's true message: seek peace with the means of peace and leave violence aside."[13]

Jesus's Nonviolent Alternative: Dramatized in His Life

It is thrilling to read the Gospels and see how Jesus dramatized the teaching of the Sermon on the Mount in his own life, including reaching out in love to those whom society treated as outcasts. For

---

[12] Benedict XVI, Angelus, St Peter's Square, February 18, 2007.
[13] Pope Benedict XVI, Good Friday Sermon, 2011.

him there are no enemies—not even Roman officials. He healed a Roman officer's servant. Not the Samaritans. Jesus celebrated that traditional enemy of the Jews as an embodiment of charity in the parable of the Good Samaritan. Not even the Pharisees and Herodians who went out of their way to trap and humiliate him. He tried very hard to turn those who thought they were his enemies into friends. He continued to reach out to them again and again—using forceful disputation, witty responses to trapping questions, appeals to their hearts, shaming examples of their contradictory teachings—hoping against hope that he would melt their hearts and change them.

In the Gospels we find examples of his personal courage and creativity in the face of violence.

When people in his hometown were so resentful and angry at him that they were about to throw him off a cliff—somehow, without violence, he walked right through their midst (Luke 4:28–30).

Consider how he dealt with a mob of men who were ready to stone to death a woman they had taken in adultery. They felt completely righteous—they felt their own law commanded them to act. First note the courage of Jesus. He did not shrink away from the scene; he walked right into the middle of it. Note his creativity. He did not use superior force to overcome their violence. He bent down in front of them and began writing in the dust—a classic diversion of attention move. They evidently cooled a bit. John's Gospel says that he then stood up. He must have looked at them but probably not in a condemnatory or angry way—that would have further inflamed the situation, probably a composed, benign face. He then put them back on their heels with a simple statement of truth: "The one among you without sin, cast the first stone." They melted away—the older ones first (John 8:4–11).

In Caesarea Phillipi, the northernmost part of the country, he decided that he needed to go to Jerusalem to confront the leaders in their own bailiwick. As Jesus set his face to Jerusalem (Luke 9:51), the disciples were afraid. He knew he was walking into the maw of state-sponsored violence. He had a vivid sense of the evil that would most likely come down on him. But he kept walking.

If we follow him through his passion we see the same centered, nonviolent way of responding to events as they unfold. The Gospels of Mark, Matthew, Luke, and John, all describe one of his disciples meeting violence with violence, taking a sword and cutting off the ear of a servant of the high priest. Luke has Jesus say vehemently: "Enough of this!" (Luke 22:51) and then healing the servant's ear. Matthew has Jesus say: "Put your sword back, for all who draw the sword will die by the sword" (Matt 26:52). Jesus certainly knew the siren song of violence. Matthew has Jesus go on to say: "Or do you think I cannot appeal to my Father, who would promptly send twelve legions of angels to my defense?" (Matt 26:53) That would be thirty-six thousand angels.

Can the sword be used in self-defense? The guards have arrived in the garden with their swords. As Dominic Crossan writes: "If opponents use violence to attack Jesus, should his disciples use violence to defend him? The answer is quite clear. Even when opponents use the sword to attack Jesus, the disciples must not use it to defend him. But if not then, when? If not then, never!"[14]

As the trial scenes unfold, Jesus continues to respond forthrightly and with dignity. When a soldier feels free to slap him for the way Jesus answered the high priest, Jesus responded calmly but assertively, "If there is some offense in what I said, point it out; but if not, why do you strike me?" (John 18:23).

In Jesus's dialogue with Pilate, he renounces the right of self-defense because he has brought into the world in his person a kingdom that is unlike Pilate's; it does not depend on violence to exert power. His kingdom is not of this world, meaning Pilate's world. His kingdom relies on the power of truth and nonviolent resistance. Jesus says to Pilate: "Mine is not a kingdom of this world; if my kingdom were of this world, my men would have fought to prevent my being surrendered to the Jews. As it is, my kingdom does not belong here" (John 18:36). He goes on to explicitly say what gives him his power: "I was born for this; I came into the world for this, to bear witness to the truth and all who are on the side of truth hear my voice" (John 18:37).

---

[14] Dominic Crossan, *God and Empire* (San Francisco: Harper, 2007), 178.

After he had been condemned to death and led to the place called, The Skull, Golgotha, where they crucified him, Jesus—consistent with his entire message concerning the way one should respond to one's so-called enemies, and consistent with his message about the centrality of forgiveness in the kingdom—said: "Father, forgive them; they do not know what they are doing" (Luke 23:24). He died as he had lived. His last words expressed love and forgiveness for those who were killing him.

Two: Jesus Worked to Relieve the Underlying Causes of the Jews' Suffering—The Structural Violence Built into Their Political System

Understanding the vision and mission of Jesus involves understanding his context, including what was going on politically and economically in his time. As Donald Senior writes: "The more we want to know about Jesus, the more we should know about his world."[15]

Rome was an occupying force demanding an ongoing stream of tribute through the king they had put in place. Their client king, Herod the Great, had spent profligately on building such magnificent structures as the Temple with blocks of stone up to forty feet long, the wonder of the world that brought people from all over the civilized world to gaze at its grandeur. He built the fortress Masada out in the Judean desert. He built a magnificent town on the shores of the Mediterranean, Caesarea, which he dedicated to the emperor, Caesar. The tax burden on the common people to support all this was beyond their strength. The high priestly family of Ananias that reigned for over sixty years had no respect from the people. The Temple revenue was directed into their family coffers.

Most important to understand was the work of the Pharisees, the lay renewal party that had come back into power under Pilate. Under Herod they had been on the outs due to their resistance to his attempts to introduce Hellenism into the country. Before Herod,

---

[15] Donald Senior, *Jesus: A Gospel Portrait* (New York: Paulist Press, 1992), 26.

under the Hasmoneans, they had enjoyed considerable influence and even had the power of the sword behind them. As John Meier writes: "They were willing to use the power of the state to impose their legal practices on the people—even to bloody vengeance on their foes."[16] Respected by the people, they were intent on seeing the practices of ritual purity and dietary laws prescribed for the priestly class apply to the people as a whole. They had a great zeal for purity. They believed that the people needed to remain pure and undefiled to be faithful to Yahweh and to renew Israel. Many things could make people impure—certain occupations such as shepherding, contact with dead bodies, contact with Gentiles, bodily fluids, lack of physical wholeness from illness, and perhaps what was most important, not keeping the rituals surrounding food and tithing according to the law.

The number of rules that grew up around eating was astounding. Of the 341 rabbinic texts attributed to the Pharisaic schools of Shammai and Hillel of the first century, 229 pertained to table fellowship—everything from meal preparation to serving to hand washing. Not to observe these rules meant a person was considered not practicing, outside the circle of faith. Just as important to them were the tithing obligations. At every stage of the food growing and production process a small fee had to be paid to the Temple. Not to pay these tithes meant that one was outside the circle of purity.[17] With this emphasis the Pharisees were intensifying the burdens on the people. To what were already insupportable burdens on the backs of the people were added these additional tithes. Religion was, in effect, further supporting what was already a very unjust social structure.

Purity reinforced separation. Separation exacerbated the view that the Gentiles were the enemy. The Pharisees believed that defending against the inroads of paganism would eventually lead to the dream of national liberation. They stoked those fires

---

[16] John P. Meier, *A Marginal Jew: Rethinking the Historical Jesus*, vol. 3 (New York: Doubleday, 2001), 331.

[17] Marcus Borg, *Conflict, Holiness, and Politics in the Teaching of Jesus* (Harrisburg, PA: Trinity Press International, 1998), 96.

of resistance and when the time came to revolt, they joined the fight against Rome—except for the faithful remnant that left for Jamnia and founded the version of Judaism that depends not on the Temple but on the study of Torah. N. T. Wright writes: "Strong evidence exists that the position of the house of Shammai, was held by the majority prior to 66. . . . The Pharisees in the period between the death of Herod and the outbreak of war in 66 were concerned with politics, not merely piety; with resistance and revolution, not merely with private holiness."[18]

What Was Jesus's Take on This Political and Economic Situation?

In the third chapter of Mark, Jesus has healed a man with a withered hand on the Sabbath. It is stunning to read what happens next: "Then the Pharisees went out and immediately began plotting against Jesus, together with the Herodians how to destroy him" (Mark 3:4). By this early in the Gospel—the third chapter!—they are ready to kill Jesus. Why? What had he done?

Jesus could not countenance an order built on exclusion. He took action to challenge structures that dehumanized and diminished and destroyed, including a system where the disabled were regarded as unholy and that healing and wholeness must be delayed.

He could not abide exclusion, separation, and hatred of the enemy—in the name of religion, in the name of their God. If there is no violence in God, only unfathomable love, that undercuts the age-old tendency of humans to label those who are outside a privileged circle as threats, as enemies, as evil—to dehumanize them and then make them objects of righteous, sacralized violence. As he read their shared history, he understood that Israel was indeed God's chosen people—but chosen as the hope of humankind. Yahweh is God of all the earth. Jesus therefore resisted with all his might the temptation to sink into tribal religion and its violence.

---

[18] N. T. Wright, "Foreword," in Borg, *Conflict, Holiness, and Politics in the Teaching of Jesus*, xii.

He was not just opposing their interpretation of their religion, a way of exclusivity that featured a hidden threat of eventual violence, he was trying to have them change the way their society was structured. The pivotal structures of their society were the Torah, the Sabbath, and the Temple. Jesus was taking issue with the ways all three were being interpreted and used. He felt that injustice was being baked into the structures of the society. He was working to change the reasons why there was so much suffering for the people. He was trying to change not just attitudes but dominating, harmful structures.

He preached and acted in ways to bring outcasts back into the fold. In his first sermon he called for a return to the Deuteronomic year of jubilee that gave a special place in society to protecting the most vulnerable: the widows, the orphans, and the sojourners. Holiness for Jesus was not purity but compassion, not exclusion but inclusion. He associated with and even ate with those who supposedly were outside the circle of faith—tax collectors, sick people, prostitutes. He healed lepers and told them to go see the priest so they could be reincorporated into the community. He declared that it is not what goes into people that makes them unclean but what comes out of their hearts—in effect denying and undercutting the entire edifice of branding people unclean through food laws.

Jesus opposed the structures that embodied unjust cultural norms and attitudes. Jesus attacked the way that the Torah had become a tool for ostracizing people, fomented a spirit of hatred for outsiders and, through the hundreds of rules governing food, had become another way to squeeze money from the poor. Jesus went to Jerusalem to oppose the way the Temple institution had become the pinnacle of a system that robbed the poor. "You have made my Father's house a den of thieves" (Luke 19:46). Even the sacred Sabbath had been made into an oppressive institution—people were afraid to do even the most obvious good for others for fear of violating the Sabbath. The fundamental problem Jesus had with the institutions of his time was that they had become buttresses of a terribly unjust social and economic system that systematically transferred wealth from the peasant class to the priestly and royal class. There can be no positive peace if the institutions have injustice baked into them.

This second contribution makes Jesus a bona fide peacemaker. Not only did he live a style of life that was nonviolent. He went further and used nonviolent action to fight for justice and peace. Why did they want to kill him so early on? Because he had upset the system. Why did he die? Because of the way that he lived.

Discipleship: Following Jesus, the Nonviolent Peacemaker

Scripture scholars make a careful point about the audience for Jesus's message of "love your enemies" and indeed of the entire Sermon on the Mount. He is addressing first and foremost the *circle of his disciples.* "Jesus saw the crowds and went up a hill, where he sat down. His disciples gathered around him and he began to teach them" (Matt 5:1–2). To follow the teachings of the Sermon on the Mount presupposes that practitioners have heard, responded to, and are leaning in to Jesus and his message. The circle of disciples however represented the whole of Israel. The message is directed not to individuals but to a community of disciples. This is why the church is so important for living this message. Only seeing others live the way of nonviolence and resistance can the individual continue to live it. It calls for continual unlearning of the usual ways of the world and continually modeling nonviolent action for one another. As Stanley Hauerwas writes: "Discipleship is not a heroic endeavor of individuals, but rather a way of life of a community. . . . The practice of peace among Christians requires constant care in our lives together, through which we discover the violence that grips our lives and compromises our witness to the world."[19]

At the same time, it is amazing how freeing and bracing is the practice of nonviolent action. Participating in the work of Christian peacemaking is to experience grace that transforms every "natural" pattern. It is to experience something of our higher

---

[19] Stanley Hauerwas, *Performing the Faith* (Grand Rapids, MI: Brazos Press, 2004), 73.

selves. Peacemaking is not a summons to follow a set of rules but a virtue to be practiced. As Eli McCarthy writes: "Virtues are habits responsive to the good rather than acting from duty or fear of punishment."[20] As we see in the following—the power of Jesus's example lights up our lives and stirs our imaginations.

Jesus's life is normative for Christians. The official creed statements, the Apostles' Creed and the Nicene Creed, jump from "he was born of the Virgin Mary and became man" to "suffered under Pontius Pilate, died and was buried." They leave out the most important part—his *life*. We cannot understand the meaning of his incarnation or his death on the cross unless we understand how he lived. He became a human being to show us the way. He died on the cross because of the kind of life he lived, a life of nonviolent, hopeful, insistent resistance to the structures of domination of his society, and arms wide-open, inclusive compassion. He was willing to risk suffering. When he asks us to take up our cross and follow him, he asks us to live life as he did. Over the centuries the words "taking up one's cross" have been emptied of their political content. The cross is not about enduring a personal tragedy or an illness or a difficult family situation—except by extension. As John Howard Yoder writes: "The cross of Calvary was . . . the political, legally to-be-expected result of a mortal clash with the powers ruling society."[21]

The Sermon on the Mount and the drama of Jesus's life give to us more than adequate guidance and inspiration for peacemaking. When the church reduced its teaching on issues of war and peace to the just war theory, it lost, or allowed to be muted, the strong, prophetic teaching of the Gospels. Rarely was the bold call to peacemaking greatness in the Sermon on the Mount heard in the church. No longer was the example of Jesus's nonviolent life held up for study and emulation. Strangled was the call to restless, creative peacemaking. As Walter Wink writes: "The removal of nonviolence from the gospel blasted the keystone from the arch

[20] Eli Sasaran McCarthy, *Becoming Nonviolent Peacemakers* (Eugene, OR: Pickwick, 2012), 32.

[21] Yoder, *The Politics of Jesus*, 129.

and Christianity collapsed into a religion of personal salvation."[22] Thank goodness we are again reading the New Testament, listening to the Sermon on the Mount and attempting to follow the arc of Jesus's courageous life of peacemaking.

Deepening the Reflection on Gospel Nonviolence

Terrence Rynne

During the second session of the April 2016 conference, Dr. Rynne, reflecting on his own article, asked why it has taken us so long? Why weren't we reading the gospels this way for 1,700 years? One reason, he said, was highlighted in an article by Karl Rahner years ago when he talked about a Christology from below that would focus on Jesus of Nazareth rather than on Jesus Christ.

"Instead of the Johannine approach—starting with Jesus's divinity and somehow work out his humanity; instead, Christology from below starts with his humanity and finds revealed there his divinity. It does focus us in a different way on his life. You know the creeds, our basic creeds: 'Born of the Virgin Mary, suffered under Pontius Pilate.' What's the gap? His life.

"Follow his life and as soon as we do that we find out just how political he was and all of a sudden we start reading with new eyes that he was trying to change the three important institutions of his religion: the Sabbath, the Temple, and the way they were reading the Torah, and so on."[23]

The other shift has been in the way we read scripture. Dr. Rynne noted in particular the work of moral theologian Bernard Häring,

---

[22] Wink, *Engaging the Powers*, 217.

[23] Terrence Rynne, Session 2 on "Jesus's Way of Nonviolence," Conference on Nonviolence and Just Peace, Rome, April 2016.

who brought scripture to the study of moral theology in his book *The Law of Christ*, and biblical scholar Sandra Schneiders, who wrote a prescient article in 1983 on reading scriptures for the sake of moral theology. Commenting on the US bishops' pastoral letter on *The Challenge of Peace*, Dr. Schneiders notes that every classic text is meant to be read in the light of the signs of the times. For example, through "that phenomenal 'sign of the times' called Mahatma Gandhi," Rynne said, we came to understand the effectiveness of nonviolent action and "people began reading scriptures in that light."

Fr. Jamal Khaddar

During the same session of the conference, Fr. Jamal Khader, rector of the Latin Seminary in Beit Jala, Palestine, said:

> "Whenever we talk about nonviolence we go directly to the teaching of Jesus to try to see how Jesus lived and his attitude, what he did and not only what he said. As Palestinians, we ask ourselves, 'What does Jesus tell us today?' Many people understand the Bible as bad news for the Palestinians with all the interpretations of texts about the Promised Land, Chosen People, etc. They interpret those texts, those prophecies, in an anti-Palestinian way, 'This is not your Land, this land was given by God to another people.' So, what did Jesus say about it? What we see in Jesus is someone who is walking with us on the road to Emmaus where beginning with Moses and all the prophets, he interpreted the scriptures. Jesus is the one who interprets the scriptures for Palestinians as Good News.
>
> "We are used to reading the Gospel, but when we go back to the context in which Jesus lived, many of the things that he did were shocking: he challenged the system, he challenged society, he challenged the way of thinking, the mentality. And this was nonviolent action. I'll give some examples:
>
> "Lepers, for Jews and for people who lived during the time of Jesus, were thought to be punished by God for their

sins. They are sinners; they are impure; they cannot participate in prayers because they are punished because of their
sins. If you touch them, you yourself will become impure.
So, when the leper asked Jesus to heal him, the first thing
that Jesus did was to approach and touch him. That should
have been shocking for them because it was against the
mentality of the whole society.

"Another example was when Jesus healed someone and
then continued the conversation with the Pharisees, 'What do
you think, should I do good on the Sabbath or not?' And then
he healed the one with the withered hand. It was not only
healing someone, it was a call to conversion for those who
are around him. When he said to the paralytic man, 'Your
sins are forgiven,' they objected, so he continued the discussion, 'What do you think, should he go back home like he is
or should you have compassion on him?' So it was always
a call to the powerful to have compassion with the poor and
the sick and the marginalized, even on the Sabbath. That's
shocking. A good Jew would never work on the Sabbath. But
for Jesus, healing someone was that important.

"So, to be on the side of those who are left back by society, those who are poor, those who are on the side of the
street, etc. In the Palestinian mentality, beggars are in the
lowest social level; beggars are near to shepherds. So, the
blind man of Jericho was on the side of the road and when
he called on Jesus, Jesus did not go to see him, he called
him in the middle. 'Your place is here, it's not on the side.
You are here in the middle because you are loved by God.'

"Eating with sinners was also shocking. How can you,
how dare you accept the invitation of Zacchaeus in Jericho,
for example? Those things were shocking, were against the
law as interpreted by the Pharisees.

"In the story of the Good Samaritan we forget about the
priest and the Levite who left the injured man—who walked
on the other side. Because according to Jewish law a priest
cannot touch a dead man, the corpse of a dead man. He will

be impure, he can no longer offer sacrifice to God. So, they left him dying on the street for religious reasons, to be pure in front of God. So Jesus was challenging also the religious system at the same time. This is a Samaritan, your enemy, the one you consider as enemy, you could help him, but you refuse to help because you want to be closer to God, offer sacrifices to God.

"And another thing is that his message is first of all to the poor and the sick, etc., but his message is inclusive. It's for everyone. It's for the poor and for the rich. For the weak and for the powerful. For conversion. . . . Now, of course, dying on the cross is the ultimate expression of the nonviolence, the active nonviolence of Jesus. He died because he said 'no' to lies, to violence. He said 'yes' to the kingdom of God. They wanted to stop him. No, he wanted to continue with his message of love and fraternity. We are all children of God. His message of good news to everyone. And because of his message, because of what he said and did, he was crucified."

Anne McCarthy, OSB

Anne McCarthy, OSB, an Erie Benedictine Sister and former national coordinator of Pax Christi USA added an extremely important and often neglected feminist perspective on the role of women in Jesus's practice of nonviolence:

"For this afternoon, I want to add three stories about Jesus—three stories that have especially spoken to people on retreats that I've led on nonviolence.

"The first story is the bent woman from Luke 13. In that story Jesus interrupts the Sabbath service, calls out, notices the woman who's bent, and has been bent for eighteen years, heals her, and then defends his action in one of the strongest challenges that he gives to the synagogue's leaders, one of the strongest challenges to their moral leadership, saying, 'You hypocrites! Which of you would not let out your ox or your ass on the Sabbath to water it? And should not this daughter of Sarah and Abraham who has been in bondage for 18 years, should not she be released, freed from her shackles on the Sabbath?' Again, it's a revolutionary act. And the woman stands up and praises God in the synagogue. And then, when she is standing and praising God with the others, the service can continue.

"Notice that Jesus interrupts the service, all are to be standing and praising God. And I think that this is Jesus's response to internalized oppression. To the people who are so bowed under oppression that they cannot stand and speak for themselves, Jesus says, 'Stop the community. Bring them forward.' Those that are wounded from all aspects of the violence cycle, call them forth, heal them until they can also bring their voice into the circle.

"Now if this story doesn't sound as familiar to us as the others, it's because this is one of the stories that is never read in Sundays in our churches. When our lectionary was set, that story was skipped. Which itself brings up the reality of some of the sexism and injustice that are part of the analysis as we consider this topic of nonviolence in our church today.

"Second story: the Syrophoenician woman who begs for her daughter whom Jesus is refusing to heal. She challenges Jesus, she stands up to him with assurance, she begs for the life of her daughter, and she converts Jesus. He doesn't plan on healing the girl, but he does anyway. Jesus is awed by her faith. Both of them are held up as models of nonviolence. Both the woman, in standing up strongly for the most vulnerable in society, and the one that she loves. And Jesus, who engages with the enemy, really listens, and converts.

"Third story is Mary of Bethany, and her anointing of Jesus. So in John, she's the one who anoints Jesus. In every Gospel there's a woman who anoints Jesus before his burial. In the Gospel of John, it's Mary of Bethany. She brings the expensive perfume and anoints his body, and Jesus receives it. In his fear, in his looking ahead at knowing where he's going, he receives her tender act. And he defends her. Several days later Jesus washes the feet of his own disciples in another very tender, beautiful act. So we have Jesus learning from Mary, learning this ritual, I think. Realizing, because he experiences it, how important it is and then sharing that with those he loves as his way of saying goodbye. And, telling them and all of us to do that for each other. It's a tender act, it's an act that forms their relationship. And it's a revolutionary act, especially when Jesus does it because, again, he's taking on the role of the servant and changing the relationships all upside down. Those are all, I think, just additional stories to this whole breadth and depth of nonviolence that the Gospels give us and that we're called to live out."

Feminist scripture scholars and theologians offer extremely important insights about women's roles and the particular nonviolent approaches and resistance practiced by women, which are often distinct from the nonviolence practiced by men (see Chapter 9).

Fr. John Dear

Finally, author and lecturer Fr. John Dear from the United States said:

"I think Jesus's life is the story of active nonviolence. In effect, he organizes the poor on a campaign of nonviolence; goes to Jerusalem like Gandhi on the salt march; enters the Temple where the religious authorities are working with the empire to oppress all the people; and does nonviolent civil disobedience. He doesn't hit anybody, hurt anybody, kill anybody, or drop any bombs. But he's not passive; he's active and daring, and if you do that you're going to get killed.

"What happens next? The Last Supper. This bread, my body broken for you, my blood shed for you. The way I look at that is this: if Jesus were a good Roman, if he were a good Nazi, if he were a good American, he should have said, 'Go break their bodies for me. Go shed their blood for me.' The Eucharist, the Gospel, only make sense in the light of nonviolence. When you participate in the Eucharist you participate in the new covenant of nonviolence. 'My body broken for you, my blood shed for you, Do this!'

"They're in the Garden of Gethsemane. Here come the Roman soldiers. What does Peter do? He is thinking: 'If violence is ever divinely sanctioned in all of human history, if there ever was a just war in all of human history, if there ever was a moment to kill for a good cause, it's here in the Garden of Gethsemane to protect our God.' And he's right. We should kill to protect the holy one. And just as he goes to kill to protect the holy one, the commandment comes down, 'Put down the sword.' Dear friends, those are the last words of Jesus to the church. It's the last thing he said to the community of men and women around him before he died. It's the last thing they heard. And, I think it's the first time they understood who Jesus is."

5

Traditional Catholic Thought on Nonviolence

Lisa Sowle Cahill

I ask God to help all of us to cultivate nonviolence in our most personal thoughts and values. May charity and nonviolence govern how we treat each other as individuals, within society and in international life. When victims of violence are able to resist the temptation to retaliate, they become the most credible promoters of nonviolent peacemaking. In the most local and ordinary situations and in the international order, may nonviolence become the hallmark of our decisions, our relationships and our actions, and indeed of political life in all its forms.

—Pope Francis, World Day of Peace Message 2017

Dr. Lisa Sowle Cahill is J. Donald Monan Professor in the Department of Theology at Boston College (USA) and author of several books, including *Love Your Enemies: Discipleship, Pacifism and Just War Theory* (Minneapolis: Fortress Press, 1994). The essay presented here was written as a background reflection for participants in the April 2016 conference. It has been slightly adapted for this volume.

Introduction: What are the roots, meaning, significance, role, and practices of gospel nonviolence in the Catholic tradition? What are its history and context, as well as its recent direction or trajectory? Lisa Sowle Cahill's essay presents an overview of Catholic thinking on nonviolence, including the dialogue between nonviolence and the just war framework in church teaching.

———————

Gospel nonviolence has been an essential characteristic of Christianity since the first century. To be a disciple of Jesus is to live out of the reign of God, as embodied in his command to "love your enemies and do good to those who persecute you . . . so that you may be children of your father in heaven" (Mt 5:44–45). The example and teaching of Jesus embody love, inclusion, forgiveness, willingness, and sacrifice. The early church excluded the shedding of blood for all his followers. Until the fourth century, nonviolence, including refusal of military service, was the Christian norm, although from the second century on, there is evidence that some Christians in fact served in the Roman army.

Just war tradition or theory began to develop in the age of Constantine, and became dominant as Christians gained access to and responsibility for government and political power, eventually even generating a crusade ideology, in which violence was claimed to serve the gospel itself. The two main shapers of Christian just war theory were Augustine (and his teacher Ambrose) and Thomas Aquinas (fourth and thirteenth centuries, respectively). Though both recognized gospel nonviolence, Augustine limited it to an inward intention of love, when establishing peace necessitates war. Aquinas thought war to defend the common good could be justified within carefully defined limits. For Aquinas, strict gospel nonviolence was to be embodied by the clergy, who imitate Christ on the altar. Nevertheless, pacifist ideals and peace movements, such as the Peace of God and Truce of God, continued throughout the Middle Ages and into the modern era. In the thirteenth century, Francis of Assisi crossed crusader lines to preach the gospel to the caliph of Egypt. In the sixteenth century, Desiderius Erasmus depicted war as inhumane and unholy, especially deplored violence by those claiming to act in God's name, and saw peace as so necessary to the blessings of life that war should be avoided at virtually any cost.

Although just war theory has historically been the most influential framework for Catholic teaching on the political use of force, it has always been secondary to the Catholic Christian commitment to peace. In fact, just war theory was and is intended primarily to restrain not validate war. Just war theory was not endorsed officially by the Roman Catholic Church until the *Catechism of the Catholic Church* (1992, no. 2309). Justification of force has been overshadowed in the tradition overall, in Catholic social thought, and in papal teachings, by exhortations to nonviolence and peace. Modern popes—including Pius IX, Leo XIII, and Pius X—have lent personal support to efforts to mediate international conflicts nonviolently. Most notable in this regard is Benedict XV, an Italian elected in 1914, just as World War I was beginning. Although the Italian episcopacy supported the war, and Catholics around the world were divided on it, Benedict used his first encyclical to deplore the horror of modern weapons. Benedict saw just war theory as merely excusing war and as unable to deal with the present-day reality of war. He called for a 1914 Christmas truce, opened a Vatican office to reunite prisoners and families, and dedicated scarce Vatican funds to relief efforts. Like his predecessors, Pius XII, pope during World War II, constantly held up the ideal of peace as growing from spirituality, justice, and charity.

In his 1944, 1948, and 1956 Christmas messages, however, Pius XII alluded to just war criteria when he asserted the right of nations to defend themselves against unjust attack. *Gaudium et spes* likewise asserts the right of governments to "legitimate defense once every means of peaceful settlement has been exhausted" (no. 79). Perhaps paradoxically, the twentieth century also saw the diminution of the just war emphasis in Catholic social teaching, especially after the Second Vatican Council (1965). Since the 1960s, official Catholic teaching has uniformly deplored the destruction and disaster of war, pressing the point that it always represents a moral failure. Although the idea and theory of a just war has not officially been repudiated, no pope since the council has approved a war, or even mounted a defense of the justice of war in principle. In fact, the criteria of just war, if applied stringently, may themselves eliminate the possibility of a just modern war. The use of force for humanitarian purposes—in cases of horrific threats to human life, human security, and social order—is still acknowledged by Catholic teaching. Yet the focus of recent official statements certainly has been on nonviolence and on the incompatibility of violence with transformational justice. Popes John XXIII, Paul VI, John Paul II, Benedict XVI, and Francis have repeatedly denounced the savagery of war. John Paul, Benedict, and Francis have all echoed Paul VI's cry, "No more war, war never again!"

Popes, other Catholic leaders, and official Catholic organizations have made the nonviolent resolution of conflict a moral and practical priority through their teachings, symbolic actions, and work to end conflicts and build peace. The Catholic Church urges the resolution of conflicts by peaceful, nonviolent, and democratic means, insisting that the way to genuine peace lies in the creation of just and participatory social, economic, and political relations and institutions. In fact, it might be said that the distinctively Catholic contribution to the Christian tradition of gospel nonviolence is to put the emphasis on constructive and practical efforts to build the conditions of peace nonviolently, in cooperation with other social entities—rather than simply to repudiate violence and refuse political participation as a countercultural act of witness. In the words of Paul VI, "If you want peace, work for justice" (1972 World Day of Peace Message).

Focus: The Priority of Gospel Nonviolence from Vatican II Onward

Both the council document *Gaudium et spes* (1965) and John XXIII's *Pacem in terris* (1963) were written at the height of the Cold War, and in light of the advent of nuclear weapons so terrifyingly balanced by the superpowers' policy of "mutual assured destruction" at the edge of planetary disaster. Both documents pose the question whether just war criteria need to be thoroughly reconsidered and contemplate a possibility that

John XXIII explicitly puts forth: "It is contrary to reason to hold that war is now a suitable way to restore rights which have been violated" (PT, no. 127; cf. GS, nos. 79–80). *Gaudium et spes* still legitimates defensive wars, and John XXIII does not definitively exclude them.

Yet they agree that modern war threatens unimaginable destruction and see the arms race as a clear and present cause of global injustice. War and preparation for war are placed under ever more stringent moral scrutiny and targeted by mounting moral disapprobation (PT, nos. 112–13; GS, nos. 80–81).

The foundation and heart of these two documents, however, is not the consideration of war. It is the proclamation of a gospel-inspired and nonviolent peace capable of engendering lasting trust among nations. Pope John appeals both to the Christian faithful and to "all men of good will," praying that Christ will banish "whatever might endanger peace" and "transform all men into witnesses of truth, justice, and brotherly love." "Besides caring for the proper material welfare of their peoples," rulers should "also guarantee them the fairest gift of peace" (PT, no. 171). *Gaudium et spes* captures the practical and social meaning of gospel nonviolence in very similar terms. Praising all who "renounce the use of violence in the vindication of their right," it calls Christians "to 'practice the truth in love' (Eph 4:15) and to join with all true peacemakers in pleading for peace and bringing it about" (no. 78). In accord with nonviolence as an authentically Christian and human mandate and practice, the council for the first time recognizes a right of individual conscientious objection to bearing arms (no. 79).

Paul VI, John Paul II, Benedict, and Francis all solidify and advance this trajectory, accentuating the tensions latent in a tradition that has historically justified war while holding up peace as its guiding social ideal. New developments include language that more strongly contrasts war and nonviolent peace, even to the point of excluding violence entirely; the marginalization and even abandonment of explicit validation of defensive war as just; the introduction by John Paul of a duty of humanitarian intervention (not excluding armed force); a strengthening and elaboration of the connection between practical work for justice ("development"), nonviolence, and peace; incorporation of environmental reasons to avoid war; the need for broad social conversion; and, with Francis, an explicit turn to interreligious as well as intercultural and international partners.

Paul VI emphasizes that "reconciliation is the way to Peace" (1975 World Day of Peace Message), declaring "No more war, war never again! Peace, it is peace which must guide the destinies of people and of all mankind" (1965 Address to the United Nations General Assembly). Not only does he hope (with *Gaudium et spes*) that war will eventually be prohibited by international law (1975 World Day of Peace Message), but he states in 1975 in no uncertain terms that "the Church cannot accept violence, especially the force of arms" (*Evangelii nuntiandi*, no. 37) and holds up Gandhi's example to urge that nonviolence can become a national and international principle of action (1976 World Day of Peace Message). Nevertheless, he does seem to accept the legitimacy of armed revolution to resist grave offenses to human dignity and the common good (*Populorum progressio*, no. 31). This pope's greatest contribution is his insistence that the only true way to peace is to engage social partners constructively to end injustice and to actualize human rights; economic justice; and stable, participatory social and political institutions. The more privileged nations and peoples have a special responsibility. "If you want peace work for justice" (1972 World Day of Peace Message; citing the 1971 Synod of Bishops' *Justitio in mundi*, no. 6). And most famously, "The new name for peace is development"—though not on a neoliberal or unrestrained market model (*Populorum progressio*, no. 87).

John Paul II announces just as clearly that "violence is evil," "a lie," and "the enemy of justice" (Homily at Drogheda, Ireland, 18–20, 1979; quoted in the 2006 *Compendium of the Social Doctrine of the Church*, no. 496). Like previous popes, John Paul sees violence as leading to more injustice, and deplores the scale of modern warfare. Combining Paul VI's distinctive contribution with his own call for solidarity as an active commitment to the common good of all, he titles his 1987 World Day of Peace Message "Development and Solidarity: Two Keys to Peace." Yet the 1990s saw humanitarian disasters in the face of international apathy or ineffectiveness in the former Yugoslavia, Rwanda, and Somalia. Hence this pope validates the new concept of "humanitarian intervention" (2002 World Day of Peace Message, no. 11). As he asserted regarding Bosnia, when "populations are succumbing to the attacks of an unjust aggressor, States no longer have a 'right to indifference.' It seems clear that their duty is to disarm this aggressor, if all other means have proved ineffective" (Address to the Diplomatic Corps, January 16, 1993).

Along the same lines, and responding again to recent events, John Paul allows for a nation's right of defense against terrorism (2002 World Day of Peace Message, no. 5), even while holding up forgiveness and interreligious cooperation as by far the better path. Yet when confronted in advance with specific military interventions such as the Gulf War and a US invasion of Iraq, John Paul rejects the possibility of war as "a decline for humanity" (Address to the Diplomatic Corps, 1991, no. 7), and "a defeat for humanity" (Address to the Diplomatic Corps, 2003, no. 4). Rejecting the inevitability of war in both cases, he urges dialogue and diplomacy in accord with international law.

Benedict XVI returns to the basic question whether a just war can even exist today, agrees that the war against Iraq was unjust, and notes that modern weapons inevitably violate noncombatants ("Cardinal Ratzinger on the Abridged Version of Catechism," Zenit, 2003). "Violence never comes from God" (Angelus Address, 2007). Specifically refusing violence and embracing gospel nonviolence, Benedict calls "love your enemies" its "magna carta." Nonviolence is for Christians not merely a behavioral strategy, much less a form of obedience to a heteronomous norm. It is "a person's way of being, the attitude of one who is convinced of God's love and power, who is not afraid to confront evil with the weapons of love and truth alone" (Angelus Address, 2007; see also Good Friday message, 2011). "Violence is contrary to the Kingdom of God" (Angelus Address, 2012). On a visit to Cameroon, Benedict asserted that all genuine religion rejects violence in any form ("The Saving Message of the Gospel Needs to Be Proclaimed," 2009).

Nevertheless, like his predecessor, Benedict endorses humanitarian intervention under the rubric "responsibility to protect." "Recognition of the unity of the human family, and attention to the innate dignity of every man and woman, today find renewed emphasis in the principle of the responsibility to protect" (Address to the General Assembly of the United Nations, New York, 2008). Like John Paul II, Benedict mentions humanitarian intervention or the responsibility to protect in international contexts such as UN intervention, or intervention by an international coalition, in which the presumable and implied means is armed force. Neither explicitly rejects this possibility. Yet, perhaps reflecting skepticism about whether violence can actually end violence, Benedict adds in *Caritas in veritate* (2009) that the responsibility to protect must be implemented "in innovative ways" (no. 7).

Benedict follows both Paul VI and John Paul II in urging economic and political "development" as a necessary part of the solution to social problems, and the best way to prevent and remedy injustices. He repeatedly confirms this aspect of Catholic social teaching in his World Day of Peace messages (2009, 2010, 2010) and makes it the centerpiece of *Caritas in veritate*, an encyclical written to commemorate *Populorum progressio.*

It will come as no surprise that Pope Francis reaffirms these same themes, often in the very same phrases. He summons international parties in conflict to seek peace by dialogue, reconciliation, negotiation, and compromise. He appeals repeatedly for nonproliferation and disarmament, especially of nuclear arms. Praying for peace in Egypt, Francis reiterates that "the true force of the Christian is the force of truth and love, which means rejecting all violence. Faith and violence are incompatible!" The way of Jesus is the way of peace, reconciliation, "living for God and for others." The strength of the Christian is "the force of meekness, the force of love" (Angelus Address, August 19, 2013). When, like John Paul and Benedict, Francis is confronted by the prospect of a military intervention in Syria by US and French "superpower," he insists: "War brings on war! Violence brings on violence" (Angelus Address, August 31, 2013).

Expanding on these themes, he adds,

My Christian faith urges me to look to the Cross. . . . *Violence is not answered with violence*, death is not answered with the language of death. In the silence of the Cross, the uproar of weapons ceases and the language of reconciliation, forgiveness, dialogue, and peace is spoken. This evening, I ask the Lord that we Christians, and our brothers and sisters of other religions, and every man and woman of good will, cry out forcefully: *violence and war are never the way to peace!* . . . War always marks the failure of peace, it is always a defeat for humanity. Let the words of Pope Paul VI resound again: "No more one against the other, no more, never! . . . War never again, never again war!" "Peace expresses itself only in peace, a peace which is not separate from the demands of justice but which is fostered by personal sacrifice, clemency, mercy and love." Forgiveness, dialogue, reconciliation—these are the words of peace, in beloved Syria, in the Middle East, in all the world! (Vigil of Prayer for Peace [in Syria], September 7, 2013)

After the publication of *Laudato Si'*, in which he connected war and ecological destruction (no. 56), Pope Francis urged the United Nations in New York to support sustainable development while protecting the environment. He decried the hypocrisy of talking about peace while manufacturing arms; and he rebuked international leaders for failing to find peaceful solutions to global conflicts, especially in the Middle East (Address to the General Assembly of the UN, September 28, 2015).

Some ambiguity in Pope Francis's position on violent force has been introduced regarding the dilemma of how to defeat the international terrorist organization, the so-called Islamic State (IS or ISIS). On August 18, 2014, in an in-flight press conference from Korea to Rome, the pope remarked informally to reporters that dialogue even with ISIS should not be considered a lost cause. "I can only say that it is licit to stop the unjust aggressor. I underscore the verb 'stop.' I'm not saying drop bombs, make war, but stop the aggressor. The means used to stop him would have to be evaluated."

Ordinarily, one would assume that stopping unjust armed aggression calls for humanitarian intervention and/or self-defense in the form of taking up arms against a very violent and very dangerous opponent. Yet, perhaps going beyond John Paul and Benedict, Francis explicitly adds that he is not endorsing bombs and war. Left unclear is whether he envisions more limited and carefully targeted uses of violence as a last resort; or whether he has in mind such measures as nonviolent peacekeeping, civil society acts of nonviolent resistance and protest, or initiatives by Islamic religious leaders and faith communities to deter membership in ISIS. In a March 13, 2015, interview with the Catholic website Crux, Silvano Tomasi, then the Permanent Observer of the Holy See to the United Nations in Geneva, did endorse military action against ISIS (but not in Syria), applying just war criteria. He urged that a political solution be sought first, yet reminded heads of state and their representatives that inaction would lead to moral culpability similar to that following, for example, the genocide in Rwanda. Tomasi cautioned that any intervention should be guided by UN authority and include the Muslim states of the Middle East. The tension continues.

A new or at least more visible dimension of the endorsement of gospel nonviolence by recent popes is their awareness that ethical analyses, Church teachings, and publicly accepted ideals and norms are one thing; commitment, solidarity, and the political will to live up to ideals and abide by norms are another. Therefore, condemning violence is not enough; a huge task remains to convert hearts and minds and to show that another way is truly possible. A similar awareness is manifest in *Laudato Si'*s use of prayer and poetry, its invocation of saints and heroes, its multiple references to local bishops conferences, its appeal to interreligious spirituality and commitment, and its accompaniment by a Vatican video illustrating the beauty and endangerment of "our common home." It is crucial to mobilize nations, peoples, communities, and members of faith traditions by awakening imaginations, inspiring new identities, and creating wider worldviews.

In this vein, it is important to note that public symbolic actions by recent popes go beyond "teaching" in the sense of pronouncements and documents. Symbolic actions and events creatively reach out to those of many faiths and span divisions that spawn violence. One example is the well-publicized prayer vigil for peace in Syria that Francis held in St. Peter's Square in September 2013. He was joined by 100,000 peace advocates, even as international leaders debated the possibility of military action. Another example is the prayer of three successive popes—John Paul, Benedict, and Francis—at the Western Wall or Wailing Wall in Jerusalem, the remnants of a platform on which the Second Temple was built. Their widely circulated and iconic images represent Christian repentance of suffering caused to the Jews, as well as hope for peace between Israelis and Palestinians. The latter message was brought home powerfully (and controversially) by Francis's additional visit to the "wall of separation" in Bethlehem.

Though the focus of this discussion has been on post–Vatican II popes, it is important to realize that the most effective "official" teachers of gospel nonviolence in local contexts are the local episcopacy, accompanied by clergy, religious, pastoral ministers, catechists, community workers, and members of base communities. Their existential perspective is frequently very different from that of high-level Vatican teachers, heads of state, and international leaders who have the power and the prerogative to deliberate about unleashing their considerable military arsenals (or even a UN peacekeeping force) against less powerful aggressors. A few illustrative examples will have to suffice.

In Medelliìn, Colombia (1968), the Conference of Latin American Bishops named the support by political authorities of an oppressive elite as a major source of violence and recognized structural injustice as a form of "institutionalized violence." They called for a church that is not only nonviolent, but in solidarity with the poor. In 1983, the bishops of the United States reflected their own cultural situation within a superpower nation when they embraced gospel nonviolence in the first half of their pastoral letter *The Challenge of Peace.* Yet in the second half they went on to endorse a policy of "strictly conditioned" nuclear deterrence that placed the lives of millions and the health of the entire planet in jeopardy. The 1993 anniversary letter, *The Harvest of Justice*

Is Sown in Peace, was more critical of just war theory, called for "peaceable virtues," and underlined the potential of nonviolence to be a principle of political debate and government decisions.

In 2009, the Episcopal Conferences of Eastern Africa (AMECEA) delegates to the Synod for Africa linked violent conflicts to religious divisions, the global economic recession, poor leadership and corruption, environmental crises, HIV/AIDS, and the lack of evangelization and spirituality with strong cultural as well as Christian roots. Simple promulgation of Catholic social teaching is hardly an adequate remedy. True evangelization must include small Christian communities, families, education, ecumenical and interfaith dialogue, and the participation of women and youth. In 2014, the bishops of Eastern Africa spoke to the crisis in South Sudan. Like recent popes they cited the Bible in support of God's mandate of peace and Christ's call to reconciliation. They called for a cessation of hostilities. But they also appealed for international humanitarian support, "intervention" on behalf of the Sudanese people whose human rights are violated, security for refugees, and participation of all stakeholders in negotiations.

In 2014, the Conference of Latin Bishops of the Arab Regions (CELRA) reported on the "horrible" conditions and levels of suffering in Syria and Iraq. Reflecting some of the tension in the papal voice on this situation, they asserted that "without true reconciliation based on justice and mutual forgiveness there will be no peace." Yet they upheld "the right of the oppressed to self-defense." Moreover, they urged "the international community" to use "proportionate force to stop aggression and injustice against ethnic and religious minorities."

Finally, the international Synod of Bishops gathered in Rome in 2015 to discuss the family issued an appeal for resolution of the situations of conflict in the Middle East, Africa, and Ukraine. They referenced "unspeakable atrocities" and "bloody conflicts" that have continued for years. But they also expressed their conviction that peace without force is possible. "Reconciliation is the fruit of fraternity, justice, respect, and forgiveness."

Much could be written about international Catholic peacebuilding organizations such as Caritas Internationalis, Catholic Relief

Services, the Catholic Peacebuilding Network, the Pontifical Council for Justice and Peace, the Community of Sant'Egidio, Maryknoll, Franciscans International, Jesuit Relief Services, Pax Christi International, RENEW International, and Peacebuilders Initiative, all united around gospel nonviolence. These too work to create the conditions of peace through justice; are committed to resourceful and practical ways of nonviolence; often work in the midst of ongoing violence; are willing to take great risks in the name of the gospel; and bridge ethnic, racial, and religious divisions. These too are embodiments of Catholic social tradition and action and are helping to define the current trajectory and future of gospel nonviolence, as well as its potential for success.

Conclusion

While recent official Catholic social teaching has certainly amplified and made central the voice of gospel nonviolence, it is clear that official teaching to date has not spoken with one voice only. This reality is *open to a variety of interpretations*. For example, (1) a simple lack of coherence in the Catholic position, deriving perhaps from different historical contexts and interests; (2) an interpretation of papal statements as rhetorically creative, pastoral interventions regarding ad hoc problems, not efforts to formulate a full theoretical analysis of ethical-political obligations and norms; (3) a deep and real "Augustinian" ambiguity within Christian social responsibility in a fallen world, reflected in the church's teaching and in its practical responses; (4) a qualified but sure endorsement of just war theory in Catholic teaching, with pleas for nonviolence a necessary reminder that the just war criteria must be stringently applied; and (5) a gradual yet sure shift from the precedence of just war theory to gospel nonviolence, though recalcitrant vestiges of the former still appear.

Without settling whether any or none of these interpretations are adequate, let me offer five *hypotheses about the trajectory and future direction* of Catholic teaching on nonviolence. These hypotheses are inferred from the present actual state of Catholic social teaching on nonviolence, not from an evaluation of desirable changes. (1) The heart of Christian identity, and hence of the Catholic message on nonviolence, is to commit wholeheartedly to *living* the gospel and the reign of God. This means to prioritize love, compassion, reconciliation, and "mercy" at the existential level; and to engage in nonviolent *practices* of justice and reconciliation. (2) Situations of conflict or injustice must be approached with the mentality of "there has to be a better way." As Francis said to Sant' Egidio in 2014, "War is never a necessity, nor is it inevitable. Another way can always be found." (3) Leave the possible use of violence *in extremis* on the table, but don't expend Christian or Catholic moral capital to debate or justify particular uses of violence (others are more than ready to do so). (4) More broadly, eliminate the elaboration or refinement of "Christian just war theory" as a Catholic social teaching project. Replace it with a theology and ethics of peace and peacebuilding (such as "just peace"). (5) Recognize that the political success of gospel nonviolence depends on broad social conversion and mobilization. Seek ways in which grassroots activism, networking, and public symbolic actions can bring that about.

Experience in Dialogue with the Tradition

Somalia

Although Bishop Giorgio Bertin, bishop of Djibouti and apostolic administrator of Mogadishu was unable to attend the conference, he wrote the following in advance of the meeting:

> I lived in Somalia, and in particular in Mogadishu, from 1978 to 1991. The country was "peaceful" though under a severe form of dictatorship in the name of scientific socialism. During the last years of the 1980s power was more and more concentrated in the clan of the ruler at that time, Mohamed Siad Barre. This prompted the birth of different

"liberation movements" practically all with a clan affiliation. When civil war broke out beginning in 1990, the country went into pieces. Since then Somalia has become a land of violence: the stronger groups or clans have been taking any law into their hands. The result is evident: a million Somali refugees in neighboring countries, and 1.2 million people internally displaced.

As church, as Caritas, we intervened in different ways. We assisted groups of journalists to organize themselves and provided them with formation on human rights. We assisted groups of Somalis with "road shows" against violence entitled "put down the gun, take the pen." We produced and broadcast special radio programs on the social teaching of the Church. We took part and invited more expert people to organize meetings among political/factional leaders. We organized prayer meetings among different religious leaders.

I think that we should work more and more through an appropriate use of liturgy (masses for peace and nonviolence). Catechesis for children and young people is very important because there we have the possibility of forming the mentality of people. Retreats and spiritual exercises can also encourage a spirituality which has a sociopolitical dimension. Campaigns against violence like Caritas Internationalis's campaign "one human family, food for all." And some of the frequent meetings of bishops and priests could be utilized to encourage nonviolence.

Philippines

Also in advance of the Rome conference, Archbishop Antonio J. Ledesma, SJ, archbishop of Cagayan de Oro, shared with other participants his reflections, "Going Beyond the Bangsamoro Basic Law," given as a baccalaureate address at Mindanao State University, Marawi, on February 3, 2016. Excerpts follow:

Last year, I presented to Christian communities ten Easter challenges for peace in Mindanao. The first one was this:

"Christianity and Islam are both religions of peace." A Muslim friend shared with me a quotation from the Koran: "If the enemy inclines toward peace, you also incline toward peace. And trust in Allah, for he is One that hears and knows all things" (Surah 8, ayah 51). For Christians, the Bible states: "Blessed are the peacemakers, for they shall be called children of God" (Matthew 5:9).

Secondly, I pointed out that the vast majority of Muslim, Christian, and indigenous people communities in Mindanao aspire for peace. Many of these communities have experienced the ravages of war, the loss of lives, and the pain of dislocation. The most vulnerable victims of armed conflict are the women and children. It is for them and future generations that we need to build structures of peace today.

Thirdly, I mentioned that all-out war is not the answer to the Mindanao situation. It has been tried and failed—in the early 1970s, and the years 2000, 2003, and 2008. There was widespread destruction and dislocation of families but no end to the armed conflict.

Then I also outlined the three major grievances felt by Muslim communities: the reduction of their ancestral territory, the erosion of their cultural identity, and the loss of self-determination in the development of their communities. . . .

Konsult Mindanaw was a project of the Bishops-Ulama Conference in 2010. More than 300 focus group discussions were conducted by the research team among Catholic, Muslim, Protestant, and Indigenous People communities throughout Mindanao. The manifold findings were summarized in six S's.

For me, the first S in importance is *Spirituality*. Participants in the focus group discussions repeatedly pointed out the need for spiritual moorings in the quest for lasting peace. A Muslim participant remarked: "Peace can be attained here on earth and in heaven when we follow the words of Allah." In the creation of our Bishops-Ulama Forum, in 1996, we religious leaders pointed out that the missing dimension in the peace process was the spiritual and transcendental values of Christian and Muslim communities—which can provide the framework for the peace process as well as a unifying vision of one God, one common origin and destiny for all.

A second S is intercultural *Sensitivity*. The *Konsult Mindanaw* report stresses that "the key to peace in Mindanao lies in celebrating diversity through respect for each other's cultural values and belief systems." One focus group discussion participant completed the statement: Peace is . . . "when people smile at me even if I am wearing the *hijab*."

When I was working on my dissertation at the International Rice Research Institute in Los Baños, I had a Muslim friend from Bangladesh who came into my room one day and saw a thick book on my desk covered by a pile of papers. He asked me about the book. I told him it was the Bible. He was shocked and told me gently that for Muslims the Koran is always put on a special place. From that incident with my Muslim friend, I learned more about the value of a sacred book like the Bible.

A third S in pushing forward the peace process is *Solidarity*. Despite cultural and religious differences, we agree on common human values. We live on one island Mindanao and in one country.

When I was the bishop of Ipil Prelature, we conducted a Culture of Peace seminar for a mixed group of Christians, Muslims, and lumads.[1] One exercise was to form separate groups of Christians, Muslims, and lumads. We asked them to list the positive and negative traits they perceived in the other groups. During reporting time, the Christians said that Muslims cannot be trusted, but that they are united and help each other during times of crisis. The Muslims said that Christians are able to follow civic regulations, but that they are land-grabbers and oppressors. The lumads said that Christians and Muslims are better educated but that they oppress the tribal minorities. Christians and Muslims also saw

---

[1] Lumads are a group of non-Muslim indigenous people in the southern Philippines.

the lumads as uneducated, but closer and more protective of the environment.

In summarizing all these stereotype images, the facilitator challenged the three groups. Can we not build a culture of peace by focusing on the positive traits of each cultural group? For example, to follow rules like the Christians, to be united and support each other like the Muslims, and to be closer to nature like the lumads? Solidarity can be forged from the positive traits of each cultural group, which are then integrated into an all-embracing culture of peace among all the groups.

The fourth S is *Sincerity*. Negotiating panels in the peace process have to show transparency and commitment in their pursuit for a just and lasting peace. The Mamasapano[2] incident has severely tested the sincerity of both sides as it has also tested the sincerity of the general public in pursuing peace. Deep-seated prejudices and biases have resurfaced, but so also has the advocacy for peace been echoed by many civil society organizations.

And this is where the fifth S needs to be stressed: *Security*. Cessation of armed hostilities has to take place. Both contending groups have to hold the peace through a ceasefire. Over the past five and one-half years, a ceasefire has actually been honored by both sides—with the exception of the Mamasapano fire fight (which for many observers was initiated by a third party, not privy to the ceasefire agreement).

The sixth S is *Sustainability,* which focuses on the need for legislation like the proposed BBL [Bangsamoro Basic Law] in order to provide the structures for a lasting peace. The Comprehensive Agreement on the Bangsamoro was

---

[2] The incident was a major clash between the Philippine national police (PNP) Special Action Force and the Moro Islamic Liberation Front (MILF) rebels in the southern Philippines that led to the deaths of over fifty people, including five civilians (https://thediplomat.com).

signed in March 2014. This still provides the framework
for a revised or resurrected BBL at the next Congress. The
key principles and aspirations summarized in the six S's
have been articulated not only for the continued work of
negotiating panels, but more so for all of us—in churches
and mosques, in academe (like Mindanao State University),
in civil society, and in the homes of lumad, Muslim, and
Christian families throughout Mindanao.

United States

Catholic thought on war and peace, violence and nonviolence continues to develop. In many ways *The Harvest of Justice Is Sown
in Peace* published by the US bishops on November 17, 1993,
the tenth anniversary of their historic document *The Challenge of
Peace*, describes well the situation in which we still find ourselves:

An essential component of a spirituality for peacemaking
is an ethic for dealing with conflict in a sinful world. The
Christian tradition possesses two ways to address conflict:
nonviolence and just war. They both share the common
goal: to diminish violence in this world. . . . Throughout
history there has been a shifting relation between the two
streams of the tradition which always remain in tension. Like
Christians before us who have sought to read the signs of
the times in light of this dual tradition, we today struggle to
assess the lessons of the nonviolent revolutions in Eastern
Europe in 1989 and the former Soviet Union in 1991, on
the one hand, and of the conflicts in Central America, the
Persian Gulf, Bosnia, Somalia, Lebanon, Cambodia, and
Northern Ireland, on the other. The devastation wrought
by these recent wars reinforces and strengthens for us the
strong presumption against the use of force, which is shared
by both traditions. . . .

Although nonviolence has often been regarded as simply
a personal option or vocation, recent history suggests that in

some circumstances it can be an effective public undertaking as well. Dramatic political transitions in places as diverse as the Philippines and Eastern Europe demonstrate the power of nonviolent action, even against dictatorial and totalitarian regimes. . . . These nonviolent revolutions challenge us to find ways to take into full account the power of organized, active nonviolence. What is the real potential power of serious nonviolent strategies and tactics and their limits? What are the ethical requirements when organized nonviolence fails to overcome evil and when totalitarian powers inflict massive injustice on an entire people? What are the responsibilities of and limits on the international community? One must ask, in light of recent history, whether nonviolence should be restricted to personal commitments or whether it also should have a place in the public order with the tradition of justified and limited war. *National leaders bear a moral obligation to see that nonviolent alternatives are seriously considered for dealing with conflicts. New styles of preventative diplomacy and conflict resolution ought to be explored, tried, improved and supported. As a nation we should promote research, education, and training in nonviolent means of resisting evil. Nonviolent strategies need greater attention in international affairs.* (emphasis added)

6

Catholic Practice of Nonviolence

Ken Butigan and John Dear

*A culture of nonviolence is not an unattainable dream,
but a path that has produced decisive results. The
consistent practice of nonviolence has broken barriers,
bound wounds, healed nations.*

—Pope Francis, personal letter to
Cardinal Blase Cupich,
April 4, 2017

*Introduction: The practice of gospel nonviolence in the Christian
community over the centuries has not always been visible, yet the
early church resolutely placed nonviolence at the center of community and individual discipleship. Many Catholics throughout
the years have believed that to be a disciple of Jesus has meant
being comprehensively nonviolent (see Chapter 4). This chapter
highlights some of the many examples of nonviolence as practiced
by the Catholic/Christian community.*

Dr. Ken Butigan is senior lecturer in peace, justice, and conflict studies at
DePaul University, Chicago, Illinois (USA). Rev. John Dear is a Catholic
priest, Christian pacifist, author, and lecturer. This chapter is based on their
essay "An Overview of Gospel Nonviolence in the Christian Tradition,"
originally published for the conference.

It is important to note that nonviolent practices in Christian history have reflected the gendered roles in society. Men's nonviolent practices often took place in the sphere of abstaining from bearing arms and from participation in war. Women's nonviolent practices more often took place in the sphere of family, community, and religious orders as they resisted direct and structural gender violence and exploitation.

In the first centuries after Jesus, the church nourished a culture of spiritually grounded nonviolence through the corporal works of mercy, the practice of forgiveness and reconciliation, resistance to the culture of violence, and preparing its members to face the consequences of their nonviolent resistance, including persecution and martyrdom. The witness of early Christian martyrs was often recorded and recited when the community celebrated Eucharist together as a way to encourage one another in their gospel nonviolence.

Moreover, feminist scholars studying early writings like the Acts of Thekla are recognizing that women's resistance even then had a form of its own:

The Acts of Thekla are an outstanding document on women's resistance during early Christianity. Although they must be regarded as a novel-like story (similar to the other Apocryphal Acts of the Apostles) and not as historical reports, they are nevertheless not to be underestimated in their relevance to the reconstruction of historical reality. . . . Thekla is— so the story goes—a beautiful virgin from an upper class family in Iconium. She is engaged to Thamyris. From a neighboring house, she hears Paul's sermon on abstinence and resurrection, which addresses women in particular. She refuses to marry Thamyris and is punished . . . sentenced to death because her refusal to marry is seen as a threat to public order. . . .

The Acts of Thekla are a unique document of the history of women's resistance. According to this text, women's resistance evolved by women refusing their role, which again and again is forced on them by agents of the patriarchal order.[1]

More familiar is the story of Christian apologist Justin Martyr, who, in the second century, wrote,

> We who were filled with war and mutual slaughter and all wickedness have each and all throughout the earth changed our instruments of war, our swords into plowshares, and our spears into farm tools, and cultivate piety, justice, love of humankind, faith, and the hope, which we have from the Father through the Crucified One.[2]

He was tried, convicted, and beheaded for his teachings by a Roman official in 165.

Many other saints and writers condemned Christian participation in killing. Among them were Tatian, Athenagoras, Irenaeus, Clement of Alexandria, Cyprian, Minucius, Felix, and Lactantius.[3]

Perhaps the most celebrated Christian in the first one thousand years of the church was St. Maximilian. In 295, this twenty-one-year-old son of a Roman veteran refused conscription into the Roman army and was beheaded. At his trial he said, "I cannot serve in the army. I cannot engage in wrongdoing; I am a Christian."[4] His testimony was read as part of the mass for centuries after his death.

When Christianity was legalized by Constantine in 313 CE and Christians, as Lisa Sowle Cahill says in the previous chapter, "gained access to and responsibility for government and political power," a just war tradition began to develop—even a "crusade ideology, in which violence was claimed to serve the gospel itself."

---

[1] Luise Schottroff, "Nonviolence and Women's Resistance in Early Christianity," in *The Pacifist Impulse in Historical Perspective*, ed. Harvey L. Dyck (Toronto: University of Toronto Press, 1966), 83, 85.

[2] Clive Barrett, *Peace Together: A Vision of Christian Pacifism* (Cambridge: James Clark and Co., 1987), 29–30.

[3] Ibid., 30–31; see also Michael G. Long, *Christian Peace and Nonviolence: A Documentary History* (Maryknoll, NY: Orbis Books, 2011), 17–24.

[4] Long, *Christian Peace and Nonviolence,* 31.

Yet thousands of Christians over the centuries have followed the path of gospel nonviolence. They have been a remnant church, a small movement.[5]

In the centuries after Constantine pockets of Christian men and women retreated to the deserts to keep the nonviolence of Jesus alive. Later, monasticism developed, with communities created for worship and study, service to the local community, and the practice of peace and hospitality. (They were largely, but not universally, nonviolent. Bernard of Clairvaux, for example, is widely known for having preached the Second Crusade.)

Other persons and movements also have pursued the path of gospel nonviolence. An important example after the Constantinian shift is the witness of St. Martin of Tours (316–97). Martin was an officer in the Roman army before his conversion to Christianity. After becoming a Christian, he felt he could no longer remain a Roman soldier. Just before a battle in the Gallic provinces, Martin told his superior officer, "I am the soldier of Christ; it is not lawful for me to fight." The commander was furious. As the saint's contemporary biographer, Sulpicius Severus, recounts:

> The tyrant stormed on hearing such words, declaring that, from fear of the battle, which was to take place on the morrow, and not from any religious feeling, Martin withdrew from the service. But Martin, full of courage . . . exclaimed, "If this conduct of mine is ascribed to cowardice, and not to faith, I will take my stand unarmed before the line of battle tomorrow, and in the name of the Lord Jesus, protected by the sign of the cross, and not by shield or helmet, I will safely penetrate the ranks of the enemy." Baffled by Martin's offer to stand unarmed in front of the battle line, the commander put him in prison and considered taking him up on his offer. Then the unexpected happened: "The following

---

[5] For the best study of this tradition, see Roanld Musto, *The Catholic Peace Tradition* (Maryknoll, NY: Orbis Books, 1986).

day the enemy sent ambassadors to treat about peace and surrendered both themselves and all their possessions."[6]

Severus connects this turn of events to Martin's nonviolent resistance: "In these circumstances who can doubt that this victory was due to the saintly man?"[7] After leaving the army, Martin lived as a hermit, founded a monastery, was installed as a bishop in Gaul, and spent his life serving the poor.

In the fifth century Pope Leo the Great saved the city of Rome by nonviolent dialogue when Attila the Hun invaded Europe and St. Severin mediated between the Germanic tribes who were threatening populations of fortified cities.[8] He successfully asked the inhabitants to enter into dialogue with the enemy, and war and destruction were avoided.

In the Middle Ages the Truce of God was instituted by the church as a measure to suspend warfare, especially the many private wars, during certain days of the week and during church festivals and Lent. The Peace of God was fostered by the church and later by civil society to protect women, priests, pilgrims, merchants, other noncombatants, and church property from violence.

In the thirteenth century Francis of Assisi was an icon of gospel nonviolence. He reclaimed the nonviolence of Jesus, pointed Christians back to the gospel, and almost single-handedly reimagined the church. As an affluent youth fighting in his local military, he was imprisoned, experienced a profound conversion, embraced life at the margins of society, and began to live a radically nonviolent life. He formed a community of practitioners of gospel nonviolence who refused to take up arms. They lived in poverty, served the poor, and greeted everyone with the phrase "Pace e Bene" (peace and

---

[6] Sulpitius Severus, *On the Life of St. Martin*, in *A Select Library of Nicene and Post-Nicene Fathers of the Christian Church*, Second Series, Volume 11 (Buffalo: The Christian Literature Company, 1894).

[7] Ibid.

[8] Hildegard and Jean Goss-Mayr, "The Gospel and the Struggle for Justice and Peace: Training Seminar" (The Swedish Ecumenical Council and the International Fellowship of Reconciliation, 1990), 20.

goodness), often being attacked as a result. Within a few years their movement began to spread. Thousands joined.

During the Fifth Crusade, Francis took bold action. He crossed contested territory and met with Sultan Malik al-Kamil, the leader of the "enemy," to make peace. Along with Clare of Assisi and her sisters, Francis and his early community offered a Christian witness of nonviolence that historians now believe helped end feudal violence.

A well-known story about Clare describes her decision to have the Blessed Sacrament placed on the walls of the convent when an attack by invaders was imminent. She told her sisters not to be afraid but to trust in Jesus. The invaders fled.

Francis forbade any follower to own a weapon, support war, or kill others. St. Francis is widely regarded as the greatest, most beloved saint in history, but he was first of all a practitioner of a deeply holistic and integral form of gospel nonviolence.

In the centuries after Francis religious orders and communities focusing on the works of mercy and charity proliferated. Moreover, after the Protestant Reformation and Counter Reformation, small "peace churches" blossomed that explicitly espoused the nonviolence of Jesus, including the Anabaptists, Brethren, Mennonites, and the Society of Friends (Quakers). These peace churches advocated for nonviolent social change. Along with powerful Christian anti-slavery and antiwar leaders such as Sojourner Truth and Frederick Douglass, the peace churches contributed vision and organization to the abolition movement that led to the end of slavery in the United States. Many of the most powerful and well-known suffragists were from these peace churches, including Susan B. Anthony, Lucretia Mott, and the Grimke sisters; their actions and writings have helped inspire and sustain other nonviolent social movements around the world.

At the beginning of World War I the International Fellowship of Reconciliation was established as one expression of a renewed attention to gospel nonviolence. As Hildegard Goss-Mayr writes,

It was the first organized and ecumenical expression of Christians who, in following Jesus Christ, are not only saying "no" to the use of violence as a means of conquering injustices and resolving conflicts, but at the same time are rediscovering the creative force of the nonviolence of God.[9]

In the United States, Ben Salmon from Denver, Colorado, gained notoriety as a Catholic conscientious objector during the First World War. Ben, who was married with four young children, believed that the war was immoral and an abuse of political power. "The Germans," he said, "are my brothers. I will not train to kill them." He was arrested, tried in a military court, though he was not in the military, and convicted of treason. Sentenced first to death and then to a reduced sentence of twenty-five years of hard labor, Salmon was sent to seven different federal prisons, where he was often paraded in chains and kept in solitary confinement. In prison he was refused access to the sacraments; was eventually ruled insane; and was sent to St. Elizabeth's Hospital in Washington, DC. On Thanksgiving Day in 1920, two years after the war ended, thanks to pressure from the newly established American Civil Liberties Union and Father John Ryan, a professor at Catholic University, Salmon was released.[10]

Also in the United States, Dorothy Day co-founded with Peter Maurin the Catholic Worker movement, a network of houses of hospitality, now present in many countries, where Catholics welcome the poor and the homeless to live with them, and where they also publicly denounce and resist war and preparations for war in obedience to the nonviolent Jesus. Day engaged many times in nonviolent civil disobedience for peace and justice.[11]

During World War II, Franz Jägerstätter of St. Radegund, Austria, was another powerful, faithful witness for nonviolence. A Catholic, Jägerstätter was ordered to join the Nazi military in 1943 but refused on the grounds that to do so would be to

---

[9] Ibid.

[10] Jack Gilroy, "Imprisoned War Resistor Rooted in Catholic Faith," *National Catholic Reporter,* July 16, 2016.

[11] For Day's life and writings, see, for example, Jim Forest, *All Is Grace: A Biography of Dorothy Day* (Maryknoll, NY: Orbis Books, 2011).

disobey Jesus's teachings in the Sermon on the Mount. He was arrested, brought to Berlin, tried, and beheaded. After the war his action and writings became known and have influenced thousands of people around the world; many who have become involved in grassroots movements for peace have cited his witness as a motivation. Jägerstätter was beatified by the Catholic Church on October 26, 2007.

When German troops occupied northern Italy in 1943, Italian men were conscripted into Hitler's army in violation of international conventions. Among them was a young man, Josef Mayr-Nusser, who was enlisted into the SS in September 1944. Deeply influenced by St. Thomas More's letters from prison and the challenge of taking a stand based on conscience, he, at the end of his training, refused to take the oath of loyalty to Hitler. "His faith and conscience would not allow it. To his comrades he explained: 'If no one ever finds the courage to tell them that they don't agree with their Nazi ideology nothing will ever change.'" He was arrested, imprisoned, and condemned to death for undermining military morale. Severely weakened by prison starvation and dysentery, he died on February 24, 1945, in the cattle wagon on his way to Dachau, where he was to be shot. Josef was beatified on March 18, 2017.[12]

As the Second World War drew to an end, Pax Christi, a Catholic movement for reconciliation between the French and the Germans, was founded in 1945 in France by a Catholic lay woman, Marthe Dortel Chaudot, and the bishop of Montauban, Pierre Marie Théas. Bishop Théas had just returned from the detention camp at Compiègne after being arrested by the Gestapo for speaking out against the persecution of Jews. The Pax Christi International movement spread quickly in postwar Europe and later throughout the world, promoting reconciliation and active nonviolence, demilitarization, social justice, and human rights.

With the atomic destruction of Hiroshima and Nagasaki by the United States during World War II, the threat of global nuclear

---

[12] Pax Christi UK, "Martyr for Nonviolence Josef Mayr-Nusser to Be Beatified on 18 March," www.nonviolencejustpeace.net.

annihilation became a possibility. With the development of grass-roots movements and the widespread legacy of Gandhi, millions of people began to awaken to the teachings and methodologies of nonviolence, helping to build a global movement that succeeded in making possible nuclear-arms-control agreements, including the 1962 Partial Test Ban Treaty, the 1968 Treaty on the Non-Proliferation of Nuclear Weapons, and the 1993 Comprehensive Test Ban Treaty signed by 183 nations that ended most nuclear testing worldwide.

Thomas Merton, the celebrated Trappist monk and author, called for the abolition of war and nuclear weapons. His book, *Peace in a Post-Christian Era*, which was banned by the abbot general of his Trappist community and finally published by Orbis Books over forty years later, in 2004, was (in mimeographed form) an important influence on the Second Vatican Council. Jim Forest's "Foreword" to the Orbis edition gives an excellent account of the impact of Merton's writing on millions of people around the world.

Following the Second Vatican Council many Catholics including laity, clergy, and religious communities, became more deeply involved in political activism for social justice and peace. For example, "while the Catholic Church as an institution never played a leading role in the civil rights movement, those black and white Catholics who participated in demonstrations and spoke out concerning Catholic social teachings helped promote the cause of equality."[13]

Encouraged by encyclicals like *Pacem in terris* (1963), Vatican Council documents such as *Gaudium et spes,* and other church documents, including the 1971 Synod of Bishops' statement *Justice in the World*, many Catholic religious communities made corporate commitments to nonviolence, peace, and social justice, and implemented those commitments through community action.

Dolores Huerta and Cesar Chavez, co-founders of the United Farm Workers, led carefully orchestrated nonviolent campaigns

---

[13] Catholic University of America, "The Civil Rights Movement—American Catholic History Classroom" (n.d.), http://cuomeka.wrlc.org/exhibits/show/pfp/background/pfp-civil.

in the United States for farmworker justice, including the Delano Grape Strike of 1965. The farmworkers' strategies reflected the dominance of the Catholic tradition among the workers and fully integrated symbols of the faith and liturgical expression into the heart of most actions.

In many Latin American countries where assassinations and disappearances in the 1970s and 1980s were a frequent occurrence, the mothers of the disappeared—the CoMadres in El Salvador, the Mothers of the Plaza de Mayo in Argentina, the Mothers and Relatives of the Kidnapped and Disappeared in Nicaragua, and the Grupo Apoyo Mutuo (GAM) in Guatemala—led powerful, persistent, public acts of resistance to brutal violence.

During the same period, the leadership of Father Miguel D'Escoto, MM, as foreign minister of Nicaragua, decidedly emphasized nonviolence, which he considered to be the "essence of the gospel." During Lent in 1985, as the war between the Contras and the Sandinistas intensified, he initiated a month-long fast, which he called an "evangelical insurrection." Then he led a two hundred mile, two week long Via Crucis (Way of the Cross) across Nicaragua to promote reconciliation and an end to the violence.[14]

In El Salvador and around the world the example of Blessed Archbishop Oscar Romero inspired a new generation of Catholic peacemakers. He was assassinated on March 24, 1980, the day after he preached in his homily that Christians were forbidden to kill and that members of the military and death squads should disobey orders to kill, quit their positions, and stop the repression in his country.[15]

Catholic religious and lay people around the world, with justice and peace departments, commissions, and committees in bishops' conferences dioceses, and parishes, were involved in nonviolent efforts to end the Vietnam war, the military dictatorships in South America, the extremely violent wars in Central America, apartheid in South Africa. Catholics led the Solidarity movement in

---

[14] Paul Wehr, Heidi Burgess, and Guy Burgess, eds.. *Justice without Violence* (Boulder, CO: Lynne Reiner Publishers, 1994), 90.

[15] Oscar Romero's *Homily,* March 23, 1980, is widely available online. See also Bishop Kevin Dowling's reflection in Chapter 1 herein.

Poland and were involved in the peace communities in Colombia and in peace zones in Mindanao, Philippines. Catholic President Julius Nyerere was the first president of Tanzania, where his vision cemented a peaceful identity for a new nation. Followers of Jesus in Northern Ireland, including Nobel Peace Prize laureates Mairead Corrigan Maguire and Betty Williams, finally brought the "troubles" to an end. Catholics in East Timor, including Bishop Carlos Belo, recipient with Jose Ramos-Horta of the 1996 Nobel Peace Prize, weathered a vicious occupation by Indonesian forces and denounced horrific human rights abuses until East Timor achieved full sovereignty in 2002.

Just as the global anti-nuclear movement has applied nonviolence to the struggle for a world without weapons of mass destruction, thousands of other movements involving followers of Jesus have been proliferating for more democratic societies, human rights, economic justice, and environmental sustainability over the past half-century using the power and methods of nonviolence for effective change. Forming broad coalitions with people of many traditions and faiths, they have successfully banned anti-personnel landmines and cluster munitions, and they have generated significant international efforts to cancel unjust and unsustainable foreign debt, promote fair trade, and end human trafficking and destructive mining practices.

Nonviolence also has characterized the courageous and important movements working within the church for an end to the violence of sexual abuse and thorough accountability for the abuse of power and the violation of confidence pervading that horrific crime against children. Also courageous and creatively nonviolent are those many women and men in the church who have been working against racism and for the full inclusion of women in the life and leadership of the Catholic community.

At the same time, followers of Jesus have played pivotal roles in developing positive, innovative approaches to addressing violence, injustice, human rights violations, and war. These include restorative justice (Victim Offender Reconciliation Program; Peace Circles); forgiveness and reconciliation training; third-party intervention and unarmed civilian protection and accompaniment

(Witness for Peace, Christian Peacemaker Teams, Nonviolent Peaceforce, Operation Dove); nonviolent communication; conflict transformation programming; trauma healing; antiracism training; and innumerable initiatives for interfaith dialogue.

Also important in recent decades is a dramatic increase in academic degree programs in peace studies in Catholic universities around the world, along with research on the core values of nonviolent change, including forgiveness, creativity, love, compassion, and empathy, as well as nonviolent civil resistance, movement building, and the dynamics and infrastructure for a culture of peace and nonviolence. Lisa Sowle Cahill in Chapter 5 refers to the Catholic Peacebuilding Network formed by many of these universities.

Mahatma Gandhi, who read the Sermon on the Mount every day for forty years, concluded that Jesus was the greatest person of nonviolence in history and that everyone who follows him is called to be a person of nonviolence. Many Christian saints, martyrs, and holy people for over two thousand years have affirmed, like Gandhi, that gospel nonviolence is the way of Jesus and have sustained a commitment to follow him in that way.

The story of the People Power movement in the Philippines is one clear example of the official Catholic Church leading the wider Catholic community to understand active nonviolence and to put the principles and practices learned into effective action at a critical time. Under the US-backed regime of Ferdinand Marcos there was much corruption and poverty, widespread human rights violations, and a lack of democracy. Systematic violence by the government was aimed at destroying the opposition, including community-based organizations and movements working for change. There was little hope for social transformation. There was a growing armed struggle led by a group called the New People's Army. At the same time, however, the Catholic Church in this predominantly Catholic country was casting about for an alternative. Was there an option to passivity on the one hand and violence on the other?

Many people were not sure. Richard Deats recalls:

A bishop said to me, "I used to believe in nonviolence, but Marcos is too cruel; only a bloody revolution will work against him." When he was asked how long such a revolution would take, he said, "Ten years."[16]

The 1983 assassination of opposition leader Benigno Aquino seemed only to confirm that gloomy assessment.

It was then that the church's leader in the Philippines, Cardinal Jaime Sin, decided to see if an alternative was possible. He put the full weight of the church behind an exploration of gospel nonviolence and how it could be applied to change the situation in his country.

Ultimately, in Manila, over one million unarmed human beings joined the self-described People Power movement and demonstrated how nonviolent people power can trump tanks and circling bombers. There were many factors to its success, but two of those included a call from the church to take nonviolent action, and the role of the church in organizing nonviolence trainings, many with Hildegard and Jean Goss-Mayr, whose account of that experience follows.

Personal Experiences of Nonviolence in Practice

Colombia and the Philippines

In 2001 Pax Christi Flanders arranged an interview of Hildegard Goss-Mayr by journalist Mark Deltour. Translated by Annemarie Gielen, general director of Pax Christi Flanders, in 2015, the interview reveals the deep wisdom and experience of active nonviolence that Hildegard and her husband Jean Goss shared with the world through their many trainings and leadership. Excerpts follow:

---

[16] Ken Butigan, "The Philippines' People Power Revolution Wins New Victory," WagingNonviolence.org, February 28, 2013.

When Hitler entered Vienna in 1942, all the schoolchildren had to welcome him. I felt lost in the crowd. Suddenly came the convoy. I felt how a force took possession of the crowd. I saw how that crowd cheered the man who was responsible for this unjust regime. I said to myself, "No, you don't have the right. You have to refuse to bring the greeting and to shout"—even if they would lynch me. I was twelve years old then and I didn't realize the extent of my deed yet. Later I discovered that only from such a moment do you realize that you are a real human being, when you refuse to take part in injustice.

In nonviolence everybody is invited to take part. Elderly, young people, children, ill people. There are so many tasks—of praying, of joining rallies, of being taken into custody. There is something to do for everybody. But every participation demands discipline. People decide together and then they stick to what has been decided. People cannot execute nonviolent actions or big projects if there is no structure—if there is no plan that is commonly elaborated.

We worked relatively long in South America in the 1970s and 1980s. We worked in the slums of Medellín in Colombia. In that particular slum, where there was no water or electricity, worked a Colombian priest. There was an indescribable poverty, unemployment was high, and many children died in these circumstances. The priest had created small base communities. There started the preparation already. In such a group two things need to happen: to discover their dignity, their power. They understood they were not slaves. The priest helped them discover God's power. It was he who invited us to help them walk the path of Jesus' liberation, the path of nonviolence. The second task for the group is to look at the reality. By making an analysis of injustice, by seeing the pillars that support the injustice, and how we, through passivity and fear, keep the injustice going.

So we worked in the slum. A group of women undertook action. They first made the analysis. From the many different ways of suffering and injustice they chose the worst: the absence of drinkable water. Many children died because of that. The women wanted to address this through a meeting with the council of this city of one million people. This city had a modern, luxurious, and well-developed center; around it are districts full of suffering. So they went to talk to the council but they were treated like dogs. They meant nothing in the eyes of the rich, who were not prepared to share their wealth. The women said, "We have to approach it differently. We have to make sure there is solidarity that will make us strong." You see how nonviolence is creative?

Illiterate women decided to go with their babies in groups of ten to the main square in the city center. There was a large fountain where water flooded day and night. The wind blew some of the water over the edge of the fountain so there were puddles in the square. One day they went to wash their babies, not in the fountain but in the muddy water in the puddles. There were always a lot of people in the square. When rich women saw these poor women do that they said they were crazy. A conversation started. The rich women became more aware of the problem. The police came to chase the poor women away in a violent way. But after ten minutes a new group came. And another. Four, five groups did the same thing. Every time more rich women stopped. When they saw how the police behaved brutally, one of the rich women stood up for them and said, "If your wife would live in the same situation, she would be part of this group."

That meant the end of the manifestation and a small committee was formed of rich and poor women. A few weeks later they went together to the city council. The difference in power wasn't so great anymore. Dialogue became possible. The poor women asked their unemployed husbands, "Why don't you offer your labor in order to help with the building of the water system? That way it will cost less money and the city council will understand that we are prepared to make efforts to solve the problem. We will share the costs." When we came back six months later there was water on the hill. On a big memorial stone was written: "In honor of the women of our district. They had the courage to fight for water."[17]

Of their work in the Philippines, Hildegard remembered in particular the significance of the sacrifice of Aquino, the leader of the opposition to Ferdinand Marcos. She describes Aquino as a "christic" figure who was prepared to give his life so that the people could become free. He was assassinated in 1983. When he gave his life, millions of people stood up and accompanied his body to be buried.

From that moment on a nonviolent movement was created, but in the beginning it was not organized. That's why we were invited to give a structure to this resistance. We gave seminars and made preparations with people on all levels—grassroots, intellectuals, even bishops. The church played a significant role in that situation. We realized together a strategy to take support from the dictatorship. Finally, the entire population was ready to say "no." A dictatorship can only exist as long as it is supported. If millions of people organize strikes and manifestations and if the church collaborates—this was the case in the Philippines where the bishops encouraged people to resist in a nonviolent way—the dictator becomes isolated and he has to go. Most beautiful were the soldiers, who were overwhelmed by the charms of the women who brought them flowers, cigarettes, Coca-Cola and who said to them: "You are the sons of our country come down from the tanks and join us." This power of the people

---

[17] Pax Christi Flanders interview with Hildegard Goss-Mayr by Mark Deltour (2001). Reprinted with permission of Pax Christi Flanders.

was really a moral force and at the same time a political force. This showed me the political dimension of the gospel in favor of liberation.[18]

United States and Guatemala

During Session 2 of the conference Nathanael Bacon, who now works with InnerChange in Guatemala, spoke about a powerful experience of working with gangs in California:

> "One of the first things that Pope Francis did really grabbed my attention. On his first Holy Thursday, if you recall, rather than celebrating at St. Peter's Basilica, he went to a juvenile hall, a juvenile prison, and washed the feet of the inmates there, including a Muslim girl. Part of the reason this impressed me is due to a personal experience which I think relates really deeply to this, to how we look at Jesus and nonviolence. My wife and I worked for fifteen to twenty years with gang members, Latino gang members in San Francisco, California. Many came to live with us, which was a tricky thing, with a young daughter and a small apartment. But God moved us to bring one young man in particular, named Antonio, into our home. After he was with us for a month, the priest at our parish very kindly suggested that we have him be one of the twelve to have his feet washed at the liturgy on Holy Thursday. We were delighted, and thought it was a great idea. And then the day came, and he was having a bad day, so he decided not to show up. It was a bummer, but right after we got home he burst through the door looking pale, and said, 'I just got shot!' He'd been out on the street where the gang hangs out when enemy gang members had opened fire with an automatic weapon. He dove behind one of those big metal garbage dumpsters, which saved his life. But one bullet caught him in the foot. So I took his shoe off, and the bullet had only grazed off the thick part of the flesh

---

[18] Ibid.

on the bottom of his big toe. He was very lucky. So guess what I end up doing? Washing his foot! Thinking, this is odd. Holy Thursday . . . he was supposed to . . . and I look at him and say, 'Antonio, this would have been a lot better in church!' And then I'm in tears and I say, 'Mijo, son, thank God you're alive.' But what he said cut us to the heart; he said, 'I wish they would have killed me.'

"Antonio grew up in Mexico in an abusive home; he was abandoned at seven years old and was on his own since eight; he crossed the border at eleven; ate out of garbage dumpsters; made his way northward; and finally a man offered to take him into his home . . . but then severely mistreated him. All of that pain inside came pouring out in a group that invited him to be part of their family, a street gang.

"We sat for the longest time, trying to understand this strange Holy Thursday message, and what we finally grasped is very core to Jesus and nonviolence: we all carry wounds. This young man had very deep wounds, like almost all the kids we worked with in the gangs. Jesus calls us to wash those wounds, communally, as family, to wash those wounds with his love. And he calls us to be the instruments of that love.

"If wounds don't get washed, they get infected and the wound begins to look like all the symptoms that you see on the outside—the violence, the gangs, the addictions, and all of that. We recognized that he would have been just a gang member, a statistic, a newspaper item—something, someone to be put in a jail or deported. But we had opened the door and let him be part of our family, so now he was our son. And so his wounds became our wounds. When he said that he wished he had been killed, we had to sit in the pain with him. Then we recognized that those wounds aren't just his and ours, they're also the wounds of Jesus.

"This whole process of nonviolent compassion is just a pouring out of this love as a salve to heal these wounds that are wounds of others, but which in solidarity become our wounds, and mystically in prayer and experience become the very wounds of Jesus.

"I carry the bullet that we removed from his shoe every-where to remind me of the challenge to love those who ap-pear to be enemies, coming close enough to recognize their wounds and to be instruments of peace in washing them."

Philippines

In the reflection paper she submitted prior to the conference, Jasmin Nario-Galace, Pax Christi-Pilipinas's leader, described the invitation to active nonviolence that she identifies with the Catholic faith tradition:

As a Catholic community, there is a need to highlight that our faith tradition has always motivated us to embrace non-violence as a pathway to peace. We can invest our energy in interfaith education, in supporting and accompanying peace processes around the world, in efforts to challenge deeply held biases against minorities, and in building bridges of friendship and understanding amongst people of differing faiths and cultures. To move towards a wider practice, we can all help popularize the Catholic social teachings related to peace and nonviolence. We can continue to organize and join nonviolent initiatives and campaigns in spaces where we are. We can write and publish stories or make video documentation of nonviolence experienced by our members worldwide. Most importantly, as members of the Pax Christi community, we must bring to light that nonviolence is not only a political tool for change but a philosophy to be lived. It is when we live it that we can convince others that there is no other way to peace but peace. As Gandhi put it, let our life be our message.

Iraq

Language-specific discussion groups met between the plenary sessions of the conference. During those conversations Sister Nazik Matty, a Dominican Sister with the Sisters of St. Catherine of Siena in Iraq, whose whole community was displaced from its center in Mosul, said:

> "When you are in trauma and pain you think others will not understand. But after this morning I understand that so many others are living this pain but they are fighting for peace. I liked what the bishop said—to be among people, with people, for people. After Daesh/ISIS, the church took responsibility for all of us. It was encouraging to see such active presence of the church, not passive, but active. We can't respond to violence with worse violence. This encourages the spiral of violence up and up.

South Sudan

Bishop Paride Taban also spoke:

> "The weapon of the church is love. The church is a mother and has a strong weapon: It is love for everybody. In South Sudan, the church has been with all the people but never ever advocated for weapons. I destroyed all my guns that I use for hunting birds. The church has to be a place where there are no guns and no fear. Not just war, but just love. Love everybody by name. Hatred jumps into our heart from the son who is not called by name. The church must call people sons and daughters, not rebel or president. When the BBC asked if I was with the SPLA, I said no, the SPLA is with me. The church should be a mother. Never advocate for weapons and call everyone by name."

Later Bishop Taban added:

> "Understanding. Discernment. Wisdom. If you are right, then you need not get angry. And if you are wrong, then you have no right to get angry. Patience with family is love. And patience with others is respect. Patience with self is confidence. Patience with God is faith. Never think hard

about the past; it brings tears. And don't think more about the future; it brings fear. Live this moment with a smile; it brings cheer. Every test in our life makes us bitter or better. Every problem breaks us or makes us. The choice is ours, whether we become victims or victorious. Beautiful things are not always good but good things are always beautiful. Do you know God created gaps between fingers so that someone who is special to you will come to fill those gaps forever?"

7

Active Nonviolence

An Effective Political Tool

MARIA J. STEPHAN

Inequality eventually engenders a violence which recourse to arms cannot and never will be able to resolve. It serves only to offer false hopes to those clamoring for heightened security, even though nowadays we know that weapons and violence rather than providing solutions, create new and more serious conflicts.
—POPE FRANCIS, *THE JOY OF THE GOSPEL*, 2013

Introduction: All across the globe, from Guatemala to Poland to Venezuela to Palestine, ordinary people are organizing and challenging systems of injustice, inequality, and oppression using weapons of will and active nonviolent means. Their struggles are part of a rich history of nonviolent movements and "people power" that includes the Mahatma Gandhi–led fight for self-

---

Dr. Maria J. Stephan is senior advisor, US Institute of Peace, and co-author with Erica Chenoweth of *Why Civil Resistance Works: The Strategic Logic of Nonviolent Conflict* (New York: Columbia University Press, 2011). This essay was originally published for the conference as "Advancing Just Peace through Strategic Nonviolent Action." It has been slightly adapted for this volume.

determination in India, the Polish Solidarity movement against communist dictatorship, the anti-apartheid struggle in South Africa, the peaceful ouster of dictator Augusto Pinochet in Chile, and recent nonviolent movements for human rights and dignity in Tunisia, Guatemala, Brazil, and elsewhere. Maria Stephan's essay highlights the importance and effectiveness of nonviolent movements, particularly in the last century.

In each of the cases mentioned in the editor's introduction to this essay, unarmed civilians used nonviolent direction action, or what nonviolent action scholar Gene Sharp describes as techniques outside of institutionalized behavior for social change that challenges an unjust power dynamic using methods of protest, noncooperation, and intervention without the use or threat of injurious force.[1] The theoretical underpinnings of nonviolent resistance, articulated by Sharp and by earlier scholars including German philosopher Hannah Arendt, holds that power is fluid and ultimately grounded in the consent and cooperation of ordinary people, who can decide to restrict or withhold that support.

Sharp identifies six key sources of political power that are present to varying degrees in any society: authority, human resources, material resources, skills and knowledge, intangible factors, and sanctions.[2] Ultimately, these sources of power are grounded in organizations and institutions, made up of people, known as "pillars of support." When large numbers of people from various pillars of support (bureaucracies, trade and labor unions, state media, educational institutions, religious institutions, security forces, and so on) use various nonviolent tactics to withhold consent and cooperation from regimes or other power-holders in an organized

---

[1] Gene Sharp, *Social Power and Political Freedom* (Boston: Porter Sargent Publishers, 1978).

[2] Gene Sharp, *How Nonviolent Struggle Works* (Boston: Albert Einstein Institute, 2013), 5–6. For a detailed description of each of these six key sources of political power, see the complete text, available at http://www.aeinstein.org/wp-content/uploads/2014/01/How-Nonviolent-Struggle-Works.pdf.

fashion, this can shift power from the oppressor to the oppressed without bombs or bullets.

Sharp identified 198 methods of nonviolent action that included peaceful marches, vigils, social and consumer boycotts, stay-aways, sit-ins, street theatre, humor, and the creation of parallel structures and institutions (included in what Gandhi referred to as the "constructive program," which focused on social uplift for the poor and marginalized).[3] The rise of social media technologies, including Facebook, Twitter, WhatsApp, and Instagram has expanded the universe of tactics even further, while offering new avenues for communication, mobilization, and peer learning across borders. Successful movements have integrated both online and offline forms of mobilization, organization, and direct action—online activism is never a substitute for nuts and bolts offline organizing.

Nonviolent struggle draws on courage, strategic planning, and, for many people involved in nonviolent resistance, on spiritual discipline and motivation. In many of the most iconic historical nonviolent movements, from the Catholic Worker movement, to the US civil rights movement, to the People Power struggle for democracy in the Philippines, to the struggles against dictatorship in Poland, Argentina, and Chile, Catholic and Christian faith communities and institutions played pivotal roles in exposing injustices, encouraging global solidarity, providing organizational strength, and offering spiritual nourishment for activists and nonviolent change agents.[4]

Despite these successes, deep economic disparities, institutionalized racism and discrimination, protracted intra-state wars, and the rise of extremist groups continue to wreak havoc on lives and livelihoods around the world. The civil war in Syria, which began

---

[3] Gene Sharp, *The Politics of Nonviolent Action: Part 2—The Methods of Nonviolent Action* (Boston: Extending Horizons Books, 1973).

[4] See, for example, Peter Ackerman and Jack DuVall, *A Force More Powerful: A Century of Nonviolent Conflict* (New York: St. Martin's Press, 2000); Stephen Zunes, Sarah Beth Asher, and Lester Kurtz, eds., *Nonviolent Social Movements: A Geographical Perspective* (Malden, MA: Blackwell, 1999); Maciej Bartkowski, ed., *Rediscovering Nonviolent History: Civil Resistance in Liberation Struggles* (Boulder, CO: Lynne Rienner, 2013).

as a nonviolent uprising against the Bashar al Assad dictatorship in 2011, has now claimed over 250,000 lives. The Islamic State of Iraq and Syria (ISIS) has used brutal tactics to take over territory in an attempt to create an Islamist totalitarian state. In Uganda, which boasts the largest per capita youth population in Africa, the thirty-year autocracy of Yoweri Museveni was recently extended another five years after elections in February marred by fraud, violence, and intimidation. In the United States structural injustices and police violence continue to adversely target African Americans, while politicians mobilize fear, xenophobia, and hatred as part of a strategy to take power.

Nonviolent Resistance Is More Effective than Violence

Despite the prevalence of these and other injustices around the world, there is reason for great hope. Catholic teachings focus on the need to avoid war and prevent violent conflict by peaceful means.[5] Fortunately, empirical data reveal that there is a force more powerful than violence to achieve social justice, which Pope Paul VI in his 1967 encyclical *Populorum progressio* called the basis of peace (no. 76). According to research that I conducted with Erica Chenoweth from the University of Denver, which culminated in our 2011 book, *Why Civil Resistance Works,* nonviolent resistance against formidable opponents, including those with predominant military power, has been twice as successful as armed struggle. We examined 323 violent and nonviolent campaigns against incumbent regimes and foreign military occupations from 1900 to 2006 and found that the nonviolent campaigns succeeded, in terms of stated political objectives, about 54 percent of the time, compared to 27 percent for violent campaigns.[6]

In addition, our study concluded that nonviolent campaigns are associated with both democratic and peaceful societies. Armed

---

[5] See US Conference of Catholic Bishops, "Seven Themes of Catholic Social Teaching" (Washington, DC: USCCB, 2005).

[6] Erica Chenoweth and Maria J. Stephan, *Why Civil Resistance Works: The Strategic Logic of Nonviolent Conflict* (New York: Columbia University Press, 2011).

rebel victories almost never produce democratic societies (less than 4 percent resulted in democracy); worse, they are often followed by relapses into civil war. The data clearly show that the means by which peoples challenge injustices and oppression strongly influence the character of the societies that follow. For a Catholic faith community that places a premium on the avoidance of war and the protection of human life as the moral foundation of society, these are significant findings.

Why has nonviolent civil resistance proven to be so much more successful than violence? In a nutshell: it's all about participation. We found that the average nonviolent campaign attracts eleven times the level of participants compared to armed campaigns. The physical, moral, informational, and commitment barriers to participation in nonviolent campaigns are much lower compared to violent campaigns, which means that young and old people, men and women, rich and poor, disabled and able-bodied, peasants and professionals can all participate in nonviolent activism. The range of nonviolent tactics is vast, facilitating participation. Sharp's list of nonviolent methods has greatly expanded with the rise of social media and new tactics invented by creative nonviolent resistors around the world. When large numbers of people from diverse societal groups engage in acts of protest, noncooperation, and nonviolent defiance, their actions create social, political, economic, and moral pressure for change. When violence is used against disciplined nonviolent protestors, the chances that the violence will backfire against the perpetrators, causing them to lose legitimacy and power, is much greater than when violence is used against armed resistors.[7]

Although nonviolent movements contain elements of spontaneity and artistry, the chance of success increases significantly if participants adhere to basic principles of strategy. Those include achieving unity around achievable goals and nonviolent methods, building capacity to maintain nonviolent discipline, focusing on expanding the diversity of participation, and innovating

---

[7] Brian Martin, *Justice Ignited: The Dynamics of Backfire* (Lanham, MD: Rowman and Littlefield, 2007).

tactically. The strategic dimensions of nonviolent resistance were first articulated by Peter Ackerman and Christopher Kruegler in *Strategic Principles of Nonviolent Action* and by Robert Helvey in *On Strategic Nonviolent Conflict*.[8] In *Why Civil Resistance Works*, Erica Chenoweth and I, building on writings by sociologist Brian Martin and others, discussed why state violence targeting nonviolent movements (versus armed resisters) is more likely to backfire against the perpetrator, leading to greater support for the movement. We highlighted the strategic importance of innovating tactically and alternating between methods of concentration (for example, street demonstrations, sit-ins) and methods of dispersion (such as consumer boycotts, go-slow actions) to reinforce movement resilience and effectiveness.[9]

The techniques-based approach to nonviolent action described by Sharp, Ackerman, and others focuses on the pragmatic, utilitarian use of nonviolent action, which is detached from religious or ideological underpinnings. This approach is distinguished from *principled nonviolence,* whose adherents reject violence on any grounds and are typically pacifists. An advantage of the technique-based approach is that it does not create a barrier to participation for those who are not pacifists (that is, most people around the world). It is possible to convince those living under profound oppression, who might otherwise take up arms or who have taken up arms, that there is a more effective way to challenge injustice—without having to first convince them that violence is always wrong. Well-known Quaker pacifist and nonviolence trainer and practitioner George Lakey famously said that "most people who participate in nonviolent campaigns aren't pacifists,

---

[8] Peter Ackerman and Christopher Kruegler, *Strategic Nonviolent Conflict* (Westport, CT: Praeger, 1994); Robert L. Helvey, *On Strategic Nonviolent Conflict* (Boston: Albert Einstein Institution, 2004). For a condensed version of strategic principles of nonviolent action, see Peter Ackerman and Hardy Merriman, "The Checklist to End Tyranny," in *Is Authoritarianism Staging a Comeback?*, ed. Maria J. Stephan and Mathew Burrows (Washington, DC: Atlantic Council, 2014).

[9] Chenoweth and Stephan, *Why Civil Resistance Works.*

and most pacifists don't participate in nonviolent campaigns."[10] On the other hand, there is tremendous value in the principled nonviolence approach which provides moral, religious, and philosophical anchors to remaining nonviolent when the going gets tough (as it often does) and the temptation to use violence is high. And nonviolence offers a long-term vision for societies, and the world writ large, that is built on nonviolent communications, peaceful co-existence and reconciliation.

In practice, the line is not so stark between the principled and pragmatic nonviolence traditions.[11] Spiritual belief and religious organizations and institutions have often played critical roles in nonviolent movements. Mahatma Gandhi himself, a brilliant strategist, devised a nonviolent resistance strategy against British colonialism that was clearly inspired by faith. He referred to Jesus as nonviolence par excellence.[12] On the most practical level it is extremely difficult for a nonviolent movement challenging entrenched and longstanding injustices to maintain morale and to sustain active participation over an extended period of time. Activists burn out. Sustained resistance becomes burdensome. In such circumstances activists and movement leaders need to be able to draw on resources that will inspire, encourage, and nourish. Their strength and resilience depend on it.

Faith communities and institutions can provide that sense of community solidarity, spiritual nourishment, and the cultivation of virtuous habits. It is difficult to imagine the US civil rights movement sustaining its vibrancy and effectiveness without the spiritual and organizational power provided by the black churches. The iconic images of the Filipino nuns, rosaries in hand and kneeling in prayer in front of dictator Ferdinand Marcos's soldiers, together with declarations by Cardinal Jamie Sin imploring justice over

---

[10] George Lakey, *Powerful Peacemaking: A Strategy for a Living Revolution* (Philadelphia, New Society Publishers, 1987).

[11] Eli S. McCarthy, *Becoming Nonviolent Peacemakers: A Virtue Ethic for Catholic Social Teaching and US Policy* (Eugene, OR: Wipf and Stock Pickwick Publishers, 2012).

[12] M. Gandhi, *Collected Works of Mahatma Gandhi*, vol. 62 (New Delhi: Government of India, May 20, 1936).

Radio Veritas, helped galvanize the popular nonviolent struggle for a democratic Philippines in 1986. Archbishop Desmond Tutu of South Africa drew on faith-based beliefs grounded in justice and reconciliation in his insistence that the struggle for a free South Africa be nonviolent, and that forgiveness be the guiding principle of the post-apartheid state. In East Timor, which gained independence in 2002 following a brutal Indonesian military occupation, Catholic priests and religious sisters from around the country spoke out against the atrocities committed by Indonesian forces and provided protection and material support to youth and others who were fighting nonviolently for self-determination.

In Liberia, a country that endured years of brutal civil war between armed rebel groups and the Charles Taylor government, a group of churchgoing women came together and organized a remarkable nonviolent direct action campaign that pressured the warring parties to sign a peace agreement in 2003. Peace vigils, sex strikes, and social pressure were a few of their tactics.[13] In Guatemala, a broad-based coalition involving peasants, students, lawyers, and religious leaders used boycotts, strikes, and protests to challenge entrenched government corruption, forcing a kleptocratic president to step down without violence in 2015. This was a remarkable achievement for a country that had endured over three decades of civil war.[14] NETWORK's Nuns on the Bus movement in the United States, founded by Sr. Simone Campbell, has used cross-country bus rides since 2012 to stand with ordinary people and provide a creative and hopeful outlet for Catholics (and all Americans) committed to economic justice, immigration reform, equality, and civic engagement.[15]

---

[13] See "Liberian Women Act to End Civil War," Global Nonviolent Action Database, 2010; "Pray the Devil Back to Hell," Gini Reticker, Director, Fork Films LLC, 2008.

[14] Azam Ahmed and Elisabeth Malkin, "Otto Pérez Molina of Guatemala Is Jailed Hours after Resigning Presidency," *New York Times*, September 3, 2015.

[15] Sister Simone Campbell, *A Nun on the Bus: How All of Us Can Create Hope, Change, and Community* (New York: HarperOne, 2014).

Catholic Teachings and Solidarity with Nonviolent Activists

Contemporary Catholic teachings on nonviolence have been animated in documents including Pope John XXIII's April 1963 encyclical *Pacem in terris*, World Day of Peace messages by Popes, and the US Catholic Bishops' pastoral letters, *The Challenge of Peace* and *The Harvest of Justice Is Sown in Peace*. The church's social justice teachings focus on the inherent dignity of the human person, the importance of participation in society, rights and responsibilities, the primacy of the poor and the vulnerable, the dignity of work and the right of workers, the importance of global solidarity, and care for God's creation. Faithful citizenship, understood in the context of Catholic teachings, includes engaging in nonviolent action to advance the rights and dignity of the most vulnerable and oppressed, including those whose basic rights to life and work are violated by unjust systems of power.

The church's social justice mission would be further strengthened through an explicit commitment to supporting those who struggle for basic human rights and dignity using active nonviolent means. Although there are sometimes tensions between perspectives that advocate "peace" and those that advocate "justice," in reality these camps ought to be bridged, as the Pontifical Council of Justice and Peace signifies.[16] There is nothing inherently contradictory in using tactics that nonviolently disrupt the status quo and those that embrace dialogue, mutual understanding, and reconciliation. In his famous April 16, 1963, "Letter from a Birmingham Jail," Martin Luther King, Jr., responded to criticisms that the sometimes disruptive tactics of the US civil rights movement were "unwise and untimely" and that he should be seeking dialogue instead:

> You may well ask, "Why direct action? Why sit ins, marches, and so forth? Isn't negotiation a better path?" You are quite right in calling for negotiation. Indeed, this is the very

---

[16] Maria J. Stephan, "The Peacebuilder's Field Guide to Protest Movements," *Foreign Policy*, January 22, 2016.

purpose of direct action. Nonviolent direct action seeks to create such a crisis and foster such a tension that a community which has constantly refused to negotiate is forced to confront the issue.

In conflicts where power is uneven and discrimination is institutionalized, those power dynamics need to shift in order for negotiation and lasting peace to have a chance. Violent extremist groups like ISIS recruit disaffected youth and others by claiming that only violence will allow them to resist injustice and exclusion. That narrative needs to be fiercely challenged. There are remarkable examples of nonviolent resistance being used against ISIS in Iraq and Syria.[17] In Kenya, militants from the extremist group Al Shabab boarded a passenger bus in 2014 and demanded that the Christians and Muslims be separated—a tactic that had been used prior to mass killings of Christians. The Muslim passengers, mostly women, refused to be separated. They insisted that the militants should shoot everyone or leave, and they put hijabs on the heads of the Christian women. Amazingly, the militants left, and nobody was killed.[18] Fortunately, powerful alternatives to violence exist, and the church can play a powerful role in spreading the message of how effective and faithful nonviolent struggle really is.

Conclusion

Through its teachings, advocacy, and support for peacebuilding and social justice endeavors globally, the Catholic Church shepherds manifold moral and material resources to promote a world without violence. Committing to supporting those around the world engaged in nonviolent resistance to advance rights, peace, and dignity—doctrinally, through Catholic teaching, education, and formation; through the policy-influencing arms of the church;

---

[17] Maria J. Stephan, "Resisting ISIS," *Sojourners* (April 2015); see also ibid., "Civil Resistance vs. ISIS," *Journal of Resistance Studies* 1, no. 2 (2015).

[18] "Kenyan Muslims Shield Christians in Mandera Bus Attack," BBC, December 21, 2015.

and through field-based programs—is a concrete and powerful way to counter violence globally. Increasing solidarity and material support to those nonviolent change agents around the world is a specific way to reduce the huge loss of life that inevitably follows when people take up arms or governments drop bombs.

Fortunately, there is an ever-expanding library of resources—books, films, nonviolent action training manuals, online courses—and a growing number of capacity-building organizations around the world that specialize in helping conflict-affected communities organize nonviolently for change. The US Institute of Peace, Rhize, the International Center on Nonviolent Conflict, Nonviolent Peaceforce, the American Friends Services Committee, Operation Dove, and Christian Peacemakers Teams are only a few such organizations. Together with remarkably active and effective organizations like Pax Christi, Mercy Corps, Caritas International, and Catholic Relief Services, expanding and deepening partnerships and synergies focused on improving knowledge and skills related to strategic nonviolent action could help prevent and mitigate violent conflict around the world. At a policy level, combining a principled denunciation of war with firm support for those nonviolently resisting injustices—and embracing the peaceful warriors on the front lines of nonviolent change—would be a profound step in realizing Pope Francis's vision of a world in which conflicts are transformed without violence.

Nonviolence More Deeply Examined

Mexico

Early in the conference Pietro Ameglio from Mexico stressed the importance of asking whether our nonviolent actions are effective:

"I think nonviolence needs a place and a time. You can't speak in the abstract about nonviolence because different situations change strategies and tactics. I learned for many years from a Maryknoll priest in Mexico about nonviolence—what la Virgen de Guadalupe said to Juan Diego, the indigenous—for me are the two main qualities of nonviolence: to be humble and to have audacity. I think it is a very big challenge, not only to churches but to many of us, to have more audacity. We can't be perfect without audacity.

"It's a different kind of nonviolent struggle. One thing we know is that nonviolent struggle has a direct relationship with the adversary. So, if the adversary is disappearing people, killing people, with no justice, we can't keep organizing marches and publishing letters in the paper because that is only 'symbolic action.'

"We do symbolic actions, but the process of war continues. We must have the courage to ask whether what we are doing is stopping the violence and dehumanization or not. In this sense, churches have a very big role because there is a tool in nonviolent struggle that is moral reserve [the moral authority of certain social actors that they are able to use as leverage in the service of the societal values that their moral authority represents]. Churches have a social force that many of us don't have. Our big challenge is how to push hierarchy into the middle of a nonviolent testimony against power. Nonviolence has a constructive program, as Gandhi said, in the social network, but it also has to challenge power using the nonviolent weapon of moral reserve—otherwise the process continues."

Lebanon

In the fourth session of the conference Ogarit Younan, founder of the Academic University for Non-violence and Human Rights in the Arab world (AUNHOR), based in Lebanon, spoke about the challenge and the promise of promoting nonviolence:

"Nonviolence for me, is not an ideology, obviously. It's not a doctrine, it's not something that's frozen, that's closed. It's a "no" that ruptures violence. . . . But I prefer using words like *action* and *fight against injustices.* We have the obligation and the responsibility to fight, by nonviolent means, to change structures, ways of thinking, education, the use of force in society. It's a fight. That's why I say if we're going to add something to the word *peace*, we should add *nonviolent fight.* If we add something to the word *war,* we add *no to war.* It's not just *just war.* . . .

"Humans aren't born nonviolent and then turn violent. No, they have both capacities . . . and it's through education and environment that we prepare them to use much less violence or more violence in their lives. So it depends on our work vis-à-vis the individual through education—all instruction, not only at school. The media, the family, religions. . . .

"I had the chance recently to start a university of nonviolence and to introduce nonviolent education in Lebanon, in the Arab countries, over the last thirty years. I have found that education is a must, it's the essence of human life. Without it we wouldn't open up to change or the possibilities of nonviolence. Without it we would be left with authoritarianism, violence, and the acceptance of violence. . . .

"Obviously, there are no models. Each country works on justice and peace. In Lebanon during the war we came up with the slogan: *partial fights to general violence.* We have global violence, economic, political, war, religious war, civil war, and so on, so we have to concretize partial fights to have results here and there to accumulate through the years. In this way we can present models of successful nonviolent fights. We need to look at nonviolence not as something that is cute or fun, though not useful or effective. We need to present nonviolent models that have the power to accomplish change."

France

Also in the fourth session French philosopher and author Jean-Marie Muller offered his thoughts on the concept of nonviolence:

"The word *nonviolence* is a word that is hard insofar as that it's a negative word . . . *non*violence. So to what does the word *nonviolence* say no? You'll say, 'to violence.' But what do we mean by violence?

"First, it's rejection of violence that kills. The basic principle of universal wisdom is 'you will not kill,' and the human person, in the end, fears more killing another person than dying—taking the risk of dying to avoid killing rather than taking the risk of killing to avoid dying. But the ideology of just war or legitimate violence is to take the risk of killing to avoid death.

"At the same time we can't content ourselves with defining nonviolence as the refusal of violence. We need a positive definition of nonviolence. We can't keep on saying that there should be no war and that there should be peace. Condemning war has never reduced war. Making promises of peace never has built peace. What we need is an alternative to violence that builds peace.

"Here we need to refer to Gandhi. Gandhi was at the same time a wise man who lived nonviolence—not only outside his society but in the heart of the conflicts in his own society. He first and foremost proposed a strategy of resistance to free India from colonial oppression by Britain. He tried to convince the Brits, to negotiate with the Brits. But that became impossible, and he finally initiated an act of civil disobedience by disobeying the law regarding salt. We have to be careful not to accept an idealized notion of nonviolence that only relies on dialogue and negotiation. . . .

"We shouldn't have an idealistic vision of nonviolence as the repudiation of conflict. I am thrilled that in the text that the cardinal read yesterday, in the text of the pope, there is a call to face conflict—to not think that nonviolence is the absence of conflict. Conflict is necessary for creating peace.[19]

---

[19] [In his letter to conference participants, reprinted in the "Preamble" of this volume, Pope Francis writes, "We must accept and tackle conflict so as to resolve it and transform it." Cf. *Evangelii gaudium* (2013), no. 227.—Ed.]

"So, we must absolutely put ourselves in a mindset to create conflict. We have to create the conditions that allow for dialogue. . . .

"Martin Luther King, Jr., tried to negotiate with whites to get justice. Dialogue wasn't possible, negotiation wasn't possible, so he went to Birmingham to perform civil disobedience. The notion of civil disobedience is central. Obedience to the state is the foundation of justice. He performed actions of civil disobedience, and he was put in jail. Then there were religious representatives, four Protestants and one rabbi, who accused him of creating disorder. When order is unjust, then actions for justice seem to be disorder. The bishops wanted to negotiate; they didn't understand that what King did was to create the conditions for dialogue, the conditions for negotiation. So Martin Luther King, Jr., replied, from prison, 'You ask why direct nonviolent actions in the streets? Why don't I think negotiations are the best way? You're right to ask for negotiations. In fact, that's precisely the goal of direct action.'[20]

"Direct nonviolent action tries to foment enough tension so that the community, at first not willing to negotiate, finally accepts it as a solution. So we need to find ways to create conditions for dialogue. Dialogue isn't the solution to conflict. We must create the right conditions for dialogue to find solutions to conflict. That means we need opposing actions. Even Gandhi couldn't dialogue with the Brits to obtain independence. He had to perform actions of civil

---

[20] "Nonviolent direct action seeks to create such a crisis and foster such a tension that a community which has constantly refused to negotiate is forced to confront the issue. It seeks so to dramatize the issue that it can no longer be ignored. My citing the creation of tension as part of the work of the nonviolent resister may sound rather shocking. But I must confess that I am not afraid of the word 'tension.' I have earnestly opposed violent tension, but there is a type of constructive, nonviolent tension which is necessary for growth. . . . The purpose of our direct action program is to create a situation so crisis packed that it will inevitably open the door to negotiation" (King, "Letter from a Birmingham Jail").

disobedience. He had the goal to create a dialogue with the Brits, but dialogue wasn't possible. So dialogue isn't the way to resolve conflicts. What resolves conflicts is opposition. Opposition to violent force."

Lisa Cahill added:

"What would be an alternative to just war that the pope or the Catholic Church could propose for everybody? I think it has to be a positive vision. One vocabulary and model that has been proposed here—not the only way to talk about it, but it's an example—is the just peace model. Concretely, many people have talked about forms of nonviolent resistance to injustice that are effective. . . . You talk about abolishing war as a legal measure, and so the question is who will do this and how will that happen? Sometimes I think it's better to speak in terms of more modest initiatives that might be more successful. For example, giving international recognition and support . . . to nonviolent movements. Maria Stephan was asking in our last group why there wasn't media attention to the nonviolent resisters in Syria before it got to a point that the United States and France were considering military intervention. So there are measures that could be taken by the international community, or some agents or networks in the international arena, not only under religious auspices."

Eli McCarthy, in Session 3, noted that we have examples of ISIS actually negotiating with other groups, for example, around hostages, prisoners, and humanitarian aid access in the areas where they are in control:

"There are a whole range of nonviolent practices such as nonviolent resistance, where you try to diffuse the sources of power . . . or you create a defection strategy where you identify defectors from ISIS who can then witness to members of ISIS and start to limit the number of people in that group. Some defectors are already drawing others out of ISIS. Also there's unarmed civilian protection. Right now Nonviolent Peaceforce and Cure Violence are training Syrians on how to do unarmed civilian protection in their neighborhoods. So that can become a piece of the puzzle. There's trauma healing that can be used in a really strategic way to help make it less likely that people will join ISIS or perhaps even build more of a pool in ISIS of people ready to leave. I don't think we have to limit ourselves to dialogue. Sometimes people aren't quite ready for dialogue, so we have to think outside of the box."

Sri Lanka

Prior to the conference, Fr. Nandana Manatunga from Sri Lanka offered the following reflection on urgent nonviolent steps toward peace in his country:

The civil war in Sri Lanka, though classified as an ethnic conflict, is also one based on sacred identities and religious separations. The mobilization of religion for ethno-nationalistic purposes plays a key role in the war's social and political history. To gain power, the early Sinhalese elite used the historical record of an ancient Buddhist heritage to unite the Sinhalese into a base of electoral support. In its rise to power the ruling Sinhalese elite tended to ignore the needs of Sri Lanka's minorities, severely damaging its relations with them.

Since religion has been so effectively tied to the ethnic conflict in Sri Lanka, it becomes particularly difficult for religious leaders who seek to be close to the ethos of their coreligionists to abandon the norm and speak for such a negotiated peace. As representatives of their group's beliefs, their public personae are subject to both external and internal pressure. There is usually more inducement to adhere to the more popular nationalist agenda, which can make it extremely difficult for religious leaders to openly support a political peace. Buddhist monks, who are the most influential on the political leadership, are also the most subject to such restraint.

On the other hand, Catholics are influential in Sri Lankan society, as Catholics are both Sinhalese and Tamils. A few Catholics have been in key positions, headed the army, or the judiciary. They are also represented in the government and opposition political parties at high levels.

The Catholic Church as an institution has always worked for a political solution to the ethnic conflict that addresses the roots of the conflict and has also opposed war and violence as a solution.

The church has played an important role in peacebuilding and has stood by the victims of war. During the war the Catholic bishops acted as facilitators carrying messages between the Sri Lankan government leaders and leaders of the LTTE. In this regard Bishop Rayappu Joseph played a vital role.

Nonviolence, in Catholic eyes, is both a Christian and a human virtue. For Christians, nonviolence takes on special meaning in the suffering of Christ, who was "led as a sheep to the slaughter" (Is 53:7; Acts 8:32). The nonviolent witness of Christians contributes to the building up of peace in a way that force cannot, discerning the difference between the cowardice which gives in to evil and the violence which under the illusion of fighting evil, only makes it worse.

In the Catholic view nonviolence ought to be implemented in public policies and through public institutions as well as in personal and church practice. Both in pastoral practice and through Vatican diplomacy, the church insists, in the face of conflict, that peace is possible. The church also attempts to nourish a culture of peace in civil society and encourages the establishment of institutions for the practice of nonviolence in public life.

On the pastoral level the Catholic theology of peace takes a positive stance. It focuses on resolving the causes of conflict and building the conditions for lasting peace. It entails four primary components: the promotion and protection of human rights; advancing integral human development; supporting international law and international organizations; and building solidarity between peoples and the nation.

We need to invest energy in grassroots peacebuilding initiatives in Sri Lanka with a deeper and wider practice of nonviolence within the Catholic community, and . . . we need to invest energy in reforming the judiciary and the policing system in Sri Lanka by motivating and mobilizing the civil society to establish the rule of law.

Countless movements around the world have shown that action which is both nonviolent and determined is often essential to overcoming the roadblocks to a just and peaceful solution in situations of oppression and violent conflict. Nonviolent action can dramatize the issue at hand and foster the creative tension that encourages all parties and the larger community to find a path to justice and peace.

But active nonviolence is also much broader than that. In the past few decades we have learned a great deal about how to build and sustain just peace—much of that body of knowledge was referenced in the High-Level Independent Panel on United Nations Peace Operations report, "Uniting Our Strengths for Peace—Politics, Partnership, and People," from June 16, 2015. The report specifically highlights a variety of nonviolent approaches, emphasizing the importance of preventing armed conflict; of mobilizing partnerships to support political solutions; of employing unarmed and civilian tools for protecting civilians; of emphasizing inclusion, healing, and reconciliation; of addressing the underlying causes of conflict; of revitalizing livelihoods in conflict-affected economies; of rebuilding confidence in political processes and responsible state structures; of reforming police; of promoting the rule of law; and of ensuring respect for human rights.

8

Catholic Just Peace Practice

Rose Marie Berger

Am I really my brother's keeper? Yes, you are your brother's keeper! To be human means to care for one another! But when harmony is broken, a metamorphosis occurs: the brother who is to be cared for and loved becomes an adversary to fight, to kill. What violence occurs at that moment, how many conflicts, how many wars have marked our history!

—Pope Francis,
"Vigil of Prayer for Peace,"
September 7, 2013

Introduction: The following essay provides an extensive overview of the just peace concept as it is developing through the work of numerous scholar and theologians, the World Council of Churches, peace practitioners, and nonviolent activists.

Rose Marie Berger is senior associate editor at *Sojourners* magazine, Catholic peace activist, and poet. The essay presented here was written for the April 2016 conference and originally published as "No Longer Legitimating War: Christians and Just Peace." It has been slightly adapted for this volume.

In these times, Roman Catholics have an opportunity to love the world in new ways and to see it through the eyes of future generations. Pope Francis models in *Laudato Si'* how a fresh approach to ancient tenets can catalyze astonishing change in our human family. As he has led on climate change and care for "our Sister, Mother Earth" (no. 1), we too can find fresh approaches to the biblical call to be peacemakers.

What Is Just Peace?

Just peace is a Christian school of thought and set of practices for building peace at all stages of acute conflict—before, during, and after. It draws on three key approaches—principles and moral criteria, practical norms, and virtue ethics—for building a positive peace and constructing a more "widely known paradigm with agreed practices that make peace and prevent war."[1] Just peace principles and moral criteria guide actions that can assist institutional change and provide a framework for judging ethical responsibility. Just peace practical norms provide guidance on constructive actions for peace, can be tested for effectiveness, and point toward a comprehensive just peace pedagogy and skills-based training. Just peace virtue ethics teaches how to change our hearts. It asks what type of people we are becoming through the virtues we cultivate and shows us how to become people of peace. These three aspects form a "head, body, heart" approach. Just peace is not merely the absence of violence but the presence of social, economic, and political conditions that sustain peace and human flourishing and prevent conflicts from turning violent or returning to violence.[2] Just peace can help Christians move beyond war.

[1] Glen H. Stassen, "Just-Peacemaking Theory," *Dictionary of Scripture and Ethics*, ed. Joel B. Green, Jacqueline Lapsley, Rebekah Miles, Allen Verhey (Grand Rapids, MI: Baker Publishing Group, 2011), 443.

[2] Part of this language came from a personal email exchange with David Cortright at Notre Dame's Kroc Institute for International Peace, March 3, 2016.

Just Peace in Biblical and Christian Tradition

Just peace is rooted in the biblical concept of shalom. Its meaning encompasses definitions such as wholeness, soundness, to be held in a peaceful covenant; to be restored, healed, and repaid. It describes both domestic tranquility and neighborliness among nation-states; both a physical state and a spiritual state. It is a quality of right relationship (see Mal 2:6). The rabbinic scholars have taught "All that is written in the Torah was written for the sake of peace" (see Midrash Tanchuma, Shoftim 18).

The phrase *Christian peacemakers* ought to be redundant. For Christians, Jesus is the incarnation of God's shalom and the manifestation of just peace. Many Christians, by the very nature of Christ's life, death, and resurrection, prioritize peace with justice and reject violence as a means toward peace, recognizing it as a failure. We are called to be courageous innovators who defend the "least of these"—without benefit of the world's weapons. The World Council of Churches (WCC) spent the millennial decade studying how to overcome violence. It produced two seminal documents: "An Ecumenical Call to Just Peace"[3] and the *Just Peace Companion*.[4] The first declared the concept and the mentality of "'just war' and its customary use to be obsolete."[5] The second offered extensive direction on implementation of just peace theology and practice. Both documents delivered a comprehensive review of scripture, ethics, values, practices, curricula, human stories, and prayer for embodying just peace within the Christian tradition and within the condition of the world in which this faith is practiced.

Every Christian is charged with resisting evil, but none is given the right to kill. On February 18, 2007, Pope Benedict XVI preached on Luke 6:27 ("Love your enemies") at his "Angeles Sermon," saying it "is rightly considered the *magna carta* of Christian nonviolence. It does not consist in succumbing to evil, as a false

---

[3] World Council of Churches, "Ecumenical Call to Just Peace" (Geneva: WCC, 2011).

[4] World Council of Churches, *Just Peace Companion* (Geneva: WCC, 2012).

[5] World Council of Churches, "Ecumenical Call to Just Peace," no. 23.

interpretation of 'turning the other cheek' claims, but in responding to evil with good and thereby breaking the chain of injustice."

Pope Francis stressed that "faith and violence are incompatible."[6]
In his June 8, 2014, address with President Shimon Peres and
President Mahmoud Abbas, Pope Francis said, "Peacemaking calls
for courage, much more so than warfare. It calls for the courage
to say yes to encounter and no to conflict; yes to dialogue and no
to violence; yes to negotiations and no to hostilities." In a June
6, 2015, interview with a journalist, Francis continued, "It is not
enough to talk about peace, peace must be made. To speak about
peace without making it is contradictory, and those who speak
about peace while promoting war, for example through the sale
of weapons, are hypocrites. It is very simple."

Just peace is an integral expression of Catholic faith and catechism[7] that can be further developed into a robust and resilient
theology,[8] theory, and praxis. If, as the US Catholic bishops wrote,
"The content and context of our peacemaking is set not by some
political agenda or ideological program, but by the teaching of his
Church,"[9] then that teaching must be full-bodied, theologically
grounded, effective, and adaptable from the local parish to the
United Nations. However, the legitimation of war in Catholic social teaching remains,[10] and according to theological ethicist Glen
Stassen, "without a widely known paradigm with agreed practices
that make peace and prevent (and defuse) war, public debate will
remain vague and unclear about the effective alternatives to the
drive to war."[11]

---

[6] Junno Arocho Esteves, "Pope Francis: 'Faith and Violence Are Incompatible,'" *Zenit,* August 19, 2013.

[7] *Catechism of the Catholic Church*, nos. 2302–2306. Available at www.
vatican.va/archive/.

[8] Fernando Enns, "Toward an Ecumenical Theology of Just Peace," in
*Just Peace: Just Peace: Ecumenical, Intercultural, and Interdisciplinary
Perspectives* (Eugene, OR: Wipf and Stock, 2013).

[9] National Conference of Catholic Bishops, *The Challenge of Peace:
God's Promise and Our Response,* Pastoral Letter on War and Peace (Washington, DC: USCCB, 1983).

[10] *Catechism of the Catholic Church,* nos. 2307–2317.

[11] Stassen, "Just-Peacemaking Theory," 443.

Three Streams of the Just Peace River

There are three broad scholarly streams that feed into the great river of just peace.

Just peace principles

The first stream identifies "principles and moral criteria" to guide action and provide a framework for judging ethical responsibility. Maryann Cusimano Love, a scholar at the Catholic University of America in Washington, DC, has spent much of her career shaping these criteria after drawing them from the practices of Catholic organizations such as Caritas Internationalis. She has also been honing their effectiveness in the highest circles of government and the military. In a formulation that is familiar from just war principles,[12] Love has identified seven just peace principles that serve as a guide for directing action:

1. *Just cause*: protecting, defending, and restoring the fundamental dignity of all human life and the common good
2. *Right intention*: aiming to create a positive peace
3. *Participatory process*: respecting human dignity by including societal stakeholders—state and non- state actors as well as previous parties to the conflict
4. *Right relationship*: creating or restoring just social relationships both vertically and horizontally; strategic systemic change requires that horizontal and vertical relationships move in tandem on an equal basis
5. *Reconciliation*: a concept of justice that envisions a holistic healing of the wounds of war
6. *Restoration*: repair of the material, psychological, and spiritual human infrastructure

---

[12] For Maryann Cusimano Love's comparison of just war principles and just peace principles, see Dr. Maryann Cusimano Love, "Drones: Ethics and Use," Center for International Social Development, Politics Department, Catholic University (Washington, DC: February 4, 2014).

7. *Sustainability*: developing structures that can help peace endure over time.[13]

Just peace principles are applied at all stages of conflict. They are not only for *responding* to violence or war. From Love's point of view, peacebuilding tools and other methods of conflict transformation and nonviolence are all tools to implement just peace, and her just peace criteria guide those practices.[14]

For example, Love has examined the work of Caritas Internationalis, a confederation of 165 Catholic relief, development, and social service organizations operating in two hundred countries. Its mission is to work for a better world, especially for the poor and oppressed. "Emergency response" to natural disaster, conflict, and climate change is one part of its work. The bulk of it, however, is the systemic building up of just societies. Caritas Internationalis and its US partner, Catholic Relief Services, have embedded Love's just peace principles into their trainings, and they practice ways of operationalizing just peace on the ground.[15]

Love's approach is relationship centered and participatory.[16] Right relationship requires high levels of participation, bringing in multiple stakeholders. "That is very different from the type of peace being built by the United Nations or the [US] Department of Defense," says Love.

They very rarely, if ever, ask for any input from the local population. If you look at the United Nations-sponsored

---

[13] Maryann Cusimano Love, "What Kind of Peace Do We Seek? Emerging Norms of Peacebuilding in Key Political Institutions," *Peacebuilding: Catholic Theology, Ethics, and Praxis*, ed. Robert J. Schreiter, R. Scott Appleby, and Gerard F. Powers (Maryknoll, NY: Orbis Books, 2010), 82.

[14] Maryann Cusimano Love specifically refers to the conflict transformation work of John Paul Lederach and Lisa Schirch and to Gene Sharp's 198 methods of nonviolence (personal email correspondence, March 2, 2016).

[15] Mark M. Rogers, Tom Bamat, Julie Ideh, eds., *Pursuing Just Peace: An Overview and Case Studies for Faith-Based Peacebuilders*. (Baltimore: Catholic Relief Services, 2008), front matter.

[16] Ibid., 5.

peace negotiations held since 1992, 98 percent have been without any—zero—participation of women. That's a pretty significant omission. And there are many other omissions, such as of civil society groups, religious groups, and youth groups. . . . Participation is not an important value for Catholic peacebuilders just because it works, but because we truly believe in the dignity of all human life. If all people have this sacred human dignity, then all people should be part of that process.[17]

Again, just peace principles are applied at all stages of conflict. They are not only for *responding* to violence or fundamental dignity of all human life.

Love's just peace criteria are particularly well suited for use with institutional change. Institutions, writes Love, "are key for new norms to take hold."[18] Institutions *do* change, but they "learn by doing."[19] She has used these principles in her work with the United Nations, the US Department of Defense, the US Department of State, and other large institutions. "The Catholic Church helped create, publicize, and institutionalize just war norms internationally,"[20] writes Love. She argues that it is an opportune time to do the same with just peace norms.

Just peace practices

The second stream identifies just peace *practical norms*. These are just peacemaking practices, available for use before, during, and after conflict, that can be tested for effectiveness, provide guidance on constructive actions for peace, and point toward a comprehensive just peace pedagogy and skills-based training.

---

[17] Maryann Cusimano Love, "Peace by Piece: On Peacebuilding with Maryann Cusimano Love," interview by the editors, *US Catholic* 76, no. 9 (2011): 12–16.

[18] Love, "What Kind of Peace Do We Seek?, 56.

[19] Ibid., 58.

[20] Ibid., 56.

Over the past thirty years, numerous scholars have contributed to honing a set of ten just peacemaking practices. Ethicist Glen Stassen at Fuller Theological Seminary in California and theologian Susan Brooks Thistlethwaite at Chicago Theological Seminary have brought significant leadership to this robust set of just peace practical norms. Stassen has described just peacemaking as "the new paradigm for an ethics of peace and war,"[21] shifting the debate away from limiting war, as just war principles do, to practicing peace.

These just peace norms have been used in a variety of settings, such as negotiations on nuclear disarmament, diplomatic intervention seeking to stop the US invasion of Iraq,[22] denominational general conventions choosing to identify as "just peace churches,"[23] interreligious and interfaith collaborative efforts to develop just peace in other traditions,[24] and intervention to combat global gender-based violence.[25]

Stassen has argued, "It is necessary to have both (1) an explicitly Christian ethic with a strong scriptural base and (2) a public ethic that appeals to reason, experience, and need, and that cannot place the same emphasis on scripture and prayer that an explicitly Christian ethic can."[26] The version of the ten just peacemaking practices below reflects both.

---

[21] Glen H. Stassen, "Winning the Peace," *Sojourners* 34, no.1 (2005): 19.

[22] Ibid.

[23] Susan Brooks Thistlethwaite, "A Just Peace Future, part 1," *United Church News* (June 5, 2011) and "A Just Peace Future, part 2," *United Church News* (June 12, 2011). For more, see the *Just Peace Church Handbook* (United Church of Christ: Justice and Witness Ministries, 2015).

[24] Susan B. Thistlethwaite, ed., *Interfaith Just Peacemaking: Jewish, Christian, and Muslim Perspectives on the New Paradigm of Peace and War* (New York: Palgrave Macmillan US, 2012).

[25] Susan Brooks Thistlethwaite, *Women's Bodies as Battlefield: Christian Theology and the Global War on Women* (New York: Palgrave Macmillan US, 2015).

[26] Glen H. Stassen, *Just Peacemaking: Transforming Initiatives for Justice and Peace* (Louisville, KY: Westminster/John Knox Press, 1992), 93–94.

Part One: Peacemaking Initiatives

1. Support nonviolent direct action (biblical basis: Matt 5:38–42).
2. Take independent initiatives to reduce threat (biblical basis: Matt 5:38–42).
3. Use cooperative conflict resolution (biblical basis: Matt 5:21–26).
4. Acknowledge responsibility for conflict and injustice and seek repentance and forgiveness (biblical basis: Matt 7:1–5).

Part Two: Working for Justice

5. Advance democracy, human rights, and religious liberty (biblical basis: Matt 6:19–34).
6. Foster just and sustainable economic development (biblical basis: Matt 6:19–34).

Part Three: Fostering Love and Community

7. Work with emerging cooperative forces in the international system (biblical basis: Matt 5:43ff.).
8. Strengthen the United Nations and international efforts for cooperation and human rights (biblical basis: Matt 5:43ff.).
9. Reduce offensive weapons and weapons trade (biblical basis: Matt 5:38ff.).
10. Encourage grassroots peacemaking groups and voluntary associations (biblical basis: Matt 5:1–2; 7:28–29).[27]

In his work Stassen notes that his team was

> aware that our social context includes a private/public dualism in which Jesus' way and also peacemaking get interpreted as idealistic and individualistic. To counter this distortion, we intentionally focused on ten practices—not

---

[27] This version of the ten peacemaking practices is adapted from Stassen, "Just-Peacemaking Theory," 443.

ten ideals—and on historical and political-science evidence showing each practice is in fact working to prevent some wars. Furthermore, with the human nature variable in mind, a realistic understanding of human sin argues that these practices need to be institutionalized in policies, international networks, and laws in order to check and balance concentrations of political, economic, and military power.[28]

Just peace virtues and ethics

The third stream is just peace virtue ethics. A virtue is a disposition to "do good." It is not just doing something good because it is required or because one can see the benefits. It is being good deep down, with an innate wisdom and intuition of what will be generative for life and flourishing. Some virtues come naturally. Others, called moral virtues, are acquired through practice, devotion, and community. Virtue ethics teaches how to create morally good cultures that foster morally good people.

Eli S. McCarthy is a Catholic theological virtue ethicist at Georgetown University in Washington, DC. He has elaborated a just peace virtue ethic by integrating the just peace approaches of Stassen, Thistlethwaite, and Love. Virtue ethics, writes McCarthy, "is focused on the character of persons, but includes concern for both acts and ends or consequences. In virtue ethics, the primary ethical question asked is 'Who are we (am I) becoming?' before, 'What is the rule?' or 'What are the consequences?'"[29]

McCarthy states that "nonviolent peacemaking ought to be assessed as a distinct and central virtue" in and of its own right. If nonviolent peacemaking is a key virtue, then other virtues, such as justice and courage, are qualified in a new way and

---

[28] Glen H. Stassen, "Transforming Initiatives of Just Peacemaking Based on the Triadic Structure of the Sermon on the Mount," paper prepared for the Society of Biblical Literature, 2006.

[29] Eli S. McCarthy, "Called to Holiness: Integrating the Virtue of Nonviolent Peacemaking," *Journal of Catholic Social Thought* 11 (Winter 2014): 67–92.

often-overlooked virtues such as "humility, solidarity, hospitality, and mercy" might be better recovered. McCarthy has developed seven practices that flow from and cultivate nonviolent peacemaking as a virtue.

1. Celebrating the Eucharist as Christ's nonviolent act of self-sacrifice,[30] with secondary components of prayer, meditation, and fasting;
2. Training and education in nonviolent peacemaking and resistance, with secondary component of forming nonviolent peacemaking communities;
3. Attention to religious or spiritual factors, especially in public discourse, and learning about religion, particularly in the form of intra-religious or interreligious dialogue;
4. A constructive program with its particular focus on the poor and marginalized;
5. Conflict transformation and restorative justice, particularly in the form of Truth and Reconciliation Commissions;
6. Unarmed civilian protection, a third-party intervention both in the form of international implementation and local peace teams;
7. Civilian-based defense, a nonviolent form of civil defense that engages the broader society against an external threat or in the overthrow of a government.[31]

McCarthy has argued that Love's just peace criteria and Stassen's and Thistlethwaite's just peacemaking practical norms have embedded in them a desire for Christians to become better and more just peacemakers. He has added to their work an "orienting virtue ethic" along with the focused question, "What kind of people are we becoming?"

---

[30] See Emmanuel Charles McCarthy, "The Nonviolent Eucharistic Jesus: A Pastoral Approach" (Wilmington, DE: Center for Christian Nonviolence, n.d.); and Raniero Cantalamessa, "Eucharist Is 'God's Absolute No' to Violence," 3rd Lenten sermon, delivered March 11, 2005.

[31] McCarthy "Called to Holiness," 67–92.

A virtue ethics approach to nonviolent peacemaking would amplify the development of character and the kind of imagination that engages and creatively applies, extends, and even corrects the practical norms of Stassen's just peacemaking. (For example, some limits to Stassen's original just peacemaking principles have been that they focus only on reducing offensive weapons and so have nothing to say about nuclear abolition. Some scholars have interpreted the principles to legitimate limited violent intervention in conflict.[32]) It would create the environment for the kinds of people who are willing to risk "unarmed civilian protection" and create the space for the practices of reconciliation, conflict transformation, and care for creation[33] through the related virtue of solidarity and nonviolent civilian-based defense.[34]

McCarthy has described his just peace approach as both a vision and an ethic. As a vision it expresses the reality of shalom and the integration of peace and justice as modeled by Jesus. As an ethic it offers a way of justice via peacemaking and peace via justice making. Here, just peace must include a "moral commitment to illuminating human dignity, but also ensuring human rights and cultivating thriving relationships," argues McCarthy. "This ethic offers a set of core virtues to form our character and shape core practices, as well as to both orient and better apply a set of just peace criteria for specific actions to engage conflict."[35]

---

[32] For more, see Martin L. Cook, "Just Peacemaking: Challenges of Humanitarian Intervention," *Journal of the Society of Christian Ethics* 23, no. 1 (2010): 241–53.

[33] *Laudato Si'* ("On Care for Our Common Home") makes it clear that care for creation is integral to human flourishing and abuse of creation leads to conflict and war. One avenue of exploration is to ask how the Earth Charter or the emerging field of earth law fit into the just peace paradigm. Restorative justice practitioner Elaine Enns uses restorative justice principles in determining moral responsibility with regard to "injured" biosystems. See Elaine Enns, "Galvanizing Will: What 'Restorative Justice' Means to the Voiceless Victims," *Sojourners* (August 2010).

[34] Eli S. McCarthy, "Summoning the Catholic Church: Turn to Just Peace" (2016), www.nonviolencejustpeace.net.

[35] Ibid.; and "Beyond Just War: Pope Francis and Justpeace," Catholic Moral Theology blog, June 3, 2014.

What Does Just Peace Look Like in Action?

Catholic communities already embody and practice just peace. Cardinal Peter Turkson said in 2013:

> From South Sudan, the Middle East, and Central America to Congo, Colombia, and the Philippines, the Catholic Church is a powerful force for peace, freedom, justice, and reconciliation. But this impressive and courageous peacebuilding often remains unknown, under-analyzed, and unappreciated.[36]

There is an opportunity for developing these significant bodies of experience, wisdom, and research into an effective and integrated just peace approach across the breadth of the church.

Having looked at three streams, let us look now at the river in action. What can be learned when just peace principles, practical norms, and virtue ethics are applied to nuclear weapons, armed drones, and civil war?

Just peace and nuclear weapons

If the Cold War is over, why do we still have nuclear weapons? Maryann Cusimano Love has argued that analyzing the Cold War through the lens of just peace teaches us that the Cold War did not end well. Not only did it leave us with nuclear weapons but also with "alert force postures and cultures of suspicion."[37] Therefore, in just peace terms, relationships are not "right." Without right relationships, reconciliation, restoration, and long-term sustainable peace are not possible. Love proves her case by applying a standard peacebuilders' tool called "disarmament, demobilization, and reintegration/reconciliation" to the relationship between the United States and Russia. She has argued that

---

[36] Cardinal Peter Turkson, "Enhancing the Study and Practice of Catholic Peacebuilding," presentation, Washington, DC, Catholic University of America, April 9–10, 2013.

[37] Maryann Cusimano Love, "Building a Better Peace: A Future Worthy of Our Faith," *America* 213, no. 3 (August 3–10, 2015).

this peacebuilding process was never completed, because the Cold War didn't end; it just changed. There was some disarmament, but without demobilization and without building deeper relationships. Love writes,

> To achieve deeper disarmament we need to build deeper relationships. To build deeper relationships, we need more people-building relationships. That means not just state government activities but exchanges between church and civil society, dialogue and engagement to broaden the work of reintegration and reconciliation. . . . [Just peace in this case means] moving away from a peace based on desolation and mutually assured destruction, and instead moving to a peace based on right relationships and mutually assured reductions of nuclear weapons.[38]

Susan Brooks Thistlethwaite has seen just peacemaking practical norms at work in the Obama administration's nuclear negotiations with Iran. "One can see how much 'multiple stakeholders' were brought in to the significant Iran Nuclear Deal," she writes, "and that is central to just peace practice #9" (to reduce offensive weapons and weapons trade). Obama's 2009 Nobel Peace Prize speech exemplifies some understanding of just peace practices.[39] However, Thistlethwaite is concerned that the Obama administration tried to "cobble together elements of both just peace and just war theory without, in fact, analyzing deeply how many contradictions are thus imported into foreign policy."[40]

Eli S. McCarthy argues that if one examines the issue of nuclear weapons in the context of the nonviolent peacemaking virtue ethic—including that the "how" of the process must be consistent in character with the "what" of the goal—then a just peace virtue

---

[38] Ibid.

[39] President Barack H. Obama, "A Just and Lasting Peace," Nobel Peace Prize lecture (December 10, 2009).

[40] Susan Brooks Thistlethwaite, personal email correspondence with author, March 2, 2016.

ethic would challenge just peacemaking practice #9 of reducing only *offensive* weapons as both an unclear distinction and an inadequate one.[41]

Just peace and armed drones

Using just war theory, the Obama administration defined US drone strikes in Afghanistan as "legal, ethical, and wise."[42] Are they? Love argues against the Obama administration's position. Proponents of drone warfare argue that use of armed drones is "more moral" than sending in ground forces or massive aerial bombing. Love says that "drones are used where the United States would never send ground troops . . . where wars have not been declared and where the United States would otherwise not intervene conventionally. Thus drones are extending, not limiting, killing." They do not build a positive peace. They do not protect the common good.[43]

Thistlethwaite also has critiqued the Obama administration's authorizing of drone strikes. Killing without risk, without humanization, she argues, greatly increases "moral hazard" and risky behavior. She has seen nations too easily tempted to use armed drones. Just peace, Thistlethwaite writes, "can offer a roadmap to create real conditions for addressing the causes of terrorism that will obviate the perceived need for drones. Just peace, in this sense, is a proposal for a counterterrorism strategy that does not involve the use of drones, or presume the necessity of force."[44]

McCarthy writes, "Just war theory doesn't prioritize or illuminate a more important *moral* question about human habits" when it comes to drones.[45] He suggests shifting the primary moral analysis

---

[41] McCarthy, "Summoning the Catholic Church."

[42] Jeff Carney (White House press secretary), press briefing, February 5, 2013.

[43] Love, "Drones."

[44] Rev. Dr. Susan Brooks Thistlethwaite, "Just War, Just Peace and Drones," Interfaith Drone Network, n.d.

[45] Eli S. McCarthy, "What Are Drones Doing to Us?" *America,* blog post, April 2, 2013.

of armed drones away from law, just war, and rights to the question of virtue and character: "What kind of people are we becoming by using armed drones?" Rather than building right relationships, drones instill fear and decrease trust. Using drones to kill people makes us the kind of people who "cultivate fear in communities as they wonder if they may be attacked just because they are in the wrong place at the wrong time."[46] Rather than respecting human dignity, drones dehumanize. Using armed drones often dictates against promoting development, practicing restorative justice, and training for nonviolent civilian resistance. Drones mask the root causes of conflict, which leads to cycles of violence. Using armed drones significantly damages our capacity for empathy, a core virtue of human flourishing. Drones drain hope—they create deep levels of anxiety in the targeted communities and erode any sense of being able to change one's situation. Drones diminish the virtues of solidarity—both with the targeted communities and within our own society where the vulnerable become a "faceless" other.[47]

Just peace and civil war in Mozambique

Peacebuilding principles, practices, and virtues can also arise from the ground in a manner that is reflective of just peace. More than one million Mozambicans died as a result of war in the years between the 1964 fight for independence and the civil war that followed it. Using a version of just peace principles, the Mozambican Christian Council (CCM) and the Mozambican Catholic Church helped end the armed conflict. Working across traditional divisions, the multidenominational Christian Council and Catholic

---

[46] Ibid.

[47] Ibid. For other examples, see Eli S. McCarthy, "Just Peace Response to Syria," *America* (February 24, 2012); idem, "Interrupting Hostilities and Seeking Justice in Syria," *America* (September 4, 2013); and idem, "Religious Leaders Urge a JustPeace Response to ISIS," *Huffington Post* (September 19, 2014).

Church adopted the following practical principles in their quest for peace:

- Look for what unites rather than what divides [right relationship].
- Discuss problems step by step [participatory process].
- Keep in mind the suffering that so many people endure as war continues [cultivate empathy and human dignity].
- Work with the friends and supporters of both sides; this is fundamental [reconciliation, right relationship, virtue of solidarity].
- Remember the deeper dimensions of peace such as forgiveness, justice, human rights, reconciliation, and trust [right intention].
- Work with other groups; the power of the churches was much increased by their inter-denominational cooperation [reconciliation, right relationship, virtue of solidarity].[48]

The Mozambican churches determined that "in working for solutions to armed conflicts, it is necessary to have patience and a method."[49] Through the virtue of patience and the method of their six just peace principles, the churches were able to adapt to the complexity of the war. Because church members had contacts on all sides of the conflict, they built up sufficient trust at the local level to travel in zones inaccessible to anyone else. In this way, the Mozambican Christian Council and Catholic Church opened up diplomatic space, provided shuttle diplomacy, and eventually brokered the 1994 Rome General Peace Accords.

---

[48] Dis S. Sengulane and Jaime Pedro Gonçalves, "A Calling for Peace: Christian Leaders and the Quest for Reeconciliation in Mozambique," in *The Mozambican Peace Process in Perspective, Accord* [An International Review of Peace Initiatives] #3 (London: Conciliation Resources, 1998), 33, http://www.c-r.org/accord/mozambique; see also Bonnie Price Lofton, "JustaPaz, 1996: Lifting Mozambique from the Rubble of War," *Eastern Mennonite University Peacebuilder* (July 28, 2015).

[49] Sengulane and Gonçalves, "A Calling for Peace," 33.

Just Peace, Just War, Just Catholic: A Conversation

In a globalized world, it no longer takes centuries for Catholic witness to reach the ends of the earth. We've moved from papyrus to @Pontifex, from frigates to Facebook. Catholic teaching on war and peace has developed slowly, over time and circumstance. In the current era the weapons of war and the communication of hate have exploded with the advance of the Internet and related technologies. There arises an opportunity to clearly communicate the Catholic faith in new ways. Does it become more important now to separate *justice* from *war and violence* in the language and witness of the church? Does just peace as language and a framework offer a positive, generative Catholic witness that, if articulated well, can take root around the world? If Catholics are called to be "first responders" in the "field hospital" of the church, what kind of training in principles, practices, and virtues does a just peace approach provide?

Just peace as the primary framework for the church?

The centuries-old just war theory sought to provide a means of determining when it was morally justifiable to break the commandment "thou shall not kill," with guidelines regarding whether to go to war (*jus ad bellum*) and how to fight war in an ethical manner (*jus in bello*). Some Catholic scholars have worked to extend just war criteria to include *jus post bellum* to guide restorative practices in a postwar context.[50]

Love asserted in an email communication that just war tradition, if anything, "tells you only how to limit war. It has nothing to say about how to build peace." She compared the applicability of just war criteria to the decline in the death penalty. "It was once thought it necessary to protect people, but now capacity has

---

[50] See Mark J. Allman and Tobias L. Winright, *After the Smoke Clears: The Just War Tradition and Post War Justice* (Maryknoll, NY: Orbis Books, 2010).

grown to protect people in other ways than the death penalty," wrote Love.[51]

Thistlethwaite wrote in an email correspondence that just peace is not just a change in terminology; instead it is "a paradigm shift away from the basic assumption behind just war criteria that war is inevitable."[52]

McCarthy argues that even a small shift in language might help delegitimize any link between "justice" and "killing," possibly opening space in Catholic imagination for relinking justice and life, justice and dignity, justice and peace. Although a shift to the language of "limited war" instead of "just war" might better illuminate some "good intentions" in the just war tradition,

> without the *turn* to a just peace approach—criteria, core practices, core virtues—then we as the Catholic Church continue to legitimate war as a practice as long as it is "limited." Such religious legitimation and more so the practice of war itself already has and will likely continue to obstruct the development of our imagination, will, and practice of just peace approaches, and thus, leave us too easily influenced and determined by those in political, economic, and military positions of power.[53]

McCarthy writes that a virtue-based approach would better prepare the Catholic Church to orient, apply, and develop Love's just peace criteria. He has advocated changing the culture of the church on war and peace by keeping its attention on these central questions: "What kind of people we are becoming?" What virtues or vices are being cultivated?

---

[51] Maryann Cusimano Love, personal email correspondence with author, March 2, 2016.

[52] Susan Brooks Thistlethwaite, personal email correspondence with author, March 2, 2016.

[53] McCarthy, "Summoning the Catholic Church."

Just peace and the Catholic Church's diplomatic work

Just war principles are deeply institutionalized in international law. If the Catholic Church adopted a just peace approach, how would it affect its diplomatic ability to persuade governments away from military action or war? Love writes that just peace principles are becoming more widely recognized and institutionalized, at the United Nations, within governments, and even in the US Department of Defense. In some cases the Department of Defense is turning away from use of lethal force and toward civilian-military relations, recognizing the need for peacebuilding over war.

> I think that much of the just war vs. just peace take down is not helpful and productive. Just war principles are deeply institutionalized in the Geneva Conventions, the US military code of justice, etc. Every arms control agreement that has ever been written has owed a debt to just war tradition's attempts to limit conflict, and limit civilian casualties. I would never want to "do away" with those normative constraints, with those limitations. But limiting conflict and trying to make war more humane is not the same as building peace.[54]

Love stresses that just peace criteria can and should be operative in every phase of conflict and conflict resolution, as well as at all levels of participation. They should entail multiple stakeholders, especially women, as well as active conflict prevention, education, economic development, and the building of participatory and transparent governance.[55] Exclusion from the process, Love argues, often fires war and lengthens it.[56] Just peace allows for a more robust intentional inclusion of women,

---

[54] Maryann Cusimano Love, personal email correspondence with author, March 2, 2016.

[55] Tobias Winright and Laurie Johnston, eds., "Just War and the Gospel Today," *Can War Be Just in the Twenty-first Century? Ethicists Engage the Tradition* (Maryknoll, NY: Orbis Books, 2015).

[56] Maryann Cusimano Love, personal email correspondence with author, March 2, 2016.

who are disproportionately affected by war. Thistlethwaite writes that sexual violence is a weapon of war and women's bodies are a strategic battlefield in any combat zone.[57] Therefore, just peace principles can address the disproportionate damage that war and violence do to women in a way that just war principles have not.

Love and others currently implement just peace criteria at the highest levels of the US government and in international and military circles. Love posits that the number of major armed conflicts in the world has declined by more than half since the beginning of the current century and that casualties in war have declined. She attributes this to overlapping trends (for example, rising number of democracies, rising economic interdependence), but also to the growing acceptance of just peace principles and a greater commitment across sectors to use peacebuilding tools to implement these principles. She observes that our overemphasis on just war since Constantine's time has caused us to miss just peace principles, which are not new, and have been hiding in plain sight.

McCarthy argues that the Catholic Church's diplomatic work would actually be enhanced by focusing on just peace principles, practices, and virtues. However,

> such impact will be truncated if the Catholic Church continues to draw on "just war" argumentation, in part because it will obstruct the development of imagination, will, and practice of just peace approaches. Further, the "just war" concept and particularly the language tends to perpetuate habits of violence in a society, thus undermining its often stated purpose of limiting war. It does this in part as an expression of Johan Galtung's "cultural violence" concept, because as a *concept* that war can be justifiable or just, it often functions as one cultural idea among many to legitimate direct and structural violence, such as large military spending and the arms race.[58]

---

[57] See Thistlethwaite, *Women's Bodies as Battlefield.*

[58] Eli S. McCarthy, personal email correspondence with author, March 14, 2016.

According to McCarthy, this is one reason why it is insufficient to say that the historical use of just war mostly to justify war is "*simply* a 'mis-use' of the approach due to human sin. The language itself functions to enable, make more likely, or perpetuate such use." McCarthy recognizes that the present legal code, both domestically and internationally, has legal limits on war which will still function. Yet, both Vatican II and Pope Paul VI have called us to go further, saying boldly it is "our clear duty, then, to strain every muscle as we work for the time when all war can be completely outlawed by international consent."[59]

Just peace and the responsibility to protect

At the UN 2005 World Summit leaders adopted a responsibility to protect populations from genocide, war crimes, ethnic cleansing, and crimes against humanity. Just war has been used to measure the moral legitimacy of this intervention in cases of "imminent threat" of lethal atrocities. How would just peace engage the responsibility to protect?

International law is relatively clear. The question here is one of ecclesial responsibility. How should the Catholic Church act? Love has written that any limited use of violence that the church might allow in cases of grave atrocity should be "more akin to policing, like Gerald Schlabach's work on just policing."[60] Schlabach has said that just policing fits well within a just peace model.

Policing seeks to secure the common good of the very society within which it operates; because it is embedded, indebted, and accountable within that community, it has an inherent tendency to minimize recourse to violence. Warfare may also seek to secure the common good of a society, of course; but because it extends beyond that society through

---

[59] Second Vatican Council, *Pastoral Constitution on the Church in the Modern World* (1965), no. 81; and Pope Paul VI, World Day of Peace Message 1975.

[60] Maryann Cusimano Love, personal email correspondence with author, March 2, 2016.

threats to other communities it has an inherent tendency to cut whatever slender bonds of accountability would truly limit its use to "last resort."[61]

Thistlethwaite reminds us that "imminent threat" is just war language, and that we must always ask who is doing the defining. Some have argued, she says, that the UN's responsibility to protect (R2P) doctrine fills a gap between just war and just peace. But Thistlethwaite suggests caution.

I think one can see that R2P gives license to a "soft interventionism." . . . R2P is an unstable mix of peacemaking and forceful interventionism. R2P incorporates "military intervention within the same norm as conflict prevention and peace support operations [and that] skews the whole R2P doctrine toward the extreme option of coercive intervention, which tends to become the center of the entire principle."[62]

McCarthy argues that, especially when a lethal threat is immediate and grave, the church—as the body of Christ—should urgently participate in just peace analysis, advocacy, intervention, and healing before, during, and after such events.

If governments or the UN decide based on present international law for military action in such atrocity cases, the Catholic Church's role is less about condemning those *persons* who took such action. Instead, the Catholic's role is to clearly name such violent *action* as a tragedy, a failure on the way of just peace, as well as inconsistent with human dignity and a culture of human rights for all.

---

[61] Gerald W. Schlabach, "Just Policing: How War Could Cease to Be a Church-Dividing Issue," *Journal of Ecumenical Studies* 41, no. 3–4 (summer-fall 2004): 412.

[62] Susan Brooks Thistlethwaite, personal email correspondence with author, March 2, 2016. She quotes from Lou Pingeot and Wolfgang Obenland, "In Whose Name? A Critical Review on the Responsibility to Protect," Global Policy Forum (May 2014).

Even more important, the church's role is to keep a just peace approach front and center in all such cases and advocate, even in the midst of violence, for actions that will transform the violence with just peace. McCarthy continues:

> During and after the violence, Catholics should be clearly taking a restorative-justice approach to all actors, which includes the human need for accountability. During and after the violence, the Catholic Church should promote public mourning rituals for the violence, advocate for addressing the root causes, and urgently call for the government actors particularly, but also the Catholic Church, to significantly increase nonviolent intervention strategies as well as investments in such training and institutions.

The Catholic Church does not need, and McCarthy suggests "should not" provide, "explicit justification or legitimation for military violence. When the level of dehumanization is so high, then what is 'necessary' is not so much lethal force, but the willingness to risk one's life for the sake of the dignity of *all* people."[63]

A Wellspring of Peace

Catholic social teaching provides a rich context in which to build a systemic body of thought and practice of Christian nonviolence. An overarching strategic objective of just peace is to develop a systematic analysis of nonviolence in order to cultivate effective approaches to addressing contemporary challenges in society through nonviolent means. Just peace can be applied at all stages of conflict, including climate change–related conflict and "resource wars." Just peace can be thoroughly integrated with *Laudato Si'* in

---

[63] Eli S. McCarthy, personal email correspondence with author, March 14, 2016. For further responses to common challenges associated with just peace, but particularly Christian nonviolence, McCarthy suggests T. York and J. Bronson Barringer, eds., *A Faith Not Worth Fighting For: Addressing Commonly Asked Questions about Christian Nonviolence* (Eugene, OR: Cascade Books, 2012).

a manner that recognizes that violence done to human communities is often accompanied by devastating environmental destruction. An integral ecology contributes to an integral just peace.

Love writes:

> For the church a tradition of just peace has been . . . given to us by Jesus. Jesus dialogued with enemies and with poor and marginalized persons, raising them up and healing impoverished, war-traumatized peoples, driving out their demons. Jesus not only had a declaratory policy urging peacebuilding, he lived peacebuilding and commissioned us to follow him.[64]

Pope Francis reminds us that out of the mystery of mercy comes the wellspring of peace. The commandment to be merciful is "a program of life as demanding as it is rich with joy and peace."[65] Reconciliation is not a theory or an approach for Catholics. It is a sacrament at the center of our lives, and it is the way of peace. Out of this wellspring comes the spiritual imagination to create just peace.

Deepening the Reflection on Just Peace

Eli S. McCarthy

In Session 3 Eli McCarthy further elaborated reasons why the church should adopt a just peace approach:

> "Just Peace is rooted in biblical shalom. The psalm (85:10) that justice and peace shall embrace reminds us that peace requires justice making, but also, peacemaking is the way to justice. Jesus modeled this approach to living under foreign

---

[64] Love, "Building a Better Peace."

[65] Pope Francis, "Bull of Indiction of the Extraordinary Jubilee of Mercy" (April 11, 2015).

military occupation. He also leads us toward restorative justice, with a focus on the harm done to relationships and how to heal. Just peace is clearly unfolding in the trajectory of contemporary popes' teaching and statements. Pope John XIII wrote about how war is not a suitable way to restore rights. Paul VI linked peace and development. John Paul II said violence is evil, it violates our dignity, it is the enemy of justice. There's no justice without forgiveness. And he calls us not to follow those who train us in how to kill. Pope Benedict called loving the enemy the nucleus of the Christian revolution. Francis has focused us on mercy, calls us to give up the way of arms, says war does grave harm to the environment, that justice never comes from killing, and that faith and violence are incompatible. He told us not to bomb or make war on ISIS. The door is always open to dialogue, he says, even with ISIS. Just peace is also being woven through ecumenical organizations and interfaith collaborations. For example, with the World Council of Churches turning to a just peace approach in 2011.

"In order to adequately develop a just peace approach I think we as the Catholic Church should no longer legitimate the just war language or appeal to the concept of justifiable war. Not only is it not true, but as we've already seen for seventeen hundred years, such legitimation will continue to constrain our just peace imagination and our will to embody just peace practices. . . . Both Vatican II and Pope Paul VI called the church to go further, saying boldly, it is 'our clear duty to strain every muscle as we work for the time when all war can be completely outlawed.'[66] In turn, the goal is to outlaw war, not to legitimate or refine the criteria for war. As Francis proclaimed, 'In the silence of the Cross, the uproar of weapons ceases and the language of . . . peace

---

[66] Second Vatican Council, *Pastoral Constitution on the Church in the Modern World* (1965), no. 81; and Pope Paul VI, World Day of Peace Message 1975.

is spoken.'[67] Therefore, I humbly suggest that the church should embody gospel nonviolence by using a just peace approach with specific criteria, virtues, and practices to prevent violence, diffuse violence, to heal well after violence, and to consistently build just peace."

Lisa Sowle Cahill

Later in the conference Boston College theologian Lisa Sowle Cahill commented:

"I think that some of the merits of the just peace model are the following: First of all, it's a positive vision. I'm not even happy with the term *nonviolence;* that's what we don't do, what we're getting away from. But what is the vision that's compelling us forward? It's to live out of the love and peace of Jesus Christ available to us in the power of the Holy Spirit. That is what we live out of, and that is what the just peace model I think captures. I also like the fact that it's a just peace, so something that we talked about in the English-language session just before this one is the interdependence, but also the difficulty, of justice, peace, and reconciliation. We really can't say there has to be peace before justice, or justice before peace, or reconciliation before justice. I think these are questions that vary a lot from particular situation to particular situation. I doubt that there is one model that everyone can adopt. I think the wisdom has to come from the local church, as well as from the Vatican or theologians, as to how to work this out, but the just peace paradigm does at least insist, as Paul VI said, 'If you want peace, work for justice' or 'development is the new name for peace.'"

Cahill also noted the importance of gender justice and the role of women in peacemaking, and many involved in the Catholic Nonviolence Initiative are convinced that women will be the

---

[67] Pope Francis, Vigil of Prayer for Peace [in Syria], September 7, 2013.

backbone of a paradigm shift away from violence that we and many others are actively promoting.

An interesting study on women, religion, and peace by the Berkley Center at Georgetown and the US Institute of Peace looked specifically at the role of women of faith in the work for peace.[68] Susan Hayward and Katherine Marshall, who led that study, noted that because religious leadership is usually dominated by men, women are often invisible. Yet they play critical roles as religious peacemakers, particularly when peace is defined in a holistic way.

Recent research is demonstrating over and over again the positive impact of women's work for peace. Inclusive Security,[69] for example, reports:

> When women influence decisions about war and peace and take the lead against extremism in their communities, it is more likely that crises will be resolved without recourse to violence. . . . Women raise different priorities during peace negotiations, often expanding the issues under consideration from military action, power and territory to include social and humanitarian needs.[70]

Jasmin Nario-Galace

The work for just peace of Miriam College and the Catholic Educational Association of the Philippines (CEAP) specifically includes a gender perspective. Jasmin Nario-Galace said:

---

[68] Susan Hayward and Katherine Marshall, *Women, Religion, and Peacebuilding: Illuminating the Unseen* (Washington, DC: US Institute of Peace, 2015).

[69] According to its website, "Inclusive Security's mission is to increase the participation of all stakeholders—particularly women—in preventing, resolving, and rebuilding after deadly conflicts."

[70] Marie O'Reilly, "Why Women? Inclusive Security and Peaceful Societies," *Inclusive Security* (October 2015).

"I am from Miriam College, one of the twenty-five-hundred member schools of the Catholic Educational Association of the Philippines, or CEAP, which has a JEEPGY program. So, JEEPGY, 'J' stands Justice and peace, 'E' for Ecological integrity, the second 'E' for Engaged citizenship, 'P' for Poverty alleviation, 'G' for Gender equality, and 'Y' for Youth empowerment.

"The JEEPGY expresses CEAP's mission of transformative education which enables individuals to participate in the fulfillment of God's intent for all peoples. A world free from war and the threat of it, a world where justice and equality prevail, a world where human rights are promoted and respected, a world where diversity is accepted and celebrated, and a world where resources of the earth are utilized with future generations in mind. JEEPGY uses a whole-school approach. CEAP encourages its Catholic member schools to integrate JEEPGY in the different facets of school life: their vision and mission, co-curricular and extracurricular programs, research, instructional adherence, and outreach projects.

"The general orientation of the JEEPGY framework is in righting relationships with God, humanity, and all of creation. The pillar programs are guided with the values of just peace, stewardship, human dignity, integrity, equality, love, dialogue, tolerance, and spirituality, among others. It takes seriously what Pope John Paul II said—that if you want to reach peace, teach peace. Many Catholic schools in the Philippines, including the school where I am from, have declared themselves zones of peace. . . . Many Catholic schools have now explicitly articulated in their vision, mission, and school philosophy the principles of just peace. Just peace principles are integrated into the curriculum of many schools.

"Miriam College, through the Peace Education Network, has successfully lobbied the Government of the Philippines to issue an executive order, which is a presidential order, mandating basic education and teacher education institutions to integrate peace education into the curriculum.

"Catholic schools have also established actual physical spaces, such as centers for peace, or justice, or the environment, or social action, or gender equality to ensure the promotion of peaceful values in the school culture. Catholic schools have also integrated just peace principles in their curricular and extracurricular activities. Student organizations promoting the principles of just peace, such as Pax Christi, have been established at many academic institutions. Catholic school outreach projects also live the by the principles of just peace. Miriam College, for example, has a twinning project with a school in Mindanao attended by Muslims, who are a minority in the country and historically the oppressed people. Students exchange letters throughout the school year and get a chance to meet and work together at the end of the year. The project is our way of accompanying the national peace process through this people to people peace process that helps build bridges of friendship and understanding between young people from two cultures and challenge historical prejudices.

"How does a turn to just peace impact the moral analysis of conflict, praxis, and engagement? If just peace means defending and restoring the fundamental dignity of all; if it means prioritizing love, compassion, reconciliation, and mercy; if it means the way of Jesus, which is loving the enemy and not winning over him or her, but winning him or her over to our side; if it means the way of Jesus, which is inclusion and not exclusion—then the way we analyze and approach conflict should be the way of nonviolence.

"The new emphasis of our peace work should be looking at and addressing the roots of conflict. Of the twenty-nine conflicts currently being waged in the world, only one is classical, according to Project Plowshares. Most are civil or internal and waged along ethnic lines. Many of these wars are waged because of experiences of deprivation, of historical injustice, of the refusal of the majority to allow the minorities to chart their political future with greater autonomy.

"The changing nature of conflict calls on us to change the way to solve them. For example, the dispossession of land of the Muslims and the indigenous peoples in the Philippines, as well as government neglect, has pushed them further into poverty. The refusal to allow them to exercise the right to greater self-determination cannot be solved by war.

"Catholic communities in the Philippines, including the predominantly Catholic security sector, are beginning to see the wisdom of targeting the root causes of the conflict, and not those who waged it. Modify the security paradigm from winning the war to winning the peace. Many Catholic educational institutions are in the forefront of supporting the peace process by lobbying for laws that will address the legitimate grievances of the people who are historically marginalized and oppressed; reaching out to those in the margins, especially the Muslim and indigenous women whose voices are otherwise not heard; and finding spaces to bring these voices to the attention of decision makers, including policymakers. Many of us are at the forefront of campaigns to end war because we know that the billions spent for war can be used to improve the lot of our country's ethnic and religious minorities. We are at the forefront of campaigns to end war because we have personally heard the narratives of victims. . . .

"Let's focus our efforts on preventing violent conflict, re-addressing the root causes of injustice, poverty and discrimination. And for violent conflicts that are already there, let us use the means already available to us, such as diplomacy, negotiation, and dialogue. Terrence Rynne said it quite well, 'The only path is to renounce violence, to begin anew with dialogue, to break the chain of injustice, that is Jesus's way, that must be our way as a Catholic faithful.'"

Francisco DeRoux, SJ

Francisco DeRoux, SJ, who worked for twenty years for just peace in Magdalena Medio, an area of Colombia where violence was rampant, spoke about his experience there:

"My contribution is about my experience in Colombia for twenty years working in the Magdalena Medio, a very violent part in my country and trying to promote just peace and sustainable human development with people, with the victims, the poor ones, the excluded. We were in the middle of a very serious conflict among the paramilitaries, the guerrillas and the military, talking to everybody, and trying to persuade everybody to change. It was a very complex, difficult process—always unpredictable. Twenty-seven of our companions were killed by the paramilitaries and the guerrillas. In the reflection paper I sent in advance of this conference, I referred to Alma Rosa Jaramillo, a very courageous lawyer. She came to work with us and was killed by the paramilitaries. When we found her, she was in the mud, dead; they had cut off her legs and her arms with a chainsaw. This was basically our daily situation in the Magdalena Medio.

"Our process was based on human dignity—the dignity we don't get from the guerrilla, or from the government, or from the military or from the paramilitary, but just because we are human beings. This is the passion of Jesus, Jesus is passionate for human dignity. This gave our people their strength to keep struggling for justice and peace.

"Now, we are in a new moment because of the dialogue between the Colombian government, the FARC guerrillas, and the National Liberation Army guerrillas. I have accompanied the victims several times to La Havana in Cuba. The presence of the victims in the dialogue was very impressive—their testimony, their decision to continue to work for peace after suffering so much. I know the peace process was transformed by the suffering of the victims.

"We are about to get a final peace agreement in Colombia with the FARC, a bilateral ceasefire agreement. But my country is totally divided. We have a lot of people who are not open to the peace process because of economic or military interests. It makes me think of Jesus telling us that

'Happy are the peacemakers,' but you're going to face con-
tradiction and opposition for what you are doing."

Marco Ghisoni

Dr. Marco Ghisoni, from Italy, represents Operazione Colomba
(Operation Dove), the nonviolent peace corps of the Pope
John XXIII community. He spoke during the third session of the
conference:

"During the last four years our group has involved more than
two thousand people, especially youngsters in their twen-
ties, mostly women, who left Italy to work in the midst of
armed conflicts. At present we have volunteers in Colombia
(Apartadò), Palestine, North Lebanon with the Syrian refugees, and Albania.

"Stopping violence without weapons is possible: this is
the point I wish to underscore, because we have experienced
it as a group, and surely many of you have also experienced
it. We work in the midst of armed conflicts, where sharing is
our way of life. We support the victims of conflicts, taking
all the risks, as a basis for building trust and credibility. This
allows external people to engage in a nonviolent struggle,
which might exist already, but without support or visibility.
Our Colombian friends say that paramilitary groups would
go to their homes intending to take their land and threatening
them with words such as, 'If tomorrow you are still here,
you'll all be killed.' The members the Colombian community, that we stand by, reply that the next day they will get
up and go to work as usual. People need to be accompanied.
We do not teach nonviolence; we learn it from them. They
only need our support.

"We are a Catholic organization with a Catholic name.
Notwithstanding this Catholic identity, volunteers and means
which support our project don't come from the official Catholic Church. Funds for our project come from Italian civil

society, which is highly sensitive to nonviolence. Ours was a spontaneous movement, but it developed a tested model, repeatedly implemented throughout these twenty-four years.

"Clearly, what human beings can do is to help stop violence. Just peace comes afterward as a result of the work done. Colombians want us to remain with them because otherwise they would be killed, but the roots of their war are to be found in our home countries—Europe and the United States of America. We need, therefore, to work in our countries where many interests are at stake (oil, production and trade in arms, drug trade, multinationals). Stopping wars is possible; stopping violence is possible. I hope that the church will come out more bravely, saying that all these people from all over the world—peace agents—are working also on behalf of the Catholic Church. I wish that all the experiences we have shared could get even more visibility and coordination. I hope that the church will create a commission, an intervention group that is able to anticipate conflicts, take preventive measures, and intervene. These are not pipe dreams. They can be done!"

9

The Church and the
Just War Tradition

*Is it possible to walk the path of peace? Can we get
out of this spiral of sorrow and death? Can we learn
once again to walk and live in the ways of peace? . . .
Yes, it is possible for everyone! . . . How I wish that all
men and women of good will would look to the Cross
if only for a moment! There, we can see God's reply:
violence is not answered with violence, death is not
answered with the language of death. In the silence
of the Cross, the uproar of weapons ceases and the
language of reconciliation, forgiveness, dialogue, and
peace is spoken.*

—POPE FRANCIS, ST. PETER'S SQUARE,
SEPTEMBER 7, 2013

The *Appeal to the Catholic Church to Re-commit to the Centrality
of Gospel Nonviolence* drafted by the Rome conference on nonviolence and just peace received immediate attention. Headlines
in the *National Catholic Reporter*, April 14, 2016, for example,
proclaimed: "Landmark Vatican conference rejects just war theory,
asks for encyclical on nonviolence."

The *Appeal* summarized the conclusions of the conference
and—perhaps even more important—urged the church to move

in the direction of a deeper commitment to learning about, teaching, and advocating for nonviolence. Although Pontifical Council for Justice and Peace staff members, including Cardinal Turkson, participated actively in many parts of the meeting, the final document was a message from other conference participants to the Vatican and was not signed or endorsed by the Pontifical Council.

The conclusion of the *Appeal* (see Chapter 1) reads:

As would-be disciples of Jesus, challenged and inspired by stories of hope and courage in these days, we call on the Church we love to:

- continue developing Catholic social teaching on nonviolence. In particular, we call on Pope Francis to share with the world an encyclical on nonviolence and Just Peace;
- integrate Gospel nonviolence explicitly into the life, including the sacramental life, and work of the Church through dioceses, parishes, agencies, schools, universities, seminaries, religious orders, voluntary associations, and others;
- promote nonviolent practices and strategies (e.g., nonviolent resistance, restorative justice, trauma healing, unarmed civilian protection, conflict transformation, and peacebuilding strategies);
- initiate a global conversation on nonviolence within the Church, with people of other faiths, and with the larger world to respond to the monumental crises of our time with the vision and strategies of nonviolence and Just Peace;
- no longer use or teach "just war theory"; continue advocating for the abolition of war and nuclear weapons;
- lift up the prophetic voice of the Church to challenge unjust world powers and to support and defend those nonviolent activists whose work for peace and justice put their lives at risk.

In every age, the Holy Spirit graces the Church with the wisdom to respond to the challenges of its time. In response to what is a global epidemic of violence, which Pope Francis has labeled a "world war in installments," we are being called to invoke, pray over, teach, and take decisive action. With our communities and organizations, we look forward to continue collaborating with the Holy See and the global Church to advance Gospel nonviolence.

While the focus of the conference was on nonviolence and just peace, rather than on just war teaching, participants explored possibilities for an articulation of Catholic teaching on war and peace that would move beyond just war language in favor of an ethical framework for engaging the violences of our world by emphasizing nonviolent conflict transformation and just peace.

Some conference participants were pacifists. Many were not; they had experience of active nonviolence but understood the legitimacy of some form of defense and the urgency of protection because they live in very dangerous circumstances. All were committed to deepening their understanding of nonviolence and just peace.

Those present generally agreed that the dominance of the just war framework in Catholic thought and teaching, as well as in ethical considerations in the political arena, was a real obstacle to the development of more and more effective nonviolent tools for protecting vulnerable communities.

As moral theologian Gerald Schlabach wrote:

The core, unassailable claim of the conference in Rome was that by focusing its teaching, pastoral counsel, chaplaincy, and advocacy on "just war," the church has paid a huge opportunity cost, to the detriment of its own nonviolent practice. When too many priests, bishops, and moral theologians continue to rely on a just-war framework, they crimp the creative imagination of the faithful and invite nationalistic manipulation of their sentiments.[1]

---

[1] Gerald Schlabach, "Just War? Enough Already, *Commonweal* (May 31, 2017).

Interventions during the conference, such as the following during Session 3 by Francisco DeRoux, SJ, had an impact on participants:

> "There is a result I am expecting from this process. It is to have the Catholic Church abandon the just war perspective. In my country, a Catholic country, it has been scandalous. Because of the just war theory, priests and nuns joined the ELN guerrillas in the 1960s and 1970s, after reading liberation theology—because of the just war paradigm, not because of liberation theology. Because of the paradigm of just war they joined the guerrillas, and it has been hell for Colombia. Our military, a Catholic military, is also trapped based on the just war paradigm. And the paramilitary, they pray to the Virgin Mary before going to kill people. This is awful. So please help us to stop, stop the paradigm and to build up a new paradigm."

The message of Ogarit Younan, founder of the University of Nonviolence in Beirut, Lebanon, who knows intimately the consequences of war and violent conflict, was even stronger:

> "From my lived experience and the pain I have lived through I propose at this conference . . . that we must absolutely stop using the term *just war.* I did some research on the terms used for war throughout history. I found twenty terms for war. Each time we go to war, we have to dress it up—twenty adjectives that we add to war so that this war becomes a necessary war. . . . We must stop using the term *just war* because *just* is one of the twenty terms. When we use the word *peace,* we don't need to add an adjective to peace because peace is peace. I propose that we don't look for an adjective for peace because the road to peace is just that. It translates itself. . . .
>
> "We must certainly speak of justice because justice fundamentally affects violence. We cannot talk about peace superficially. We have to talk about the foundations of violence that are economic and political. . . .

"The legacy of just war is not only a legacy of the church and Christians. Christian theologians gave a methodology to just war—five principles that are now the principles of international humanitarian law that ask if war is for peace, if war is being authorized by the right authority, if it has the chance of being successful, if it's proportional, if it's the last option. . . .

"I invite the church to make a decisive turn from the legacy of just war. But we also should change a law that's been adopted at the highest international levels and the United Nations. The right for war exists in our world. That's what's scary and dangerous. Countries, the strongest countries, have the right to go to war if it complies with the five principles in international law. So we must renounce war individually, as believers we must renounce war, as a church, the pope, must renounce 'just war,' but also in international law, we must work so that war is never accepted as a just war."

The message of the *Appeal* on the concept of just war was very clear. It said: "We believe that there is no 'just' war," an assessment repeated frequently by Catholic authorities in recent decades and confirmed by the strict application of the just war criteria.

The *Appeal* continued, "Too often the 'just war theory' has been used to endorse rather than prevent or limit war. Suggesting that a 'just war' is possible also undermines the moral imperative to develop tools and capacities for nonviolent transformation of conflict." Therefore, the *Appeal* asked the church to "no longer use or teach 'just war theory.'"

The concern was very real among participants that maintaining just war language and reasoning as the central frame for Catholic thought on war and peace enabled the human community to invest heavily in preparations for war while giving very little time and attention to possibly effective nonviolent ways to engage potentially or actually violent situations. Even though most contemporary just war theorists intend to use just war criteria to prevent or restrict movement to war—and have been developing peacebuilding strategies in that frame—many conference participants hoped for a new approach more fitting to the twenty-first century context and less likely to risk the possibility of war.

Clear ethical criteria are necessary for addressing egregious attacks or threats in a violent world, as well as for guiding any intervention (including sanctions, shaming, and other forceful actions) by the international community in the affairs of a state failing to protect its own people.

Conference participants hoped that moral theologians and other Catholic thinkers would explore new ways to describe such criteria unencumbered by just war language. The Catholic Church's multidimensional work for peace; presence in every corner of the world, especially among those most harmed by war and violence; and efforts to understand the gospel and follow Jesus could give the church the capacity to imagine and encourage the creation of more effective nonviolent strategies for protecting vulnerable communities, dealing with conflict, and stopping overt and institutionalized violence.

In addition, perhaps that effort would be enhanced if ethical insights and peacebuilding strategies that have been developed within the just war frame, such as *jus ante bellum* and *jus post bellum*, were explored more expansively through, for example, a "sustaining peace" frame.

Discussed at some length in the report for the 2015 Review of the United Nations Peacebuilding Architecture, the concept of *sustaining peace* has been further developed by the International Peace Institute, which describes the conceptual shift from peacebuilding to *sustaining peace*:

> Although conceived as a comprehensive process, peacebuilding has come to be narrowly interpreted as time-bound, exogenous [from the outside] interventions that take place "after the guns fall silent" in fragile or conflict-affected states. *Sustaining peace* seeks to reclaim peace *in its own right* and detach it from the subservient affiliation with conflict that has defined it over the past four decades.[2]

---

[2] International Peace Institute, "Sustaining Peace: What Does It Mean in Practice?" (April 2017).

The conference asked the Catholic Church worldwide to invest in peace "in its own right"—to do what national and international political leaders have thus far failed to do—precisely, perhaps, because so many governments have invested heavily in preparations for a just war.

An Ongoing Challenge

References to the just war theory in the *Appeal* provoked many different, often vehement, responses—some enthusiastic, others critical, many insightful. In reality, this exchange was a small sampling of what continues to be a rich and dynamic conversation in the Catholic community and beyond. While not the focus of the conference, the effort to move the just war tradition "off center stage" was an inevitable and probably essential component of pursuing a deeper commitment to active nonviolence in the Catholic community.

In an interview for *OSV Newsweekly,* Gerard Powers, director of Catholic Peacebuilding Studies and coordinator of the Catholic Peacebuilding Network at the University of Notre Dame's Kroc Institute for International Peace Studies, said:

> "There are two things going on here. One is a more narrow debate—it's a very important debate but a narrower, age-old debate—about whether the church should be like the Quakers and the Mennonites and be principled pacifists versus upholding the 'just war' tradition, which has been the teaching of the church since at least Augustine. Part of this conversation, it seems to me, was reviving that debate about which of the two traditions, both of which are legitimate, should prevail in Church teaching. And the conference clearly calls for an end to the teaching of the 'just war' tradition and for a focus on principled nonviolence as the Christian imperative. That's a very important debate, one which I don't think is going to be resolved by this conference or anytime soon. The second thing that's going on is a wider debate about what it

means to be a 'peace Church'—and I don't mean to become Quakers and Mennonites—but what it means to be a Church whose sense of Christian vocation is that we are called to be peace-builders. The pope uses the word peacemakers. I think that is central to our Christian vocation, (and), like Catholic social teaching generally, it's one of the best-kept secrets of the church. . . .

"When you look at official Catholic social teaching, that amazing body of work, you have a 'just peace' theory. The vision, the principles, the criteria for moral action constitute the substance of a 'just peace' theory, in my view. The central challenge is for the Catholic community to take seriously the church's social teaching. We really don't, as a Catholic community, act in our daily life as if peacebuilding is central to our Christian vocation. That, I think, is the fundamental problem. . . .

"Every aspect of the Catholic community's life needs to integrate Catholic social teaching and peace-building. (But) I don't think the solution is to just stop teaching the 'just war' tradition. I would argue that, especially since the Second Vatican Council, but going back even further, official Church teaching and practice have embraced a very restrictive interpretation of the 'just war,' which says that you can only justify war for extraordinarily strong reasons. And that's very different from the much more permissive approach which uses 'just war' to make it easy to justify war. That's what the Pax Christi statement is focusing on—that too often the "just war" theory has been misused to endorse, rather than to prevent or limit war. And that's absolutely true. But that hasn't been how the Catholic Church has used or taught the tradition, or applied the tradition in most of the past century. . . .

"The Iraq War in 2003 is a great example. The Vatican and the US Catholic bishops—and virtually every Catholic bishops' conference in the world—were opposed to the war. They often used, as the US bishops did, the highly restrictive approach to 'just war' to counter the Bush administration's highly permissive approach. Just because the 'just war' has been misused, as it was in that case by the Bush administration, doesn't mean that you have to throw out the whole tradition. It was used correctly, I think, by the Vatican (and) by the bishops' conferences around the world as a form of conflict prevention. Pacifist arguments were not a major part of that debate. . . .

"I think the highly restrictive interpretation of 'just war' compels you to find nonviolent alternatives to resolve conflicts because it's hard to justify using military force under modern Church teaching. The highly restrictive interpretation is not opposed to peace-building, but presumes a need to continue to develop our teaching and especially our practices of peace-building. . . .

"The bigger challenge is to become more of a peace-building Church by taking seriously our rich Catholic social teaching and reflecting on it in light of what we can learn from the amazing peace-building practices around the world. The Catholic community around the world . . . is doing courageous work for peace in some of the world's most war-torn places, but it tends to be unheralded, unknown, and underanalyzed. We need to have a lot better understanding of what the Catholic community is doing in the area of peace-building writ large. The peace-building that we're talking about is not just the nonviolent civil resistance of Martin Luther King or Mahatma Gandhi, but it is a much broader set of principles and practices related to the hard work of finding nonmilitary alternatives to conflict in the world—through diplomacy, strengthening international law and international institutions, working for economic justice, working on environmental concerns. The Vatican conference addressed many of these broader aspects of peace-building. . . .

"I think a document that would reflect on the church's long-standing teaching on war and peace and peace-building in light of current challenges would be very helpful. It might be framed as peace-building is our vocation as Catholic Christians."[3]

Responding to the *OSV Newsweekly* interview, Eli S. McCarthy agreed with many of Powers's observations but added several points:

> Scripture scholarship is basically unanimous that Jesus models a way of nonviolent love of friends and enemies. The call to love our neighbor must always be consistent with how Jesus loved (John 13:34), and our perceived enemies always remain our neighbors. Recent Popes have confirmed this reality about Jesus, and the conference builds its appeal consistent with this realism about Jesus.
>
> . . . I agree that Catholic social doctrine certainly has elements of a just peace theory. But Catholic social doctrine has yet to explicitly identify, explain, and prioritize a just peace theory/approach. For instance, the conference alluded to seven specific just peace criteria to guide moral action across all stages of conflict, including during violent conflict. These criteria and this method of application have not yet been affirmed in Catholic social doctrine. There are also specific virtues, such as the virtue of nonviolent peacemaking, which were discussed as part of a virtue-based, just peace approach consistent with Gospel nonviolence. . . .
>
> . . . It may be true that the "highly restrictive" version [of just war theory] is better than the less restrictive version. However, either version which includes the suggestion that war may be justifiable, still cultivates social conditions (ex. heavy preparations for war) that also make it more likely our society will make choices that undermine the development of nonviolent capacities. Further, even an emphasis on the "highly restrictive" version has in the concrete undermined

---

[3] Gerard Powers, in an interview by Gretchen R. Crowe [editor-in-chief], "Powers: Catholic Social Doctrine Is 'Just Peace,'" *OSV Newsweekly* (April 20, 2016).

the formation of Christian peacemakers or "peacebuilders." For instance, we see how rarely we, including Catholics, speak about or promote nonviolent resistance (esp. boycotts, strikes, civil disobedience, etc.) to injustice and violence. We see how minimal resistance is mounted by most leaders, including Catholics, to enormous military spending, primarily in countries with large militaries such as the US. We see how little we hear from leaders, including most Catholics, or key advocacy organizations on the proven practice of unarmed civilian protection (25+ years old). We see how little we hear from leaders, including Catholics, about the need to humanize or illuminate the dignity of our enemies, especially regarding people in groups like ISIS. . . .

The interview cites the Iraq war of 2003 as a good example of the "highly restrictive" use by the Catholic Church. Pope John Paul II was certainly strong in saying no to war as a practice itself, i.e. "always a defeat for humanity." The US Catholic Bishops wisely raised questions of concern but did not clearly conclude the war was unjust; except for one Romanian, Bishop Botean in Ohio, who also called on all Catholics in his diocese to not participate in the war. . . . The war proceeded and the devastating impacts [such as ISIS] continue today.

Let's imagine for a moment if the Catholic Church were to shift to an explicit just peace approach consistent with Gospel nonviolence. . . . When the Pope said not to "bomb or make war" on ISIS, Catholics would be further energized and organize around creative, effective nonviolent resistance practices. Instead, with a just war infused mentality, most US Catholic press and leaders focused their discussion on the possibility of some military action and how much made sense. Therefore, the conference appeal was proposing a new moral framework, not the withdrawal of moral judgment about war, and addressing all versions of the just war concept not simply the more "permissive use."

. . . Gandhi was clear that his approach to nonviolence or Satyagraha (truth/soul-force) consisted of both a constructive

and obstructive program (civil resistance), which enabled
each other. For Gandhi, the former is the more important,
which includes social uplift and the constructive "creation
of alternatives to armed conflict [peacebuilding]." . . .
MLK was building off Gandhi's Satyagraha approach but
oriented by his Christianity. This is important because it
illuminates how turning to an explicit just peace theory
consistent with Gospel nonviolence is central to incorpo-
rating both the constructive and obstructive programs, i.e.
more fully becoming "peacebuilders" or as Pope Francis
says "peacemakers."[4]

Some commentators rightfully noted that many just war thinkers today are committed peacemakers, not apologists for political
realism. As a result, they said, the just war teaching that the *Appeal*
wishes to abandon is not the just war teaching with which most
contemporary Catholic moral theologians are now working. There
has been a lot of rethinking of just war teaching, including with
regard to *jus ante bellum* and *jus post bellum*. Emphasis has been
given especially to *jus ante bellum* (just peacemaking) practices
in order to make just war truly a last resort.

Others said that if there are no moral norms like those tradition-
ally called just war norms to govern the use of armed force, then
there are no criteria by which we can hold political or military
authorities and others (such as ISIS) accountable for their unjust
uses of force. Just war reasoning has had a positive influence on
how armies conduct themselves in battle, so established criteria
for the conduct of war remain important.

On the other hand, while *jus in bello* criteria have restrained
some actors in war and have helped outlaw some particularly
egregious weapons systems, which is a good thing, the gains
achieved by limiting some actions in war are overtaken by the
suffering caused by ongoing wars, resources given to preparing
for war, continued development of weapons of mass destruction,

---

[4] Eli S. McCarthy, "Shifting the Lens: Just Peace and Nonviolence,"
Huffington Post, August 2, 2016.

the arms trade, and a war system embedded in the global economy and international politics.

Still others said:

- There are still circumstances when the use of violent force is justified, even necessary. For example, to ensure security from external and internal threats so that all people can reach their potential and flourish as persons; to halt genocide and mass atrocities; to resist invasions; to combat terrorism; and more.
- The church needs to build on the solid foundation of just war teaching rather than discard it and, in particular, to incorporate new moral criteria for postwar requirements.
- The just use of force and creative nonviolence belong together as essential tools in building a just peace.
- Nonviolence isn't an all-purpose strategy for "making a difference" in the world. It can work in some situations, but in the overwhelming majority of conflicts, nonviolence simply isn't an option that will make things better. In many if not most cases, it could well make them worse.

Several people noted that the limited use of force for humanitarian purposes or multilateral international police action may be a category of action distinct from war.

Although the experience of communities of color in the United States might find it very difficult to imagine such a concept, the work of Gerald Schlabach, Tobias Winright, and others on just policing as "an alternative to passivity, on the one hand, and militarism, on the other"[5] might help stir creative thinking about nonviolent strategies in a violent world, particularly in conversation with the British experience with unarmed policing. For many years these moral theologians have been exploring the significant

---

[5] Tobias Winright, "R2P and Just Policing: A Roman Catholic and Yoderian Perspective," International Ecumenical Consultation on the Responsibility to Protect, Evangelische Akademie Arnoldshain, Frankfurt, Germany, November 16–18, 2007.

differences between policing and war as an approach to bridging the chasm between pacifists and just war theorists. Schlabach describes some of the important differences:

- Political leaders draw on the rhetoric of national pride, honor and crusading to marshal the political will and sustain the sacrifices necessary to fight wars. . . . Police officials by contrast appeal to the common good of the community to justify their actions, seeking to defuse the emotions that lead to violence.
- . . . Police officers are expected to use the minimum force needed to achieve their objective, and are judged harshly if there is collateral damage of the kind that routinely occurs in warfare.
- . . . In good policing the arresting agent is not the same as the judging agent, but in war those two are the same. . . .
- We have words like *frenzy* and *berserk* in our vocabulary because our ancestors noticed that in the heat of battle irrationality sets in. . . . Police officials by contrast go to great lengths to prevent this phenomenon; and when it occurs, we condemn it as police brutality.[6]

Recent popes have repeatedly condemned war and promoted the primacy of nonviolent action, as well as peacemaking (peacebuilding) efforts. Yet they have been somewhat ambiguous about the possibility of limited, armed, multilateral humanitarian interventions in extreme cases.

In 2008 Benedict XVI strongly supported the principle of the responsibility to protect,[7] warning nations about indifference and encouraging the development of clearer rules and norms of conduct (with a footnote referring to the traditional just war criteria for defending the innocent and "limiting the damage as far

---

[6] Gerald Schlabach, "Just Policing, Not War," *America* (July 7, 2003).

[7] Pope Benedict XVI, Address to the United Nations, New York, April 18, 2008.

as possible"[8]). In the same address he said, "What is needed is a deeper search for ways of pre-empting and managing conflicts by exploring every possible diplomatic avenue, and giving attention and encouragement to even the faintest sign of dialogue or desire for reconciliation."[9] Yet, soon afterward, perhaps reflecting skepticism about whether violence can actually end violence, Benedict added in his 2009 in *Caritas in veritate* that the responsibility to protect must be implemented "in innovative ways" (no. 7).[10]

Significant debate about the responsibility to protect continues—perhaps less about the responsibility itself than about the mechanisms of protection and who decides when and how they are used, and how we might actually transform the conflict.

On August 18, 2014, in an in-flight press conference from Korea to Rome, the pope remarked informally to reporters that dialogue even with ISIS should not be considered a lost cause. "I can only say that it is licit to stop the unjust aggressor. I underscore the verb 'stop.' I'm not saying drop bombs, make war, but stop the aggressor. The means used to stop him would have to be evaluated."

Moral theologian Ken Himes noted four important points in Pope Francis's longer statement:

> First, as Francis himself emphasized, he used the word "stop" not "make war." There is a humanitarian crisis, and the cause of that crisis, the aggression of the Islamic State ought to be stopped. Second, the means to be used must be "evaluated." Third, in the past there have been alleged humanitarian interventions that served as cover for wars of conquest. Finally, the determination to intervene should not be done unilaterally, but through the UN. . . . Francis

---

[8] Pope Benedict XVI, "The Human Person, the Heart of Peace," World Day of Peace Message 2007.

[9] Benedict XVI, Address to the United Nations, New York, April 18, 2008.

[10] Lisa Sowle Cahill, "Official Catholic Social Thought on Gospel Nonviolence," background paper for Nonviolence and Just Peace Conference, Rome, April 2016.

affirmed the fundamental idea of a duty to assist innocent victims of a humanitarian crisis, but he was hesitant to conclude armed intervention as the most appropriate response. Instead he called for an evaluation of the proposed means of intervention.[11]

Similarly, in a March 13, 2015, interview with the Catholic website Crux, Archbishop Silvano Tomasi, then ambassador of the Holy See to the United Nations in Geneva, said, "What's needed is a coordinated and well-thought-out coalition to do everything possible to achieve a political settlement without violence, but if that's not possible, then the use of force will be necessary."[12]

In reflecting on such messages from the Vatican, Lisa Sowle Cahill asks how we would know when the bounds of a "limited, precise, restricted" humanitarian intervention involving some use of force have been exceeded and the action has become the "war" that their teaching consistently condemns? I think this is still rather unclear."

Gerald Schlabach encourages a step back to see the larger moral framework, asking what space the just war theory was meant to fill. What ways of filling that space make war less exceptional, and what ways might make it more exceptional? How should or shouldn't Catholic discourse addressing war and violence differ when addressing the Christian community itself, as compared to the larger social order or the international community?

Many just war thinkers have emphasized that *just* may be better understood as *justified.* In fact, in recent decades the Vatican has tended to replace just war language with "legitimate defense," which helps keep open the possibility that we would defend and protect using other tools than war—possibly even more effective, nonviolent tools.

---

[11] Kenneth R. Himes, OFM, "Humanitarian Intervention and the Just War Tradition," in *Can War Be Just in the Twenty-first Century? Ethicists Engage the Tradition*, ed. Tobias Winright and Laurie Johnstown (Maryknoll, NY: Orbis Books, 2015), 60.

[12] Silvano Tomasi, in John L. Allen, Jr., "Vatican Backs Military Force to Stop ISIS Genocide," Crux, March 13, 2015.

Clearly, more attention needs to be given to how the terms *war* and *violence* are being used and to closing the loophole—whether language or concept or both—through which too many political decision makers find excuses for war.

As long as we rely upon the just war frame, the excellent and important work that is being done to prevent mass atrocities without resort to military action and to build sustainable peace are likely to be overshadowed by the huge financial, intellectual, and psychological investment in preparation for a "just" war. Given the reality of the world in which we live and the overwhelming consequences of almost any war (in human life, spiritual degradation, moral injury, environmental destruction, infrastructure destruction, psychological damage, financial costs, and more), the conclusion of the conference was unsurprisingly that war (per se) is not a just way to deal with conflicts or the need for protection.

In an interview with the *National Catholic Reporter* on September 20, 2016, Cardinal Turkson said:

> "Pope Francis would say: 'You don't stop an aggression by being an aggressor. You don't stop a conflict by inciting another conflict. You don't stop a war by starting another war.' . . . It doesn't stop. We've seen it all around us. Trying to stop the aggressor in Iraq has not stopped war. Trying to stop the aggressor in Libya has not stopped war. It's not stopped the war in any place. We do not stop war by starting another war. . . . The participants at the conference promoted 'another thinking': gospel nonviolence, or "nonviolence as Jesus was nonviolent." People think that this is Utopian, but Jesus was that. . . .
>
> "Turkson . . . also said that international responses to unjust aggression by nation-states or other actors do not always need to involve violence. 'There are several diplomatic means we can use to stop aggression,' said the cardinal. 'If nothing else at all, stop that with which people cause the aggression. Why don't you talk about curtailing arms trafficking? The really big instruments of war come from factories

and industries which produce weapons and some of these weapons are now in these theatres of war.'"[13]

In the previously cited examples of Pope Francis and Archbishop Tomasi calling for an international response to extremist violence in the Middle East, both sought "other means" than bombing or war to stop the aggression. While Archbishop Tomasi, in particular, admitted that armed force might be necessary, they both echoed the repeated plea of religious leaders and communities of faith around the world for more effective nonviolent tools for the international community to use to prevent and resolve violent crises.

Participants in the conference were tired of being told that the nonviolent alternatives to war were underdeveloped or ineffective—in other words that the nonviolence "toolbox" for governments or the international community to use in crisis situations was almost empty while the military "toolbox" was brimming with the latest weapons and strategies for almost any imaginable level of armed, military action.

The discussion and discernment around just war teaching will go on, with particular attention to humanitarian intervention and policing, but most of those at the conference were convinced that the institutional Catholic Church and Catholic communities around the world could make a tremendous contribution to the development of knowledge and practical capacity for dealing with violence nonviolently.

In conversation after the conference, participant and theologian Lisa Sowle Cahill framed the crucial question well: "What is the distinct contribution that the Christian story can make to the ethics of the use of force in the task of peacemaking?"

To those who interpreted the outcome of the conference as an attempt by pacifists to do away with just war theory, Terrence Rynne responded:

---

[13] Joshua McElwee, "Cardinal Turkson: 'We Do Not Stop War by Starting Another War,'" *National Catholic Reporter*, September 20, 2016.

The tired debate [between pacifism and just war theory] has long been superseded. When participants at the conference talk about gospel nonviolence, they are describing so much more than pacifism, the stance that rejects violence. They are describing brawny, risk-taking action that confronts violence, uses the power of noncooperation, persuasion, deft undercutting of support for the offender, continuing loving outreach, selective civil disobedience, developing structures for cooperative action, reaching the enemy with the power of self-suffering to make the enemy into a friend. Unlike the just war theory which attempts to talk with everyone, offering a rational set of principles that all can agree upon, gospel nonviolence is for those who are captured by the example and teaching of Jesus, who experience the fact that they are loved and that they have the power therefore to reach out to so called enemies with love.[14]

The commitment of the Catholic Nonviolence Initiative—a project of Pax Christi International, in collaboration with many other Catholic communities and organizations—following the Rome conference is to engage as fully as possible in support of continued development of Catholic social teaching on nonviolence and to advocate for the promotion of nonviolent practices and strategies that can more adequately respond to the monumental crises of our times—in our own communities, in Burundi and Syria, in Iraq and South Sudan, in Israel and Palestine, and in other corners of the world where violence constantly begets violence, and prepare us to more humanely engage the crises of the future.

---

[14] Terrence Rynne, unpublished response to *Commonweal* article by Peter Steinfels. An abbreviation version is on the *Commonweal* Facebook page (June 5, 2017).

10

World Day of Peace Message 2017

Pope Francis

MESSAGE OF HIS HOLINESS POPE FRANCIS
FOR THE CELEBRATION OF THE
FIFTIETH WORLD DAY OF PEACE

1 JANUARY 2017

Nonviolence: A Style of Politics for Peace

1. At the beginning of this New Year, I offer heartfelt wishes of peace to the world's peoples and nations, to heads of state and government, and to religious, civic and community leaders. I wish peace to every man, woman and child, and I pray that the image and likeness of God in each person will enable us to acknowledge one another as sacred gifts endowed with immense dignity.

In response to an invitation from Cardinal Turkson, the Catholic Nonviolence Initiative (Pax Christi International's project that emerged from the conference) proposed nonviolence as the theme for the World Day of Peace message in 2017. Pope Francis accepted the proposal and wrote a remarkable document.—Ed.

Especially in situations of conflict, let us respect this, our "deepest dignity,"[1] and make active nonviolence our way of life.

This is the fiftieth Message for the World Day of Peace. In the first, Blessed Pope Paul VI addressed all peoples, not simply Catholics, with utter clarity. "Peace is the only true direction of human progress—and not the tensions caused by ambitious nationalisms, nor conquests by violence, nor repressions which serve as mainstay for a false civil order". He warned of "the danger of believing that international controversies cannot be resolved by the ways of reason, that is, by negotiations founded on law, justice, and equity, but only by means of deterrent and murderous forces". Instead, citing the encyclical *Pacem in Terris* of his predecessor Saint John XXIII, he extolled "the sense and love of peace founded upon truth, justice, freedom and love".[2] In the intervening fifty years, these words have lost none of their significance or urgency.

On this occasion, I would like to reflect on *nonviolence* as a style of politics for peace. I ask God to help all of us to cultivate nonviolence in our most personal thoughts and values. May charity and nonviolence govern how we treat each other as individuals, within society and in international life. When victims of violence are able to resist the temptation to retaliate, they become the most credible promotors of nonviolent peacemaking. In the most local and ordinary situations and in the international order, may nonviolence become the hallmark of our decisions, our relationships and our actions, and indeed of political life in all its forms.

A broken world

2. While the last century knew the devastation of two deadly World Wars, the threat of nuclear war and a great number of other conflicts, today, sadly, we find ourselves engaged in a horrifying *world war fought piecemeal.* It is not easy to know if our world is presently more or less violent than in the past, or to know whether

---

[1] Apostolic Exhortation *Evangelii Gaudium,* 228.
[2] Paul VI, Message for the First World Day of Peace, 1 January 1968.

modern means of communications and greater mobility have made us more aware of violence, or, on the other hand, increasingly inured to it.

In any case, we know that this "piecemeal" violence, of different kinds and levels, causes great suffering: wars in different countries and continents; terrorism, organized crime and unforeseen acts of violence; the abuses suffered by migrants and victims of human trafficking; and the devastation of the environment. Where does this lead? Can violence achieve any goal of lasting value? Or does it merely lead to retaliation and a cycle of deadly conflicts that benefit only a few "warlords"?

Violence is not the cure for our broken world. Countering violence with violence leads at best to forced migrations and enormous suffering, because vast amounts of resources are diverted to military ends and away from the everyday needs of young people, families experiencing hardship, the elderly, the infirm and the great majority of people in our world. At worst, it can lead to the death, physical and spiritual, of many people, if not of all.

The Good News

3. Jesus himself lived in violent times. Yet he taught that the true battlefield, where violence and peace meet, is the human heart: for "it is from within, from the human heart, that evil intentions come" (*Mk* 7:21). But Christ's message in this regard offers a radically positive approach. He unfailingly preached God's unconditional love, which welcomes and forgives. He taught his disciples to love their enemies (cf. *Mt* 5:44) and to turn the other cheek (cf. *Mt* 5:39). When he stopped her accusers from stoning the woman caught in adultery (cf. *Jn* 8:1–11), and when, on the night before he died, he told Peter to put away his sword (cf. *Mt* 26:52), Jesus marked out the path of nonviolence. He walked that path to the very end, to the cross, whereby he became our peace and put an end to hostility (cf. *Eph* 2:14–16). Whoever accepts the Good News of Jesus is able to acknowledge the violence within and be healed by God's mercy, becoming in turn an instrument of reconciliation. In the words of Saint Francis of Assisi: "As you

announce peace with your mouth, make sure that you have greater peace in your hearts".[3]

To be true followers of Jesus today also includes embracing his teaching about nonviolence. As my predecessor Benedict XVI observed, that teaching "is realistic because it takes into account that in the world there is *too much* violence, *too much* injustice, and therefore that this situation cannot be overcome except by countering it with *more* love, with *more* goodness. This '*more*' comes from God".[4] He went on to stress that: "For Christians, nonviolence is not merely tactical behaviour but a person's way of being, the attitude of one who is *so convinced of God's love and power* that he or she is not afraid to tackle evil with the weapons of love and truth alone. Love of one's enemy constitutes the nucleus of the 'Christian revolution'".[5] The Gospel command to *love your enemies* (cf. *Lk* 6:27) "is rightly considered the *magna carta* of Christian nonviolence. It does not consist in succumbing to evil . . . , but in responding to evil with good (cf. *Rom* 12:17–21), and thereby breaking the chain of injustice".[6]

More powerful than violence

4. Nonviolence is sometimes taken to mean surrender, lack of involvement and passivity, but this is not the case. When Mother Teresa received the Nobel Peace Prize in 1979, she clearly stated her own message of active nonviolence: "We in our family don't need bombs and guns, to destroy to bring peace—just get together, love one another . . . And we will be able to overcome all the evil that is in the world".[7] For the force of arms is deceptive. "While weapons traffickers do their work, there are poor peacemakers who give their lives to help one person, then another and another and another"; for such peacemakers, Mother Teresa is "a symbol,

---

[3] "The Legend of the Three Companions," *Fonti Francescane*, No. 1469.
[4] Benedict XVI, *Angelus*, 18 February 2007.
[5] Ibid.
[6] Ibid.
[7] Mother Teresa, Nobel Lecture, 11 December 1979.

an icon of our times".[8] Last September, I had the great joy of proclaiming her a Saint. I praised her readiness to make herself available for everyone "through her welcome and defence of human life, those unborn and those abandoned and discarded. . . . She bowed down before those who were spent, left to die on the side of the road, seeing in them their God-given dignity; she made her voice heard before the powers of this world, so that they might recognize their guilt for the crimes—the crimes!—of poverty they created".[9] In response, her mission—and she stands for thousands, even millions of persons—was to reach out to the suffering, with generous dedication, touching and binding up every wounded body, healing every broken life.

The decisive and consistent practice of nonviolence has produced impressive results. The achievements of Mahatma Gandhi and Khan Abdul Ghaffar Khan in the liberation of India, and of Dr Martin Luther King Jr in combating racial discrimination will never be forgotten. Women in particular are often leaders of nonviolence, as for example, was Leymah Gbowee and the thousands of Liberian women, who organized pray-ins and nonviolent protest that resulted in high-level peace talks to end the second civil war in Liberia.

Nor can we forget the eventful decade that ended with the fall of Communist regimes in Europe. The Christian communities made their own contribution by their insistent prayer and courageous action. Particularly influential were the ministry and teaching of Saint John Paul II. Reflecting on the events of 1989 in his 1991 Encyclical *Centesimus Annus*, my predecessor highlighted the fact that momentous change in the lives of people, nations and states had come about "by means of peaceful protest, using only the weapons of truth and justice".[10] This peaceful political transition was made possible in part "by the non-violent commitment of

---

[8] Meditation, "The Road of Peace", Chapel of the *Domus Sanctae Marthae,* 19 November 2015.

[9] Homily for the Canonization of Mother Teresa of Calcutta, 4 September 2016.

[10] No. 23.

people who, while always refusing to yield to the force of power, succeeded time after time in finding effective ways of bearing witness to the truth". Pope John Paul went on to say: "May people learn to fight for justice without violence, renouncing class struggle in their internal disputes and war in international ones".[11]

The Church has been involved in nonviolent peacebuilding strategies in many countries, engaging even the most violent parties in efforts to build a just and lasting peace.

Such efforts on behalf of the victims of injustice and violence are not the legacy of the Catholic Church alone, but are typical of many religious traditions, for which "compassion and nonviolence are essential elements pointing to the way of life".[12] I emphatically reaffirm that "no religion is terrorist".[13] Violence profanes the name of God.[14] Let us never tire of repeating: "The name of God cannot be used to justify violence. Peace alone is holy. Peace alone is holy, not war!"[15]

The domestic roots of a politics of nonviolence

5. If violence has its source in the human heart, then it is fundamental that nonviolence be practised before all else within families. This is part of that joy of love which I described last March in my Exhortation *Amoris Laetitia*, in the wake of two years of reflection by the Church on marriage and the family. The family is the indispensable crucible in which spouses, parents and children, brothers and sisters, learn to communicate and to show generous concern for one another, and in which frictions and even conflicts have to be resolved not by force but by dialogue, respect, concern

---

[11] Ibid.

[12] Address to Representatives of Different Religions, 3 November 2016.

[13] Address to the Third World Meeting of Popular Movements, 5 November 2016.

[14] Cf. Address at the Interreligious Meeting with the Sheikh of the Muslims of the Caucasus and Representatives of Different Religious Communities, Baku, 2 October 2016.

[15] Address in Assisi, 20 October 2016.

for the good of the other, mercy and forgiveness.[16] From within families, the joy of love spills out into the world and radiates to the whole of society.[17] An ethics of fraternity and peaceful coexistence between individuals and among peoples cannot be based on the logic of fear, violence and closed-mindedness, but on responsibility, respect and sincere dialogue. Hence, I plead for disarmament and for the prohibition and abolition of nuclear weapons: nuclear deterrence and the threat of mutual assured destruction are incapable of grounding such an ethics.[18] I plead with equal urgency for an end to domestic violence and to the abuse of women and children.

The Jubilee of Mercy that ended in November encouraged each one of us to look deeply within and to allow God's mercy to enter there. The Jubilee taught us to realize how many and diverse are the individuals and social groups treated with indifference and subjected to injustice and violence. They too are part of our "family"; they too are our brothers and sisters. The politics of nonviolence have to begin in the home and then spread to the entire human family. "Saint Therese of Lisieux invites us to practise the little way of love, not to miss out on a kind word, a smile or any small gesture which sows peace and friendship. An integral ecology is also made up of simple daily gestures that break with the logic of violence, exploitation and selfishness".[19]

My invitation

6. Peacebuilding through active nonviolence is the natural and necessary complement to the Church's continuing efforts to limit the use of force by the application of moral norms; she does so by her participation in the work of international institutions and through the competent contribution made by so many Christians to the drafting of legislation at all levels. Jesus himself offers a

---

[16] Cf. Post-Synodal Apostolic Exhortation *Amoris Laetitia*, 90–130.

[17] Cf. ibid., 133, 194, 234.

[18] Cf. Message for the Conference on the Humanitarian Impact of Nuclear Weapons, 7 December 2014.

[19] Encyclical *Laudato Si'*, 230.

"manual" for this strategy of peacemaking in the Sermon on the Mount. The eight Beatitudes (cf. *Mt* 5:3–10) provide a portrait of the person we could describe as blessed, good and authentic. Blessed are the meek, Jesus tells us, the merciful and the peacemakers, those who are pure in heart, and those who hunger and thirst for justice.

This is also a programme and a challenge for political and religious leaders, the heads of international institutions, and business and media executives: to apply the Beatitudes in the exercise of their respective responsibilities. It is a challenge to build up society, communities and businesses by acting as peacemakers. It is to show mercy by refusing to discard people, harm the environment, or seek to win at any cost. To do so requires "the willingness to face conflict head on, to resolve it and to make it a link in the chain of a new process".[20] To act in this way means to choose solidarity as a way of making history and building friendship in society. Active nonviolence is a way of showing that unity is truly more powerful and more fruitful than conflict. Everything in the world is inter-connected.[21] Certainly differences can cause frictions. But let us face them constructively and non-violently, so that "tensions and oppositions can achieve a diversified and life-giving unity," preserving "what is valid and useful on both sides".[22]

I pledge the assistance of the Church in every effort to build peace through active and creative nonviolence. On 1 January 2017, the new Dicastery for Promoting Integral Human Development will begin its work. It will help the Church to promote in an ever more effective way "the inestimable goods of justice, peace, and the care of creation" and concern for "migrants, those in need, the sick, the excluded and marginalized, the imprisoned and the unemployed, as well as victims of armed conflict, natural disasters, and all forms of slavery and torture".[23] Every such response,

---

[20] Apostolic Exhortation *Evangelii Gaudium*, 227.
[21] Cf. Encyclical *Laudato Si'*, 16, 117, 138.
[22] Apostolic Exhortation *Evangelii Gaudium*, 228.
[23] Apostolic Letter issued *Motu Proprio* instituting the Dicastery for Promoting Integral Human Development, 17 August 2016.

however modest, helps to build a world free of violence, the first step towards justice and peace.

In conclusion

8. As is traditional, I am signing this Message on 8 December, the Solemnity of the Immaculate Conception of the Blessed Virgin Mary. Mary is the Queen of Peace. At the birth of her Son, the angels gave glory to God and wished peace on earth to men and women of good will (cf. *Luke* 2:14). Let us pray for her guidance.

"All of us want peace. Many people build it day by day through small gestures and acts; many of them are suffering, yet patiently persevere in their efforts to be peacemakers".[24] In 2017, may we dedicate ourselves prayerfully and actively to banishing violence from our hearts, words and deeds, and to becoming nonviolent people and to build nonviolent communities that care for our common home. "Nothing is impossible if we turn to God in prayer. Everyone can be an artisan of peace".[25]

From the Vatican, 8 December 2016

FRANCISCUS

Responses to "Nonviolence: A Style of Politics for Peace"

Terrence Rynne

Following publication of Pope Francis's message, Terrence Rynne, an active participant in the conference and in the Catholic Nonviolence Initiative, reflected in an essay titled "Why Pope Francis's World Day of Peace Message Is Such a Breakthrough" on the importance of Pope Francis's message:

---

[24] *Regina Coeli*, Bethlehem, 25 May 2014.
[25] Appeal, Assisi, 20 September 2016.

That Pope Francis consciously chose nonviolence as the theme of his message to the world on New Year's Day 2017, is in itself a powerful fact. The pope unabashedly pointed out that nonviolence is what Jesus taught and modeled and said, "To be true followers of Jesus today also includes embracing his teaching about nonviolence" (no. 3). The pope is signaling a true return to the sources for the Catholic Church: Sacred Scripture and the traditions of the early church. Just as the return to the sources (*resourcement*) by theologians such as Henri de Lubac, Yves Congar, and Karl Rahner fueled the renaissance of Catholic theology and the magnificent documents of the Second Vatican Council, so also today the pope is returning in a fresh way to the sources.

First, he is reading the Gospels attentively and finds his inspiration there. Pope Francis is not using natural law theory as the basis of the church's teaching on war and violence, he is going straight to the Gospels.

Second, he reflects on the lived tradition of the early church and how its members confronted persecution with courageous nonviolence and how they stunned the world, prompting massive conversions to Christianity.

The third source of inspiration for Pope Francis is the living witness of believing, nonviolent Christians across the world. He says:

> Nor can we forget the eventful decade that ended with the fall of Communist regimes in Europe. The Christian communities made their own contribution by their insistent prayer and courageous action. Particularly influential were the ministry and teaching of Saint John Paul II. Reflecting on the events of 1989 in his 1991 encyclical *Centesimus Annus*, my predecessor highlighted the fact that momentous change in the lives of people, nations and states had come about "by means of peaceful protest, using only the weapons of truth and justice." (no. 4)

At the conference that led up to the pope's World Day of Peace message, eighty people from around the world gathered to share their experiences with violence and nonviolence—for Pope

Francis's sake and for one another. One person after another shared how violence, in his or her own experience, failed, and how nonviolence overcame violence. For example, Archbishop John Baptist Odama from Uganda explained how through patient nonviolent action he came to be able to negotiate between the Lord's Resistance Army and the president of Uganda. Francisco DeRoux, SJ, told how he and other committed Christians, some of whom lost their lives in the struggle, persevered in grassroots nonviolent reconciliation efforts between the rebels and the Government of Colombia, finally bringing them to the peace table and a declaration of peace after forty years of carnage. John Ashworth and Bishop Paride Taban of South Sudan told of their grassroots negotiation among key tribes, how they brought two hundred representatives of two tribes to a new mud-hut village constructed just for the occasion to spend protracted time together to discuss differences and brainstorm solutions. They signed a reconciliation agreement in their own blood and brought peace to one region of their country. The pope heard about these and many other examples. It is impossible to hear stories of the successes of nonviolent action on the ground by such heroic people and not be moved to see nonviolence as a practical alternative to war and violence. As a result, Francis says, "The Church has been involved in nonviolent peacebuilding strategies in many countries, engaging even the most violent parties in efforts to build a just and lasting peace" (no. 4).

As the pope reclaims Jesus's teaching on nonviolence, he is saying that in the face of violence and war, no more quiescence, no more anguished acceptance, no more standing on the side wringing hands. Instead, get in the middle of the fray and fight violence with the "weapons of truth and love" (no. 3). He underlines the teaching with the penetrating words of Benedict XVI on February 18, 2007: "Love of one's enemy constitutes the nucleus of the Christian revolution" (*Angeles*)

The second striking fact about the pope's message is that it is not a simply "religious" appeal. The title of the message is "Nonviolence: A Style of Politics for Peace." The pope is making nonviolence not just the keynote of a Christian's faith in Jesus, but he is saying that nonviolence is effective in the real world of politics—in fact superior to and more effective than violence. The world never gets to peace through violence and war but only begets more violence and war.

William James wrote an important article in 1910 entitled "The Moral Equivalent of War."[26] In it he elaborated on the positive features of war that had made it so popular through the ages. He wondered if the virtues of "hardihood" that war brought forward such as courage, discipline, oneness in a cause larger than oneself, high adventure, deep soldierly affection and serious purpose, could be maintained if war was to somehow disappear. He wondered if humans would become flabby, weak, and pusillanimous. In addition, he explained the role of war in politics—pointing out that war in human history has always served as the only and final arbiter of intractable conflicts between people.

Walter Lippman echoed James when he wrote: "Then the abolition of war depends primarily upon inventing and organizing other ways of deciding those issues which hitherto have been decided by war."[27]

The third reason why the pope's message is such a breakthrough is that he is proclaiming that the world has discovered what the world has been looking for, a substitute for war. Nonviolent direct action is that substitute for war.

Most people at this point in our history recognize the horrors of war—the death, destruction, and irrational brutality of any and all wars. Nonetheless, many people are still dedicated to war and few believe that war will ever disappear. The surprising thing is that there have been many other institutions of violence in human history that people have accepted as givens, the way things are, and that have nonetheless disappeared.

Recently David Carroll Cochran wrote an enlightening book entitled *Catholic Realism and the Abolition of War.*[28] In it he de-

---

[26] William James, *The Moral Equivalent of War*, 27th Publication of the American Association of International Conciliation (February 1910), 17–18.

[27] Walter Lippman, "The Political Equivalent of War," *Atlantic Monthly* (August 1928): 181.

[28] David Carroll Cochran, *Catholic Realism and the Abolition of War* (Maryknoll, NY: Orbis Books, 2014).

scribes how in recent centuries other institutions of violence that were thought to be givens by society have been eliminated. He describes how trial by combat had been the accepted way of determining guilt or innocence—until a new consciousness arose and a new institutional solution was brought forward—evidence-based police work and trial by jury. Suddenly trial by combat vanished. He explains how pervasive dueling was in our country. So accepted that Alexander Hamilton thought it a matter of honor to accept Aaron Burr's challenge to him—even though Hamilton's own son had been killed on a similar field of "honor." Once libel laws came into existence and adequate libel courts, dueling vanished.

Slavery, which had been accepted as a natural institution for centuries, was fought tooth and nail by people of conscience until society changed its mind. He sees the same thing happening with war—if consciousness continues to change and an institution can be found which serves as a substitute.

The United States Conference of Catholic Bishops has realized that the attitude of many people toward the death penalty has changed and that there is an alternative to the death penalty, namely, life in prison without parole. Consequently, in 2005, the USCCB issued the statement "A Culture of Life and the Penalty of Death," which stated, "It is time for our nation to abandon the illusion that we can protect life by taking life." The death penalty, another violent technique, formerly assumed to be necessary for society's protection, is on the way out.

Unlike the examples above, the consciousness about war has not adequately shifted for war to disappear. But like the above examples, a substitute institution has come to the fore—nonviolent direct action. When conflicts between peoples, or countries, or groups become intractable, unable to be solved through the rational give and take of negotiation or arbitration, and if they are serious issues, humankind now has an alternative—either choose violent direct action and/or war or choose nonviolent direct action.

The pope does not fully develop why and how nonviolent direct action works. We hope he will do so in a future extended teaching on nonviolence in the form of an encyclical. He does, however, hint at the further depths of his thinking by those he holds up as exemplars of nonviolence: Mahatma Gandhi, Ghaffar Abdul Khan, Martin Luther King, Jr., and Leymah Gbowee.

What does the example of Mahatma Gandhi show us? Gandhi was convinced that nonviolent direct action or the name he gave to it, Satyagraha or soul force, could work wonders in any and every situation of conflict, whether it was economic, political or social, and he demonstrated it again and again. That is why so many, eventually millions, embraced Satyagraha and joined the most challenging cause of all—liberating their huge country from the most powerful imperial force in the world—the British Empire. He proved it first in localized struggles such as the 1917 struggle of the indigo farmers resisting the high taxes demanded by the plantation owners.

In 1924 Gandhi worked with the untouchables in the Travancore area to gain access to a road. The Brahmins feared contamination from just being in the vicinity of the untouchables and consequently barred them access. Access to the road would save hours each day in travel to their work. They endured terrible suffering including standing in flood waters up to their shoulders as they nonviolently tried to reach the hearts of the Brahmins. Eventually not only were the untouchables able to access the road, but they were invited into the temples as well.

The common people across the length and breadth of India, especially those in the 700,000 small villages, came to know and revere Gandhi. When he said, "How is it that 100,000 English can keep 250,000,000 Indians (now over a billion) in bondage? The answer—because we let them."

He called the masses to support first a nationwide noncooperation movement—teachers in the government schools left and started their own. Headmen and magistrates in the British-dominated political establishment left their posts and hamstrung the government. People refused to buy imported cloth from England. They boycotted liquor and tobacco shops and sent revenues to the Raj plummeting.

Later he called them out to civilly disobey the unjust salt and forest laws. The whole country rose up and willingly endured the consequences. Hundreds of thousands willingly went to jail. When the jails were filled, the British started hammering crowds with lathi [baton] charges and then began firing their rifles into the resisting people. The British were revealed clearly to the world and to the Indian people for who and what they were—not the civilized masters they pretended to be but rapacious, violent dominators who were in India for the natural resources and the sweat labor of the population. The veil fell away.

Gandhi's theory of power—that power rises, that those at the top have power only if the people give it to them and cooperate with them—was verified. One huge country defeated another country—in fact the mightiest imperial power in the world. Surely that is the definition of what war is supposed to accomplish. But in this case it was accomplished not through violent direct action, war, but through nonviolent direct action. The world has seen graphically that there is a real alternative to war—nonviolent direct action.

Since then, of course, we have seen many, many examples of the power of nonviolent direct action. Erica Chenoweth and Maria Stephan completed a recent research study of 343 serious conflict situations—meaning resistance to domination by a dictator or an occupation by an army—and found that nonviolent resistance was twice as effective as violent resistance. Moreover, nonviolent revolutions were nine times as likely to produce a peaceful follow-on society.[29] Gandhi's victory, for example, was a double victory. Not only was India freed, but Britain departed in peace.

Pope Francis does not elaborate on all that Gandhi's example illustrates. He does not, for example, explain that nonviolence is not just an inner attitude but a collection of interrelated strategies that cumulatively put pressure on an adversary until he or she returns to the negotiating table. In sequence, the nonviolent campaign moves from negotiation to noncooperation to creatively bringing attention to and sympathy for the cause through demonstrations and protests, through boycotts, through civil disobedience and the willingness to suffer, which generates its own kind of power. Instead of inflicting suffering through violence, the nonviolent

---

[29] Erica Chenoweth and Maria Stephan, *Why Civil Resistance Works: The Strategic Logic of Nonviolent Conflict* (New York: Columbia University Press, 2011).

protagonist endures suffering—all the time showing respect for the adversaries and trying to reach not just their minds but their hearts.

In an extended treatment of nonviolence in an encyclical the pope will no doubt point out how strangely alike nonviolent direct action is to violent direct action, that is, war. For example, they are alike on the virtue of courage. We have seen for ourselves how Gandhi's followers, attempting to take over the Dharsana Salt Works, endured beatings with steel-tipped clubs from the native police, going down like ten pins with broken skulls and fractured shoulders and still continued to come forward wave after wave. We have witnessed Archbishop Oscar Romero continue to speak out and protect his beloved *campesinos* until he was shot down. We have seen the religious sisters in the Philippines kneel in prayer before Marcos's tanks and offer rosaries to his soldiers.

Nonviolent direct action features all the "hardihood" virtues previously associated with war: involvement in a cause greater than oneself, deep fellow feeling, heroism, discipline, and courage.

The pope will point out that effective nonviolent direct action campaigns utilize the same strategies as military strategists such as Napoleon and Clausewitz: Concentrate force at the weakest link. The moral factor is superior to material resources. Maintain surprise. Keep the initiative. Don't do what the opponent expects you to do. Endure.

The pope knows that many people equate nonviolence with passivity. He, on the other hand, knows nonviolence to be a positive, aggressive, creative stance toward violence and evil. He says in his message: "Nonviolence is sometimes taken to mean surrender, lack of involvement and passivity, but this is not the case. . . . '[It] requires the willingness to confront conflict head on, resolve it and to make it a chain in a new process'" (nos. 4, 6).[30]

He points to other exemplars of this very rich, potent method of conflict resolution. He points to Martin Luther King, Jr., who dramatically orchestrated the full panoply of strategies of nonviolent direct action, who demonstrated the power of self-suffering, who demonstrated that power does indeed rise up from the people,

---

[30] The quotation the pope uses is from *Evangelii gaudium*, no. 227.

that one does not have to break one's opponent—it is enough to change the opponent, and that the nonviolent soldier is every bit as brave as a soldier of violence.

He holds up for study Ghaffar Abdul Khan. The pope is not pretending to be politically correct in mentioning the Hindu Gandhi and the Muslim Khan in the same breath. He knows Khan was Gandhi's most effective and loyal collaborator. He knows that Gandhi came from an Indian culture that had studied and embraced *ahimsa* (nonviolence) for centuries. As a result, Gandhi could tap that culture and produce a massive outpouring of support. But Khan's example shows that nonviolent direct action can be embraced by cultures with very different traditions. Ghaffar Khan was a Pathan. Pathans were the tribe of violence and revenge in the Northwest Territories of India, even now the trouble spot on the border between Afghanistan and today's Pakistan. Nonetheless, Khan embraced nonviolence as an even more effective force than violence and he inspired a hundred thousand young Pathans to join his nonviolent army, the Khudai Khidmatgars, to work for their people and resist the British.

The final active peacemaker the pope points to is Leymah Gbowee, the Nobel Prize winner from Liberia. Her story also deserves full study. She organized pray-ins and nonviolent protests that resulted in high-level peace talks to end the second civil war in Liberia. Nonviolent direct action is becoming even more potent with the full involvement of powerful women. Africa is the locale of much of what Pope Francis refers to as a "world war fought piecemeal." The contributions of such women as Gbowee in Liberia and Marguerite Barankitse in Burundi are showing the way to the eventual cessation of violence and the dawning of peace in Africa, the continent of the future.

We are grateful to Pope Francis. Each document of the Catholic Church relating to peace and war—from Pope John XXIII's *Pacem in terris*, through Vatican II's *The Church in the Modern World*, to the US bishops' letters *The Challenge of Peace* and *The Harvest of Justice Is Sown in Peace*—has given progressively more space to the issue of nonviolence. In the pope's 2017 World Day of Peace message, nonviolence is given pride of place and the spotlight.

We look forward to the pope giving us a fuller teaching, a fuller development of the meaning, the practice, the requirements and the potential of nonviolent direct action—the long yearned-for substitute for war.[31]

Gerald Schlabach

Conference participant, moral theologian, and author Gerald Schlabach discusses additional important dimensions of Francis's World Day of Peace message on his blog:

Anyone who reads Catholic Church documents learns to recognize a certain kind of savvy rhetorical strategy. The Vatican's carefully finessed language may sometimes be frustrating in its nuance, but can also serve to balance considerations and forge consensus in a complex global community. Pope Francis thus exercises an appropriate Vatican savvy as he alludes to the possible use of "just war" criteria in his World Day of Peace message, yet leaves the theory unnamed—for now, neither rejected outright nor defended.

What Pope Francis names instead is the space that the Vatican and Catholic moral traditions have hoped the "just war" theory would fill. Section 6 of the World Day of Peace message begins this way:

Peacebuilding through active nonviolence is the natural and necessary complement to the Church's continuing efforts to limit the use of force by the application of moral norms; she does so by her participation in the work of international institutions and through the competent contribution made by so many Christians to the drafting of legislation at all levels.

Now because "just war" theory has long provided the framework for those efforts of the church to "limit the use of force by

---

[31] Terrence Rynne, "Why Pope Francis's World Day of Peace Message Is Such a Breakthrough," Peace Stories (a project of Pax Christi International), April 21, 2017. The essay has been slightly adapted for this volume.

the application of moral norms" (and indeed helped build the architecture for international law along the way) this sentence might seem to validate its continued use. And yet the papal restraint that left "just war" theory here unnamed also recalls the unease that once prompted Cardinal Joseph Ratzinger—later Pope Benedict XVI—to wonder out loud whether "today we should be asking ourselves if it is still licit to admit the very existence of a 'just war.'"

After all, . . . what Pope Francis does next in section 6 of his World Day of Peace message is breathtaking. He insists that "Jesus himself offers a 'manual' for this [integrated] strategy of peacemaking in the Sermon on the Mount." Two things are going on here.

First, calling the Sermon on the Mount a "manual" is a most intriguing word choice. "Manualism" was the neo-Scholastic mode of Catholic moral deliberation ascendant from the 17th century until the Second Vatican Council. . . . Whatever its virtues, it tended therefore to de-emphasize biblical sources and thus offered a comfortable home for "just war" casuistry. To now, instead, call the Sermon on the Mount (Matthew 5—7) the church's manual for peacemaking hardly seems an accident.

In any case, a second signal is unmistakable: After reflecting briefly on the Beatitudes as a template for the virtues that any authentic peacemaker will embody, Pope Francis describes the Sermon on the Mount and the Beatitudes as "also a programme and a challenge for political and religious leaders, the heads of international institutions, and business and media executives" to apply amid "the exercise of their respective responsibilities." The manual that the Sermon on the Mount provides, in other words, is not just for the personal lives of particularly saintly Christians. It applies to the public realm. It elicits, as the World Day of Peace title has already announced, a "style of *politics* for peace."

Here, though, is where we must especially anticipate the challenge of reception. . . . Serious biblical exegesis recognizes these teachings as paradigmatic models . . . for a sophisticated practice of active nonviolence that counters injustice with the creativity needed to transform social processes. It is not simply protest and certainly not passivity. Yet the unformed, uninformed, assumption of many is going to be that practicing the Sermon on the Mount in public affairs is a lofty but idealistic notion, no more. . . .

At various points throughout the document Pope Francis argues for active nonviolence by citing cycles of violence and the need to escape them. . . . The pope does not deny that war may sometimes respond to injustice. Yet, he asks, "Where does this lead? Does violence achieve any goal of lasting value?" No, it leads "to retaliation and a cycle of deadly conflict" rather than any "cure for our broken world" (section 2). That is why "the force of arms is deceptive" (section 4). Gospel nonviolence is the truly revolutionary alternative, therefore, because "responding to evil with good" rather than "succumbing to evil" by responding in kind means "thereby breaking the chain of injustice" (section 3). . . .

Catholic peacebuilders can be grateful that the Vatican is listening, but we should also learn from Pope Francis's pedagogically savvy rhetorical strategy. If we expect the pope to take down the "just war" theory at one fell swoop in an eventual encyclical we may be inviting disappointment. Everything in church history and the development of doctrine suggests that the magisterium is loath to say that great Christian authorities of the past were outright wrong. Rather, popes and church councils look for other clever ways to simply move on. My prediction is that the "just war" theory will be damned with faint praise, or killed with a thousand cuts. Our best and quite realistic hope is that "just war" will go the way of capital punishment, which Pope John Paul II did not quite reject in theory but did reject for modern societies (*Evangelium vitae,* no. 56). . . . Pope Francis's 2017 World Day of Peace message, and section 6 in particular, is exactly what that process is going to look like. The job of Catholic peacebuilders is to amplify its signals.[32]

---

[32] Gerald W. Schlabach, "Pope Francis's Peacebuilding Pedagogy: A Commentary on His 2017 World Day of Peace Message" (January 2, 2017), online.

Conclusion

Continuing the Conversation

Clearly the conversation will continue. The April 2016 Rome conference galvanized participants to create the Catholic Nonviolence Initiative, a partnership of Catholic networks worldwide, to implement the *Appeal to the Catholic Church to Re-commit to the Centrality of Gospel Nonviolence.*

Sister Lynette Rodrigues, PBVB

Sister Lynette Rodrigues from Zambia shared in a preconference paper the following thoughts about where the Catholic community needs to invest energy in moving toward a deeper and wider practice of nonviolence.

- We need to look at the theology we practice as church community. What is our experience of God today? What is our image of God? We need to question our dualistic thinking and approach. We need to think holistically.
- We need to be committed to inclusion, sacredness of the body, to defense without violence, to spiritual integrity. We need to look at the rules and doctrines which do not serve anymore, which do not promote the experience of God.
- We need to question the separateness of body and soul. Feminism, with its awareness of the wholeness of creation and its valuation of the female on equal terms with the male, offers us a chance to look again at the sacredness of

the body, of all bodies—the bodies of women everywhere; the bodies of Syrian children; the bodies that are abused sexually; the bodies of persons who are trafficked for the sexual pleasures of men and the greediness of a few; the bodies of unborn babies; the bodies of men who are used on the battlefields of the world to maintain the systems of the world against the people of the world. When the body is valued for its sacredness, aggression against it has no place.

Pope Francis's 2017 World Day of Peace Message demonstrates that the Catholic Church is opening to the rich possibilities of nonviolence. In that message Francis said, "In the most local and ordinary situations and in the international order, may nonviolence become the hallmark of our decisions, our relationships and our actions, and indeed of political life in all its forms." These words were reaffirmed in Pope Francis's address to the Corps of Diplomats on January 9, 2017, when he appealed to all religious authorities to join in reaffirming unequivocally that one can never kill in God's name.

The Catholic Nonviolence Initiative is a partnership of prominent Catholic organizations already deeply engaged in peacebuilding, with networks of thinkers and peace practitioners around the globe who strongly believe in a renewed Catholic social teaching on nonviolence and a recommitment of the Catholic Church to gospel nonviolence.

On February 18, 2007, Pope Benedict XVI, speaking at the Vatican, described "Jesus true message: to seek peace with the means of peace and leave violence aside." Nonviolence, he said, "does not consist in surrendering to evil . . . but in responding to evil with good (Romans 12:17–21), and thus breaking the chain of injustice." The Catholic Nonviolence Initiative promotes active nonviolence as a way of life—as a positive and powerful force for social change that recognizes the humanity of every person, even in the context of terrible violence, and actively promotes the in-breaking reign of God.

Strategic nonviolent practices include organized forms of resistance, restorative justice, trauma healing, unarmed civilian protection, conflict transformation, diplomacy, atrocity-prevention policies, peacebuilding strategies, peace education, and more. These strategies have been proven effective in many situations of potential or actual violent conflict.

Yet worldwide investment in the development of effective non-violent practices is sorely lacking. Creative thinking, significant financial allocations, training that has proven effective, the commitment of large numbers of people, and well-placed and well-timed action are all essential to expanding the development and application of nonviolence in justice and peace work throughout the world.

The Catholic Church, with its diplomatic presence in almost every country and at all major multilateral organizations, has a well-developed network of universities, seminaries, religious communities, parishes, publications, and media outlets; a membership of over one billion people; and rich spiritual and theological resources. These could make a tremendous contribution to the development and acceptance of nonviolent approaches to a more peaceful world. And at this moment, with Pope Francis as the pastor of the church, the opportunity for the church to lead a global conversion to active nonviolence is enormous. His moral voice is a powerful advocate to promote nonviolence. When the Catholic Church commits itself to nonviolence as the means most likely to be effective and sustainable for preventing or ending violent conflict and for protecting vulnerable communities, civil society at large will have added leverage to promote creative alternatives to armed intervention and to build just peace solutions.

The Catholic Church can help lead the world away from perpetual violence and war by an expanded investment of its intellectual, pastoral, academic, diplomatic, and financial resources in developing and promoting nonviolent practices and strategies. Essential to this effort is education of Catholics and society at large about active nonviolence as a practical and effective tool for building peace within families, local communities, nationals, and throughout the globe.

Maria Stephan

Maria Stephan urges the church to put into practice a vision very similar to that articulated by Pope Francis in his 2017 World Day of Peace message.[1] The church, she says, should prioritize investment in teaching and training that brings together dialogical and action-oriented nonviolent approaches.[2] She asks what would happen if the church galvanized support for those Syrians who have, since March 2011, been committed to nonviolently challenging both dictatorship and violent extremism. What if the church really challenged political leaders to consider new options?

> The church should work with academics and practitioners to establish a firm evidence base for these nonmilitary interventions; and then advocate for them locally, regionally, and internationally. That would be a concrete way to put meat on the bones of "just peace," while mainstreaming the principles, tools, and approaches at all levels of the church—from the Vatican to national bishops' conferences to dioceses and local parishes. Further, Catholic universities and peace-building organizations like Pax Christi, Mercy Corps, Caritas International, and Catholic Relief Services are well-placed to integrate dialogue with nonviolent collective action approaches in their education and field operations. They could ally with umbrella organizations like the Alliance for Peacebuilding, plus nonviolent action and movement-building organizations like Rhize and the International Center on Nonviolent Conflict, and civilian protection organizations like Nonviolent Peaceforce that are advancing effective nonmilitary solutions on the ground. If the church joined forces with other Christian denominations, along with Muslim and Jewish leaders and institutions, to prioritize

---

[1] Maria J. Stephan, "What Happens When You Replace a Just War with a Just Peace," *Foreign Policy* (May 18, 2016).

[2] Maria J. Stephan, "Peacebuilder's Field Guide to Protest Movements," *Foreign Policy* (January 22, 2016).

areas of collaboration focused on Abrahamic peacemaking, the effect would be even more powerful.[3]

Anne McCarthy, OSB

Anne McCarthy, in her reflection prior to the conference, wrote:

Teaching, reflection, and preaching on gospel nonviolence is needed at all levels, including seminaries. In order to reach the general Catholic population, as well as spiritual seekers everywhere, a spirituality of nonviolence is foundational. Sharing the stories of the saints, the nonviolent elders, and mentors and guides in our long history will capture the imagination of people of all ages. Stories of nonviolent movements around the globe need to be told and shared. Their stories connect with ours and draw out our own experiences of times fear and hatred were overcome by compassion and love.

Along with sharing the stories, rituals and liturgies draw people into prayer experiences that help them move beyond fear to grow in compassion. Often our liturgies and hymns focus on our individual sinfulness and personal salvation. Liturgical experiences that move us to nonviolence need to be developed, fostered, and spread. Retreats can help individuals and communities address and heal from violence in all forms and explore gospel nonviolence. These also need to be developed and fostered.

Popular pieties have supported nonviolent movements globally: rosary marches, processions, fasts, anointing and blessing of protestors, washing the feet of refugees and prisoners, even eucharistic liturgies in places of violence. Our Lady of Guadalupe led every United Farm Workers march. The nonviolent revolution in the Philippines was especially strong with visible Catholic symbols.

---

[3] Stephan, "What Happens When You Replace a Just War With a Just Peace."

It is also important to examine and reject our church's pact with violence. Horrible violence has been blessed and sometimes enabled by the ignorance, greed, and hatred of us all and in the church as an institution. Catholic chaplains, employed by the military, are one example; ROTC[4] on Catholic campuses another. A sharp turn from the just war theory and from support of war and violence is needed.

Nonviolence is learned primarily by practice. Nonviolence training offered at a parish or regional level could be a basic foundation for other action. Catholic participation in nonviolent campaigns and even in an interfaith peace force would counter the long history of visible participation in war and violence.

The global climate crisis creates an opportunity for the worldwide church to act nonviolently together and unleash amazing creativity. Imagine a coordinated and sustained campaign with the universal Catholic Church praying and acting together nonviolently to protect the planet. It would embed nonviolence in the Catholic psyche at a deep level.

Rania Murra

Rania Murra from the Arab Educational Institute in Bethlehem, Palestine, and a member of the board of Pax Christi International, described the hopeful possibility of *Sumud,* which is Arabic for *steadfastness*. *Sumud* refers to an active, nonviolent lifestyle in which one neither becomes resigned to injustice or oppression— such as the occupation of Palestine—nor becomes absorbed by hatred toward the enemy. *Sumud* is a third way in which one keeps head and dignity high; stays actively connected to the land and community; and challenges the oppression by a peaceful lifestyle with preparedness to suffer. *Sumud* is about being tested as Jesus was tested in Gethsemane and afterward. It's a concept that gives space to stories and voices of individual woman, families, and

---

[4] The Reserve Officers' Training Corps (ROTC) include college-based programs to train commissioned officers for the United States Armed Forces.

communities. Jesus, Gandhi, and King are all examples of the
personal leadership of *Sumud.*

Sumud implies a solid strategy, living by example. *Sumud*
means that we have to work on educating and liberating people, and especially raising the voice of women. Women have
to participate and present their stories, but they should also
be decision makers in their communities. Each woman has
her own way to make a difference. This has also a personal
and family dimension. It is about raising your children in the
spirit of *sumud*, against the occupation, against despair and
emigration, against the bare survival. In the case of women's
rights, you are trying to build your country in a way that
aims at ending the occupation. When I fight what are called
"honor killings," it is not only a fight for humanity but also
a fight against the occupation because you make your people
and community stronger.

I believe that we have several strategies available to
deepen and widen the practice of nonviolence in the worldwide Catholic community. All require our energy:

- Living by example; working with Catholic communities
  on local and global issues of justice, inequality, discrimination, poverty, and peace—and showing the many
  linkages between the different issues in an increasingly
  interconnected world. A practice of nonviolence can only
  be fostered by working together on real world problems.
- Working together; increasingly involving lay people in
  the church. Conversely, it is helpful to have more clergy
  involved in directly dealing with real life problems.
- Approaching world problems nonviolently; working on
  peace and nonviolence education; enabling people to raise
  their voices in different forms and genres.
- Working with women on issues important for protecting
  their human security and rights; promoting women's participation in society, including participation in the church.

- Strengthening ecumenical Christian dialogue and interfaith dialogue across borders to build a broad-based, global, nonviolent peace movement.
- Making a direct connection between the example of Jesus's life of suffering, *sumud,* and nonviolent approaches to present-day world problems. Symbols referring to Jesus's life of struggling nonviolently for a just peace are meaningful; showing the life of the Virgin Mary and the life stories of saints in appealing forms and designs can help to illustrate a nonviolent life style. Some spiritual traditions of the church are inspired by nonviolent approaches including indigenous traditions in newly established churches in Africa, Asia, and Latin America.
- Last but not least, it is extremely important that the church itself give a good example of nonviolence, including preventing the abuse of children in its own ranks.

The *Appeal to the Church to Re-commit to the Centrality of Gospel Nonviolence* (see Chapter 1) proposed that the Catholic Church, "develop and consider shifting to a Just Peace approach based on Gospel nonviolence." Since the Rome conference, thousands of individuals and organizations have endorsed the *Appeal*, in essence committing themselves "to furthering Catholic understanding and practice of active nonviolence on the road to just peace."

Many members and friends of Pax Christi around the world have adopted the tradition of making a vow of nonviolence each year, often with others as a form of public witness in their parish or religious community.[5] Such a practice would be an excellent idea for the Catholic community worldwide to consider in the coming years, as the church, both the institution and the people of God, reaffirm the centrality of active nonviolence to the vision and message of Jesus, to the life of the church, and to the long-term vocation of healing and reconciling both people and the planet.

---

[5] The vow's most familiar form, written by John Dear and Eileen Egan, was initiated by Pax Christi USA in 1985.

Index